CHINOISERIE

CHINOISERIE

DAWN JACOBSON

To John, with love and gratitude

Phaidon Press Limited
Regent's Wharf
All Saints Street
London N1 9PA

First published 1993
First paperback edition 1999
© 1993 Phaidon Press Limited
ISBN 0 7148 3836 5

A CIP catalogue record for this book
is available from the British Library

Library of Congress Cataloging in
Publication Data available

Printed in Hong Kong

Cover: illustration: Sir Jeffrey
Wyatville, *Design for a Fishing
Pavilion at Virginia Water*, *c.*1825.
(British Architectural Library,
RIBA London)
Page one: Decoration for
a Drawing Room in the
Chinese taste by George
Smith, 1807.
Page two (frontispiece):
The White Bridge, a Chinese
bridge in the grounds of the
Palace at Worlitz, Germany.
Page three: Design for a
Chinese Temple. From a
book of Oriental Designs by
G. Landi, *c.*1810.
Opposite: Design for a
Chinese Table by William
Chambers, 1757.

Contents

Chinoiserie is an oddity. It is a wholly European style whose inspiration is entirely oriental. True chinoiseries are not pallid or incompetent imitations of Chinese objects. They are the tangible and solid realizations in the West of a land of the imagination: an exotic, remote country, fabled for its riches, that through the centuries remained cloud-wrapped, obstinately refusing to allow more than a handful of foreigners beyond its gates.

Those few travellers to make the long voyage to Cathay, as China was known in the Middle Ages, returned with tales that surpassed the imaginings of their fascinated audience in Europe. This fanciful vision of a quasi-mythical land was fuelled by the inimitable nature of those few objects brought to the West by the returning adventurers who had penetrated Cathay's mysteries. The notion that China was a land unlike any other, inhabited by people whose manners and conduct were unknown elsewhere, found fertile soil in the western mind. In the seventeenth century, evidence of the Orient's prodigious wealth buttressed western imaginations. Porcelain, lacquer, ivory and silk, unloaded from the great ships of the East India Companies, filled the wharfs and warehouses of Europe's maritime powers.

To meet the growing demand for Eastern imports, inventive artists and craftsmen from all over Europe began to produce their own alternatives – chinoiseries – which while evoking the products of China did not imitate them. Indeed the means for imitation were not at hand. So, pottery factories throughout Europe strove to produce versions of blue-and-white Ming porcelains, local 'japanners' lacquered furniture with wayward designs, English needlewomen reproduced the Indian Tree of Life design in crewel embroideries, and imaginative tapestry makers represented the life of the Chinese emperor. The taste for chinoiserie became ubiquitous and affected every area of the decorative arts from complete interiors to needle-cases. Its motifs could be painted on walls as successfully as on porcelain, while its ornament proved equally suitable for furniture or garden follies.

Eighteenth-century rococo taste saw chinoiseries become an integral part of fashion. Furniture altered its character, porcelain factories arose in the grounds of princely estates, pagodas shimmered on drawing-room walls. That grand phenomenon, the Anglo-Chinese garden, combined the kiosks and summer houses of Cathay with the landscape arts of England to transform the parklands of the rich from Naples to the Gulf of Sweden. Chinoiseries became a key element in furnishing and design, successfully surviving even the return to Classicism of the latter part of the eighteenth century. In the nineteenth, chinoiserie's high point was furnished by the Prince Regent's Royal Pavilion at Brighton, and the adoption of the style by the new middle classes invigorated and extended its role.

Chinoiserie continues to flourish. Its ability to bob along with the changing tides of fashion has made it an abiding, if often unrecognized, leitmotif in the design of everyday objects. When we drink tea from a blue-and-white china cup, choose paeonies and plum-blossom to flower on our curtains, or conceal the television set behind a lacquered screen, we are its unconscious heirs, followers of the passion for the arts of China that consumed the West for hundreds of years and led its artists and craftsmen in an exhilarating pursuit of its charms.

Dawn Jacobson

Plate from Owen Jones,
***Examples of Chinese Ornament*, Part II, 1867.**

The origins of chinoiserie

Let us now … travel into Cathay, so that you may learn something of its grandeurs and its treasures.

Marco Polo, *Travels, c.*1305

Chinese silk embroidery, late seventeenth century. *A ten-inch 'mandarin square', the official badge of a high-ranking civil servant. China was known to the Romans as the 'land of silk'. The fabric was unique to that country and remained so until the eggs of the mulberry silk moth were smuggled into Rome in the sixth century AD.*

Pottery tomb figures of princesses. T'Ang dynasty (618-906). *China continued to surprise up to modern times. It was not until the early twentieth century that the first T'Ang dynasty ceramics became known in the West.*

Porcelain plate. Ming dynasty (1368-1644). *(far right) Blue-and-white Ming ware provided the model for all the attempts to produce a European version of porcelain. The phoenix was to turn into the long-tailed bird still preening on dinner services today.*

Cathay, the old name for China, and the land of chinoiserie, consists of palaces and pagodas, ragged trees and rainbow-hued plants, fiery dragons and long-legged birds. Its climate is kind, its landscape abounds in watery vistas and pointed mountains, its forests in small and gnarled trees, its meadows in large and exotic flowers. The countryside is populated by little figures: children with round faces and tiny mouths, men with wispy beards and lampshade hats, and women whose patterned robes are moulded to delicate limbs and swaying forms. They are found in bamboo pavilions perched on the slopes of rocky mountains, or by the side of wriggling streams, whiling away the hours in placid irresponsibility: drinking tea, flying kites, or fishing with slender rods at pools fringed with willows. The inhabitants of this miniature world of fancy, conjured out of travellers' tales and the careful scrutiny of lacquer screen and porcelain tea-cup, were well known in salon and *schloss*, its pavilions were copied from the Gulf of Finland to the shores of the Hudson River, and its flora and fauna provided a source of decorative fantasy still popular today.

For centuries China has fascinated the imagination of the West. For a long time there were only the haziest ideas of where China was, who lived there or how they lived. Those few travel-stained merchants who penetrated its shores returned to Europe with silk, porcelain, tea, lacquer: inimitable products fabled in the West, whose extraordinary qualities were augmented by heavily embellished tales of their home country. These ingredients conjured up the land of Cathay: a recipe for romantic speculation, creating fantastic visions of luxury and refinement, pleasure and abundance.

The spell persisted. Even such a modern, sober source of information as the *Encyclopaedia Britannica* succumbed to the charms of this land. As late as 1929 the entry on China writes of its 'woodland of peculiar richness and variety … the supreme expression of the cool, temperate, broad-leaved deciduous forest', of its 'profusion of growth' with 'nine thousand flowering plants' and 'fauna of great diversity' and goes on to catalogue the survival there of animals elsewhere extinct or unique to China: pandas, laughing thrushes and salamanders. The illustrations chosen to depict this enchanted place reveal a world of 'wayside shrines', 'mandarins', and 'Chinese girls in richly embroidered robes', all of them images that might be found on a piece of soft-paste porcelain, or a royal trinket of the eighteenth century.

The West has always prized China's goods. Great quantities of Chinese silk were carried along the caravan trails of Central Asia in the days of the Roman Empire. The Romans valued the trade but had little idea of where the silk originated, judging by the speculations of an anonymous Roman writer of the first century AD who provides the earliest description in European literature of the route to China: 'The sea comes to an end somewhere in Thin; and in the interior of that country, somewhat to the north, there is a great city called Thinae, from which raw silk, and silk thread and silk stuffs are brought overland through Bactria and Barygaza, as they are on the other hand by the Ganges river to Limyrice.' Unsurprisingly, the writer observes: 'It is not easy, however, to get to this Thin, and few and far between are those who came from it.' It was an observation that would go unchallenged for centuries.

By the end of the third century Barbarian
incursions rendered the Silk Route insecure.
Trading conditions, already precarious, grew even
more difficult as a result of the rise of Islam. From
the seventh century both sea and land routes to
China became effectively barred to western traders,
who seldom penetrated beyond the Black Sea. And
in 878 China closed its doors on all foreigners, to
remain secret and sealed for centuries. So it was
when the nomads of the Central Asian steppes met

Portrait of a Mandarin.
Portrait of a Tartar Lady.
*The enchanted vision of China
held by the West persisted for
centuries. In these nineteenth-
century watercolours by an
unknown artist, the scrupulous
detailing of the gorgeous robes
and the aloof visages of their
wearers enhance the sense of
mystery and charm.*

on the plains of Karakorum in 1206 and elected as their leader the legendary Genghis Khan. Within twelve years Genghis and his Tartar army had conquered the whole of China, and the Tartar capital moved from the barbarous wastes of Mongolia to the cultured and civilized city of Peking. With China theirs, the Tartars had acquired a taste for conquest. As Marco Polo explained in his *Travels*, they 'made up their minds to conquer the world'; and indeed they did, creating the greatest empire ever seen, stretching across the landmass of central Asia and Russia as far west as Hungary.

The great mercantile republics of Pisa, Genoa and Venice – who had been trading with the Infidel across the Mediterranean since the seventh century – still held a virtual monopoly of trade in the thirteenth century. They took advantage of the *pax Tartarica*, to return to direct trade with China, particularly in silks. Other European powers awoke to the possibilities of trade with the new regime now ruling Cathay. In the mid-thirteenth century both the Pope and Louis IX of France despatched envoys to the court at Karakorum. Both offered baptism and alliances; neither received much encouragement.

Around the same time – in 1245 – two Venetian brothers, Niccolo and Maffeo Polo, set sail from Constantinople for the Crimean port of Sudak, where a colony of Venetians was already established and where their elder brother had a house. An adventurous pair, they traded up the Volga until the activities of the local warlords forced them to take refuge in Bukhara. There they learned sufficient Tartar to join a diplomatic mission from the Khan of the Levant to his overlord, the great Khan of all the Tartars, Kublai Khan, who lived, by Marco Polo's

calculations, 'at the ends of the earth in an east-north-easterly direction'.

Kublai Khan was enlightened, courteous and energetic. Curious to learn what he could of the oddities of the world he had once sent a mission to Madagascar, 5000 miles away, for information about the fabulous *rukh* or gryphon, a bird which was rumoured to reduce an elephant to pulp by picking it up in its talons and hurling it down on the earth. In much the same spirit, the great Khan despatched Niccolo and Maffeo to ask Pope Clement IV to send a hundred Christian savants to his court to convince him of the virtues of Christianity. The Polos set off, but the enterprise was frustrated by the inconvenient death of the Pope in 1268, and they returned to Kublai's court bringing with them Niccolo's 17-year-old son, Marco, who was to serve the Khan for 20 years.

The Mongols had only recently conquered the Chinese. Kublai Khan, reluctant to fill the senior positions in his Yuan dynasty's civil service with the vanquished Chinese, realized that a foreigner could be a useful go-between. The 17-year-old from Venice became his trusted servant, and travelled all over China and the Mongol empire for the Khan. Many of the places he visited were closed to Europeans until the nineteenth century, and some remained unseen by western eyes until the building of the Burma Road during the Second World War.

It was Marco Polo who provided the world with its first vision of Cathay. Imprisoned in a Genoese jail at the end of the thirteenth century he was fortunate to find himself with a cell-mate who was a practised writer of romances, one Rustichello of Pisa, to whom he was able to dictate an account of his travels. The resulting book, *The Travels of Marco Polo*, published early in the fourteenth century, presented a most tantalizing account of Cathay, as China was known to the medieval world, a land of wise government and elaborate courtesy, teeming with exotic natural phenomena and bursting with treasures. His book enshrined and distilled the fabulous vision of the East held by generations of Europeans, and played a starring role in the creation of chinoiserie, a style whose very being depended on an imperfect and romantic understanding of China.

The *Travels*, Polo modestly suggested, comprised a description of the world, for he had travelled more extensively than any man since the Creation. His book certainly describes a surprisingly large part of it, from the polar sea to Zanzibar. Much of what he wrote was accurate, but some facts seemed so incredible that it was hard to distinguish them from fable. To the thirteenth-century Venetian, the men with tails or with dogs' faces that Marco Polo said he had been told about – he never actually claimed to have seen such things for himself – seemed no more outlandish than his description of a serpent ten paces long and able to swallow a man in one gulp (the crocodile). Little wonder that he was known to his contemporaries as *Il Milione*, a reference to the number of lies he told.

Following Marco Polo, other westerners travelled to China and they too reported on what they had seen. A Franciscan missionary, Friar Odoric, spent three years in Peking in the early fourteenth century and wrote an account of his travels on his return to Italy. Odoric, more observant of everyday matters than Marco Polo (who seemed to spend his time dashing about escorting princesses and attending hunting parties) bequeathed to us some of the most enduring images of Cathay: it is from him we learn that Chinese women bound their feet, that mandarins grew their fingernails to extravagant lengths, and that cormorants were trained to fish.

Then, in the middle of the fourteenth century, a medieval bestseller appeared: the *Travels* of Sir John Mandeville, originally published in French and subsequently translated into ten languages. This book played a leading role in consolidating the fabulous myth of Cathay, and it is entirely suitable that it should, for both travels and author were complete works of fiction. The author's extravagant tales were cobbled together from a whole variety of sources, and his claims of noble lineage mere invention. 'Sir John' had the luck of good timing to aid his success as a best-selling author, for the doors of the Far East were about to close again. The open-minded reign of Kublai Khan and his descendants was now at an end. From 1368 the xenophobia of the Ming dynasty, which succeeded it, ensured that no more foreigners entered the country. Astonishingly, Sir John's *Travels* became the authoritative account of the region for the next two hundred years.

The route Sir John Mandeville took to Cathay set the tone for the discoveries he would make there. Despite the calm statement in *The Merchant's Handbook* of 1348 that the road from the Black Sea to Cathay is 'perfectly safe, whether by day or night', Sir John found himself having to traverse an archipelago of islands inhabited by a bewildering variety of monsters: some with ears which hung down to their knees, some with lips so pendulous they could serve as sombreros, some with no heads at all. In the centre of the archipelago was the Orient, and

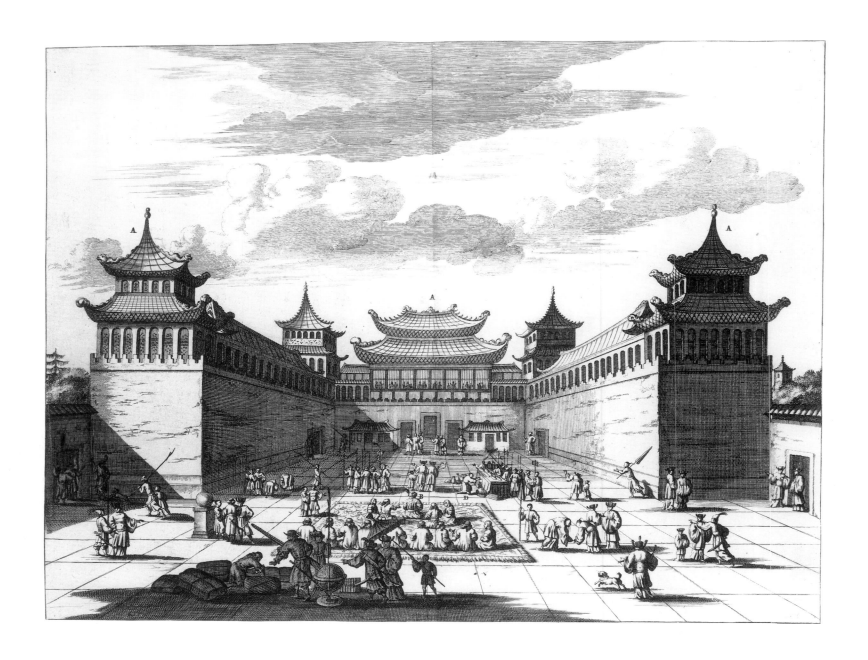

in the centre of that was Cathay, and at the heart of Cathay was its ruler, the Great Chan.

Sir John described the palace of the Great Chan in terms calculated to make the medieval reader's eyes bulge. Red panther skins lined the walls, pure gold formed its pillars (silver was only used for pavements and steps) and a ceiling covered with a golden vine bore clusters of grapes fashioned from precious stones. But this fictional account was remote from the truth. Marco Polo had devoted pages to describing – more or less accurately, as far as can be established – Kublai Khan's palaces and gardens, both at Kanbalu (Peking) and at Shang-tu (Xanadu). These rather prosaic descriptions were later to produce the magical images of Xanadu in Samuel Taylor Coleridge's poem *Kubla Khan*:

> *In Xanadu did Kubla Khan*
> *A stately pleasure-dome decree:*
> *Where Alph, the sacred river, ran*
> *Through caverns measureless to man*
> *Down to a sunless sea.*
> *So twice five miles of fertile ground*
> *With walls and towers were girdled round:*
> *And there were gardens bright with sinuous rills,*
> *Where blossomed many an incense-bearing tree,*
> *And here were forests ancient as the hills,*
> *Enfolding sunny spots of greenery.*

While Coleridge's poem explores the natural beauties and mysterious qualities of Cathay, Marco Polo devoted much of his book to stressing the prodigious riches of the East, a land of precious gems and spices and cloth of gold and gorgeous silks. There were sound economic reasons for his emphasis on the Orient's riches. The costs of trading were so high that only goods that weighed little and were worth

much made the enterprise worthwhile. And when the Mongol Empire disintegrated in 1368 and the fortunes of Islam revived, travel beyond the Christian world grew ever more perilous. Moreover, the resurgence of Chinese nationalism made foreigners unwelcome once again. There would be no further direct trade between Europe and the Indies until Vasco da Gama's voyage to Calicut in 1498 led to the opening of a sea-route to India.

Successive Chinese dynasties sanctioned a limited trade with the West while discouraging any other contact with the outside world. Now and then a few missionaries or the members of a tribute embassy were allowed to pass beyond Canton to the court at Peking. There their gifts would be received and they were granted the privilege of making a *kow-tow*, a custom that involved the individual so honoured by the Son of Heaven to kneel before him and, in a ritual of servility, knock his forehead on the ground nine times. Once safely restored to their native land these travellers, bowled over by what they had seen, would add their reports to those compiled centuries before by Marco Polo and Friar Odoric and invented by Sir John Mandeville. Thus Lorenzo de' Medici learned in 1515 that not only was Chinese silk superior, but that its makers were men to be reckoned with too: 'They are people of great skill, and of our quality, though of uglier aspect with little bits of eyes.' This view of the Chinese as being different, but in no way inferior, helped to sustain the myth of Cathay, and the vision of a culture that was profound as well as peculiar.

An Augustinian friar, Juan Gonzalez de Mendoza, a member of yet another unsuccessful embassy to the Court of Heaven (this time by Spain)

The Emperor Receiving the Dutch Embassy at his Palace in Pekin. **Seventeenth-century engraving.** *Throughout the seventeenth century the great mercantile powers of Europe made fruitless attempts to gain trading bases in China by despatching envoys to the Court of Heaven at Peking.*

fitted more of the jigsaw into place. His *Historia …
del gran Reyno de la China* was published in
Rome and, as seems *de rigueur* for books on China,
translated into seven European languages and
reprinted 46 times. Before being hustled out of the
country the friar was able to see some of the houses
of the provincial governors. Mendoza did not provide
the kind of technicolour extravaganzas of jewelled
interiors and staggering riches that had enlivened
the descriptions of Sir John Mandeville. Nevertheless
his account of the 'superbious and admirable'
accommodation of the Chinese he encountered must
have impressed any seventeenth-century man of
letters. Brushing the soot from his cuff, the reader
would have taken up his candle to read of houses
as large as an entire village in Europe, with walls as
'white as milk', paved floors and painted wooden
ceilings, three courts filled with flowers and herbs
and a pond stocked with fish, all standing in grounds
that extended to encompass woods and lakes, water
ponds and gardens.

　　The European who knew the most of China
at this time was Matteo Ricci, a Portuguese Jesuit
priest who lived in China for more than a quarter
of a century, dying in Peking in 1610. Ricci not
only learned the language and mastered the
elaborate rigmaroles of etiquette required by the
Chinese court, he studied Confucian philosophy –
no doubt to indulge in Jesuitical debate – and his
translations of the great philosopher's writings,
disseminated by the Society of Jesus, made
Confucianism known to the West. Yet even Ricci
was affected by the persisting image of a legendary
land. When he finally reached Peking in 1601, after
19 years in Macao and Nanking, he took a good

**The Sheng Xin Lou, or Tower
of Introspection, inside the
Great Mosque at Xi'an.
Founded in 742.** *So few
travellers to Cathay were
allowed to pass beyond Canton
that exaggerated tales of
strange buildings and peoples,
of awesome splendour and
wealth, fuelled the imagination
of the West.*

look round and politely enquired where he could find Cathay. It took some persuading to convince him that he was already there.

The Portuguese had established a foothold in Goa more than a century before, in 1510, and had encountered Chinese traders for the first time at Malacca. But Portuguese attempts to forge closer links with China had proved a dismal process. Their first embassy to Canton, in 1517, resulted only in the imprisonment of the unfortunate envoy, and this after a two-year wait for an audience. This established a pattern in China's relations with the West that was to become depressingly familiar. As the decades passed, however, the Portuguese were allowed to rent the town and harbour of Macao, situated on a desolate promontory in the estuary of Canton, and they started trading in earnest with China and Japan. Profits from the trade were enormous, and Lisbon rapidly became one of the greatest cities in Europe. No wonder that trade with the East became a matter of importance to the other European countries.

In England Queen Elizabeth I took the prudent course of licensing privateers to plunder the Spanish galleons and Portuguese carracks sailing back to Europe laden with treasure. In 1592 the *Madre de Dios* was captured off the Azores and taken to Dartmouth where its splendours were brought up and displayed. 'Upon good view,' wrote the geographer Richard Hakluyt,

> *it was found that the principal wares after the jewels (which were no doubt of great value though they never came to light) consisted of spices, drugges, silks, calicos, quilts, carpets, and colours &c. The spices were pepper, cloves, maces, nutmegs, cinamon, green ginger; the drugs were benjamin, frankincence, galingale, mirabolans, aloes, zocotrina, camphire; the silks damasks, taffetas, sarcenets, altobassos, that is, counterfeit cloth of gold, unwrought China silke, sleaved silke, white twisted silke, curled cypresse. The calicos were book-calicos, calico launes, broad white calicos, brown course calicos. There were also canopies and course diaper towels, quilts of course sarcenet and of calico, carpets like those from Turkey; whereunto are to be added the pearle, muske, civet and ambergriece. The rest of the wares were many in number but less in value; as elephant's teeth, porcellan vassels of China, coconuts, hides, ebenwood as black as jet, bedsteads of the same, cloth of the rinds of trees very strange for the matter, and artificiall in workmanship. All which piles of commodities being by men of approved judgement rated but in reasonable sort amounted to no less that 150,000 li. sterling which being divided among the adventurers (whereof her Majesty was the chiefe) was sufficient to yield contentment to all parties.*

Although perfectly in tune with the adventurous spirit of the age, piracy could not be considered a secure method of trade, however spectacular the booty. In 1600 Queen Elizabeth granted a charter giving a monopoly on trade with India and the Far East to a new joint-stock company, the East India Company. This move above all others served to establish England's influence in the development of chinoiserie. The East India trade fundamentally altered the drink, dress and artistic taste of the well-to-do classes in England and on the Continent. It

**Detail from a scroll painting
showing the Dutch Factory
on the Island of Deshima.
Nagasaki School, c.1700.** *The
Dutch East India Company,
established in 1602, scored a
great trading victory when it
was allowed a monopoly on
the establishment of trading
stations or 'factories' in Japan.*

permanently affected art and design, as European and English craftsmen were inspired to emulate the materials and patterns of the objects imported and to produce their own version of what they saw: in short, to create chinoiserie.

At first the East India Company established trading stations (or 'factories' as they were called) on land assigned to them by the native princes in Madras and Bombay. These traded with China in the only manner allowed, through the port of Canton. They built their own forts and establishments and manufactured their own armaments. Their ships, the great 'East Indiamen', were built and manned both for commerce and for war, since the Royal Navy could not protect them so far from home. Over the years the company prospered, making fortunes for its shareholders. By the 1680s it was paying a dividend of 20 per cent of profits and importing 14 per cent of the total value of all goods imported into the realm.

The other great seventeenth-century maritime power, the Dutch, was neck-and-neck with the English in the race to trade with the East. The Dutch fleet reached Canton in 1600. Two years later, the Dutch East India Company was established with bases in the Pescadores and later in Formosa. Not to be outflanked, the English East India Company extended its hold on the area by setting up a trading base in Siam in 1612. The Dutch traded with China, but their great coup was to establish trade with Japan. In the usual manner, the Dutch created a monopoly which made them almost entirely responsible for the Japanese lacquer and porcelain imported into Europe in the seventeenth and eighteenth centuries. France was the last great power to reach the East. The other European states kept her

ships out of Chinese waters for as long as they could; until 1678 the French were prevented from trading freely even in the Indies.

Following the collapse of the Ming dynasty in 1644 and the succession of the Manchu dynasty, the western powers made a fresh attempt to establish relations with China's new rulers that would allow them trading bases in China itself. The Dutch were first off the mark, and in 1656 despatched an embassy to Peking bearing gifts of toys, clocks, astronomical instruments and guns. The new Manchu emperor, Shun Chih, received them in much the same way as might his Ming predecessor, with exquisite politeness but utter firmness. His mandate to the Dutch embassy leaves his attitude in no doubt:

> *The distance that divides Holland from China is so great that regular intercourse between the two countries is hardly practicable. Indeed there is no record of any previous Dutch embassy. Aware of the long and arduous journey of the present Ambassadors, WE were happy to give them audience and receive their tribute-presents. In earnest of our good-will WE returned them gifts of suitable value. But when WE think of the danger of storm and shipwreck that besets the passage hither, WE are too solicitous of the welfare of the Dutch people to do more than permit them to send ships to China once in eight years, what time they may sell four cargoes and bring presents to OUR COURT.*

However disappointing the effect on trade, the entire evolution of chinoiserie benefited from the unsuccessful embassy. Johan Nieuhoff, steward to the ambassador, was a most observant man with an

Mandarins Having a Feast in a Boat. **Engraving from Johan Nieuhoff's** ***Travels*,** **1665.** *By providing the first images of China to be seen in the West, Nieuhoff's book profoundly influenced the West's view of China and consequently the evolution of chinoiserie.*

Interior of a warehouse for the East India market. *Travellers' tales of the prodigious riches of the East were made flesh by the inimitable lacquer and porcelain objects imported by the East India Companies to the avid collectors of Europe.*

additional talent: he could draw. Travelling along the great rivers from Canton to Peking, Nieuhoff had kept his eyes open and his pencil busy. He wrote down all his observations, from the importance of philosophy in Chinese culture to the 'cats with long hair' that the ladies of the court kept as pets – a somewhat undignified description of the Pekinese, that most unruffled of dogs. He drew the porcelain tower of Nanking which became the best-known Chinese building in Europe, and the imperial gardens at Peking, the prototype of innumerable chinoiserie garden designs in the eighteenth century. Descriptions had their place, but illustrations showed what the wonderland of Cathay – never before seen in the West – actually looked like. In 1665 Nieuhoff's account with more than a hundred engravings was published in Dutch. Very quickly it appeared in Latin, French and English; an edition of 1669 had the original plates copied by no less an artist than Wenceslaus Hollar. The entire publication was of vital importance to the European reconstruction of Cathay. The book, grandly titled *An Embassy from the East-India Company of the United Provinces to the Grand Tartar Cham Emperor of China*, but commonly known as the *Travels*, became the staple of the endlessly popular compilations of travels in China that were published in the seventeenth and eighteenth centuries. Over the centuries, designs derived from its engravings found their way into architecture and all the decorative arts from interiors to porcelain, profoundly affecting the evolution of chinoiserie.

If publications were a vital ingredient in the development of the style, the goods that were imported stimulated the development of chinoiserie even more directly. The English East India Company limited its own purchases to tea, silk (largely raw) and porcelain, in that order, but its policy was to allow its employees, from captain to crew, to trade privately. It was this private trading – in furnishing textiles, dress fabrics, wallpapers, ceramics, lacquer ware, silver and gold, ivory and fans – that brought Chinese objects to Britain. At first only a handful of objects found their way from the East to Europe, and these were so highly prized they seldom entered the open market. Even in the great houses furniture was scant, often clumsily made and heavily ornamented with bulbous legs and crude carving. No wonder that the arrival of one of their East Indiamen would bring the directors of the newly established East India Company hastening to the docks to grab what they could of the goods brought back. Even when trade increased, the small amount imported from the East made for high prices. As demand by far outstripped supply, European craftsmen were bound to attempt local imitations of Chinese wares.

The manufacture of silk, from a series of nineteenth-century engravings. *Clockwise from top left: Silk Farms at Hoo-Chen; Feeding Silkworms and Sorting the Cocoons; Destroying the Chrysalides and Reeling the Cocoons; Dyeing and Winding Silk. From the time of the Han dynasty (220 years BC), the silk of the mulberry silk moth of China, then unknown in the West, was carried on the Silk Route overland to Europe.*

Italian brocade in gold metallic thread. Fourteenth century. *By the fourteenth century chinoiseries had made a tentative appearance in Europe, as Italian silks incorporated Chinese motifs of swooping phoenixes, lion-like dogs and formalized flowers.*

Silk production had responded early to Eastern influence. The *pax Tartarica* established by Kublai Khan allowed bales of Yuan dynasty silk to be transported across Asia to the Middle East, and from there to Europe. These fabrics, bedecked with dragons, phoenixes and lions, were often used to adorn the Catholic clergy, and their designs and patterns were so well known that by the mid-fourteenth century the weavers of Lucca were freely imitating them.

The creation of lacquer in Europe was less straightforward. There were two problems, both major ones: the material and the ornament. A central difficulty was that the key ingredient for making true lacquer, the sap of the tree *Rhus verniciflux*, would dry out on the long journey west, and therefore could

not be imported. Local equivalents were inferior, lacking the lustrous quality that Nieuhoff so admired and which made the houses 'shine and glister like Looking-glasses'. And local craftsmen were evidently perplexed by the problem of ornament.

Small wonder that the first attempts to produce lacquer were not wildly successful. The earliest surviving examples – two boxes owned by the Saddler's Company, a ballot box dated 1609, and another containing roundels – have nothing markedly oriental about them. Both are oak, heavily covered with black varnish and ornamented, probably by the same hand, with gold and silver painted decoration. A cabinet of the same period in London's Victoria and Albert Museum does have some vaguely exotic aspects to the scenes depicted, but the chinoiserie style was in its infancy and the general effect is still uncertain.

France was as eager to acquire lacquer as England. Marie de Médicis, Queen until 1610 and thereafter Regent, not only placed a seller of Chinese wares conveniently close at hand in the gallery of the Louvre, but she also employed a French cabinet-maker to produce work in the *façon de la chine*. In Italy, too, craftsmen were able to produce some kind of lacquer imitation. In these early days, the only European countries that seemed immune to the challenge of producing lacquer were the two most directly associated with the Far Eastern trade: Spain and Portugal. Perhaps their carracks and galleons transported enough of the real thing to meet local demand.

Porcelain posed problems of imitation as daunting as any found with lacquer. They could make earthenware in the West, and decorate it finely, but they had no idea of how to make porcelain, which had been manufactured in China since the ninth century. As early as the Middle Ages small quantities of porcelain had made their way into Europe. In the fifteenth century it had been among the gifts given to the Doges of Venice by the Sultans of Egypt and had appeared in paintings of the period, where its rarity made it a fitting embellishment to scenes of the Holy Family or of pagan gods. Naturally all the crowned heads could boast of owning porcelain: Philip II of Spain had three thousand pieces, Henry VIII of England, one. Once the sea-route to the Indies was opened quite large quantities of porcelain began to enter Europe. The pieces were considered precious and given mounts of silver-gilt to protect them. The material itself was rumoured to have magical properties – it would repel poison, or resist fire – and how on earth was it made?

Marco Polo gave a somewhat garbled description of porcelain manufacture:

> They collect a certain kind of earth, as it were from a mine, and laying it in a great heap, suffer it to be exposed to the wind, the rain and the sun, for thirty or forty years, during which time it is never disturbed. By this it becomes refined and fit for being wrought into the vessels above mentioned. Such colours as may be thought proper are then laid on, and the ware is afterwards baked in ovens or furnaces. Those persons, therefore, who cause the earth to be dug, collect it for their children and grandchildren.

Others had different explanations: the time it was left undisturbed was a hundred years; the ingredients were eggshells, the shell of 'umbilical fish', bones and 'a certain juice which coalesces underground'.

Byzantine ivory casket. First half of the twelfth century. *(opposite) The phoenix, one of the four symbolic guardians of the Celestial Empire, rises for the first time in Europe.*

Detail from *The Adoration of the Magi*. Andrea Mantegna, c.1490. *The rarity of Chinese porcelain in Europe, coupled with wild stories of its manufacture and belief in its magical qualities, made it the obvious choice to contain the rare and precious gifts from the Magi.*

No one knew that the secret of true porcelain lies in a mix of felspar with clay and a kiln capable of firing at extremely high temperature. True porcelain would not be made in Europe until the middle of the eighteenth century.

The first attempt was made much earlier than that, however, in Florence in about 1575. The project was initiated by the Grand Duke Francesco I, the first in a long line of princely porcelain factory owners. The experiment produced a soft-paste porcelain made from a cocktail of ingredients that included sand, glass, powdered rock-crystal and two kinds of clay. Only a handful of pieces were made, presented by the Grand Duke to highly favoured grandees. They looked nothing like oriental porcelain, behaved badly in the kiln and so were rather misshapen, but they were all decorated in blue on a white ground, like the contemporary Ming porcelain, and the designs all derived from Chinese prototypes.

In the following centuries Europe was to become flooded with porcelain produced both in China and Japan, much of it manufactured specifically for export. By 1580 Lisbon's smartest shopping street, the Rua Nova dos Mercadores, had six shops selling porcelain. Some of Portugal's imports, no doubt intended to grace the tables of the Portuguese aristocracy, fell into the hands of privateers: a Portuguese carrack, the *Catharina*, captured by the Dutch in 1604, was carrying a cargo of 100,000 pieces of porcelain. The newly established Dutch East India Company soon gained a legitimate ascendancy in the porcelain trade. By 1638 it had shipped over three million pieces to Europe. These were mainly decorated with Chinese motifs in blue and white on a wide variety of European shapes.

This mingling of styles was to become typical of chinoiserie. Chintz – painted cotton imported into Europe from India in the sixteenth and seventeenth centuries – formed part of the growing vogue for Eastern fabrics. These were imitated both in England and in France, where they were described under the generic title *façon de la chine*, although the imports came from India as well as from China. In 1643 the English East India Company complained sharply to their factors at Surat for sending *pintadoes* (painted cloths) that were not to English taste, and set about organizing their textile trade to produce fabrics abroad specifically to be sold in England. Their complaints were quite particular:

> Those which hereafter you shall send we desire may be with more white ground, and the flowers and branch to be in colours in the middle of the quilt as the painter pleases, whereas now most of your quilts come with sad red grounds which are not so well accepted here, and therefore let them be equally sorted to please all buyers.

By 1662 the London directors, no longer content with generalized descriptions, were sending their own patterns for chintz out to India. As the fashion grew at home for hanging fabric as though it were a kind of wallpaper so the directors kept their factors abroad informed. As one director put it:

> Now of late, they are here in England come to a great practice of printing large branches for hangings in Rooms, and we believe that some of our Calicoes painted after that manner might vent well, and have therefore sent you some patterns, of which sort we would have you send us 2,000 pieces.

These were not the patterns seen on the English tapestries and embroideries of the period: rabbits and roses, or gentlemen in puffy trousers. They were essays in eastern design, or rather, English designs in the Chinese taste. It appears that as early as the mid-seventeenth century the idea of what eastern fabrics should look like was already some considerable distance away from the actuality. Confusions multiplied as the patterns sent out were themselves re-interpreted by the Indian craftsmen who did not copy them exactly. And a final twist was given to the tale when the chinoiserie design had grown so far away from its origins that the Chinese were able to import it from India and copy it without recognizing it as their own invention in the first place, like the now-famous Tree of Life design.

The case of the Tree of Life pattern was not unique. In the coming centuries, chinoiserie was to move further and further away from an exercise in reproduction to an original reworking of Chinese themes, from the *façon de la chine* which might have brought a supercilious smile to the lips of a Chinese connoisseur to those chinoiserie wares that he would be baffled to hear were intended to reflect something of the spirit of his land. For chinoiserie is western, it is a purely European vision of China; a fantasy based on a China of the imagination, the fabulous Cathay invented by the medieval world.

Ming dynasty blue-and-white porcelain ewer with English sixteenth-century silver-gilt mounts. *After the 1520s a great deal of Ming porcelain was brought to England where it was regarded as a magnificent luxury and often embellished with mounts of silver or gold.*

China comes to Europe

I'll have them fly to India for gold, Ransack the Ocean for Orient pearl.

Christopher Marlowe, *Dr Faustus*, 1604

Detail of japanned lacquer chest. English, *c.*1720. *Picked out in gold relief on a red ground, an elegantly-dressed, turbanned woman, inexplicably holding a fluttering pennant, surveys her face in a mirror held by a page boy.*

Tankard and two-handled porringer. English, *c.*1685. *The English use of chinoiserie decoration seems to have been light-hearted from the outset. To decorate silver with exotic easterners, birds and flowers was an entirely original concept. These are true chinoiseries for which there were no imported prototypes.*

A Paris chez I. Mariette rue S. Iacques aux colonnes d'Hercules avec privilège du Roi.

***Habit d'un Mandarin chinois.*
Design for a masquerade
costume, Jean Berain, *c.*1700.**
*From 1674 Berain was in
charge of providing the
costumes and settings for
royal festivities at the court
of Louis XIV.*

**Early European chinoiserie
design. Valentin Sezenius,
*c.*1620.** *(opposite) The design
was probably for enamelling.*

By the second half of the seventeenth century the *beau monde* of Europe was gripped by a craze for the Orient and all things Chinese. Impassioned collectors waited avidly for the galleons and carracks and the great East Indiamen to arrive bearing embroidered silk hangings, lacquer cabinets and screens, gold filigree, and blue-and-white porcelain vases. Chinese entertainments and masques were fashionable and pointed hats and mandarin moustaches a chic alternative to the costumes of Harlequin or Pierrot. Contemporary accounts describe the King of France himself appearing at a ball dressed in '*un habit, moitié à la persienne, moitié à la chinoise*', while Monsieur, his brother, always inclined to go the whole hog, fluttered through a series of costume changes at a carnival ball in 1685 to emerge finally, '*vêtu en Grand Seigneur chinois*'.

On a less exalted level, gentlemen tired after a day's hunt could while away their evenings leafing through one or other travel book on the splendours of the East, where the occasional accuracy and unbridled romance of the text combined to intrigue and amuse, and the engraved illustrations provided inspiration for those craftsmen whose task it was to transfer the images depicted on the page to the possessions of the gentry. The ladies of the household, newly clad in the soft fabrics and brilliant colours of the East, whose long hours were spent among the sewing silks and Venice gold of the embroiderer's craft, had their range of subjects enlarged from the 'sundry sorts of spots, as Flowers, Birds and Fishes' recommended in *Schole-house for the Needle* of 1624, to the landscapes, flowers and peaked pavilions of chinoiserie.

To the seventeenth-century eye 'the East' was an entity, a single source of bizarre customs and fabulous treasure. A general geographical confusion, an uncertainty regarding what was where, and where was what, persisted until the end of the century, and there was little attempt to distinguish imports from the East on stylistic grounds. Goods from China, Japan, Siam and India were assigned random attributions in a spirit of topographical indifference engendered by the belief that it was all so outlandish out there that little purpose would be served by precision. A late seventeenth-century operatic version of *A Midsummer Night's Dream*, called *The Fairy Queen*, was set in a Chinese garden, described as a place where 'The Architecture, the Trees, the Plants, the Fruit, the Birds, the Beasts [were] quite different from what we have in this part of the World'. When such a combination of vagueness and exoticism was called on to provide a repertoire of ornament one could expect some fairly rum results.

But imports from the East were not sucked into a stylistic vacuum. The Baroque was in full fig in Europe, and although it was a classically-derived style, its exuberant decoration, expansive forms and overall air of opulence and grandeur could comfortably accommodate those Chinese imports whose 'baroque' qualities of glitter, extravagance and luxury were valued. In fact Chinese potters and textile producers were perfectly content to produce wares intended solely for export to the West, decorated in a way that a western connoisseur would find acceptable, but which might well appear garish and overdone to an Easterner. When these objects arrived in Europe they were easily incorporated into the baroque decorative schemes then fashionable. So the fine clear colours and handsome shapes of the porcelain vases were displayed in a quite un-eastern fashion, towering and clustering on cabinets and chimney-pieces, or mounted in silver or ormolu. The glowing hues of the embroidery were hung on bedsteads which rose to the height of the ceiling and were capped with great plumes of feathers, while at Versailles, where Louis XIV was able to collect oriental works on a vast scale through the *Compagnie des Indes*, the glitter of lacquer, 'varnish more glossy and reflecting than polisht marble' was used to replace the silver furniture that had been melted down to finance the king's disastrous wars.

Under Louis XIV the French court at Versailles became the vortex of fashion, not just for France but for all Europe. There chinoiserie was given the royal imprimatur, and from there it spread as a court style to Germany and further north, to the Scandinavian countries and later to Russia. In Holland, where much fine chinoiserie was produced, the court was not fashion's arbiter; here the new taste for chinoiserie was not identified exclusively with the aristocracy but was generally popular. In England,

meanwhile, the turmoil of Civil War, Commonwealth and Restoration had dampened the power of the court to set a style.

The Restoration of 1666 brought Charles II and many of his courtiers back to England after decades dawdling round the courts of Europe. There they had acquired a taste for luxury, although many lacked the means to put it into great effect. In any event, opulence was viewed equivocally in a country with a strong puritan tradition. The diarist, John Evelyn, an ardent royalist, was shocked to see the silver furniture in the apartment of the Duchess of Portsmouth, the king's mistress, and his verdict on Charles II's entire reign – that it had ushered in a 'politer way of living which passed to luxury and intolerable expense' – was as prim as any puritan's.

Although England's taste was influenced by the Continent, it never followed that of Europe absolutely, and chinoiserie developed its own particular, English, quality: less reverential in its imitation and less high-flown in its application. In general the baroque style, which was closely identified with propagandizing Catholicism and the doctrine of Absolutism, could be expected to undergo a certain transformation in English hands.

The grandeur was certainly acceptable, but its underlying principles were discounted. No Versailles was built for the King of England, and much of the aristocracy, impoverished by the Civil War and its aftermath, patched and refurbished their dilapidated houses rather than rebuild them from scratch. But Chinese imports could provide interiors with some of the sheen and glitter known abroad, and lacquer – which had already established itself in the early part of the century – was soon back in high favour.

Design for a Chinese cabinet, c.1700. *This highly fashionable interior was designed by Daniel Marot, Jean Berain's pupil and chief designer to William and Mary.*

The Porcelain Pagoda, Nanking. Illustrated and described in Nieuhoff's *Travels*, 1665. *The most famous Chinese building in Europe, this nine-storey pagoda, constructed of glazed and painted tiles and crowned by a golden pineapple, was the prototype of innumerable chinoiserie designs.*

Ironically, it was the Glorious Revolution, which put in place a constitutional monarchy, that saw the building of great baroque palaces like Blenheim and Chatsworth and the setting of new standards of luxury and formality. Within these great houses the stiff-necked grandeur of the enfilade of gilded and painted rooms was eased with small dressing-rooms and closets, used for the expensive and fashionable pastime of taking tea: a ceremony which demanded the beguiling acquisition of Coromandel cabinets, high-backed japanned chairs and masses of blue-and-white porcelain ranged above the fireplace or glowing on the tops of the cabinets.

But the China-mania of the seventeenth century had its critics in France and in England. The 3rd Earl of Shaftesbury, the patron saint of Palladianism in England, declared Chinese taste effeminate and overly luscious, and feared – correctly as it turned out – that classical appreciation would become corrupted. French voices were raised in opposition too, although it should be noted that the sharpest attack was prudently penned a good distance from Versailles. Writing from Peking in the 1690s, Père Louis le Comte roundly condemned Chinese architecture. He found 'the apartments ill-contrived, the ornaments irregular', and a general lack of the great organizing principle of classicism: uniformity. He concluded: 'In a word, there is, as it were, deformity in the whole, which renders [Chinese architecture] very unpleasing to foreigners, and must needs offend anyone that has the least notion of true architecture.' Le Comte's strictures did affect the course of orientalism in architecture in France, but by the time he wrote these words the brief

The Trianon de Porcelaine, Versailles. Engraving *c*.1675. *Designed by Louis Le Vau and undoubtedly inspired by the Porcelain Pagoda at Nanking, this was the first of the exquisite, ephemeral garden buildings that were to arise in the parklands of Europe.*

existence of the first chinoiserie building in Europe, the Trianon de Porcelaine at Versailles, had already come to an end.

Inspired by the engraving of the Porcelain Pagoda at Nanking that had appeared in Johan Nieuhoff's publication of his *Travels*, and built very quickly in the park of Versailles in the winter of 1670-71 only a few years after the French edition of the *Travels* had appeared, the Trianon de Porcelaine was conceived as an architectural trinket for the king's current mistress, Madame de Montespan. It was designed by Louis Le Vau, the leading baroque architect in France and the creator of the Louis XIV style at Versailles. Nieuhoff would no doubt have been surprised to be told that Le Vau's pavilion and the Nanking pagoda he had seen were brothers under the skin. According to Nieuhoff the latter stood on an octagonal base and rose nine storeys, each one

diminishing slightly and each one hung with golden bells. Its top was crowned with a golden pineapple and the entire exterior was covered by glazed and painted porcelain tiles. The Trianon de Porcelaine comprised three separate single-story pavilions and a pair of lodges, all looking perfectly at home in the formal gardens that surrounded the courtyard in which they stood. They were built in an unmistakably baroque and European manner with pediments, giant pilasters and double sloping mansard roofs. What then distinguished them from any other building, and made them so deliciously Chinese? The answer is their ornament. The Trianon de Porcelaine's great novelty was that its balustrades were loaded with Chinese vases, its roofs covered with blue-and-white faience tiles and its somewhat chilly interiors decorated with blue-and-white chinoiseries and filled with furniture 'in the Chinese manner'.

The whole thing was described in a suitably reverential manner by Jean-François Félibien in his *Description sommaire du château de Versailles* written in 1674. According to him the Trianon was '*un petit palais d'une construction extraordinaire*' and its interiors '*travaillé a la manière des ouvrages qui viennent de la Chine*'. However the painting which decorated the faience roof tiles was completely classical and of western subjects: hunting putti, and a variety of naturalistically painted birds.

Peering at the engraving that is the sole survivor of Louis XIV's '*petit palais*', one would struggle to see it as Chinese. This is a chinoiserie of the mind. As with all products of the Louis XIV style the symbolic content is pre-eminent. One of the engravings in Nieuhoff's *Travels* was of the Emperor of China with the Nanking pagoda in the background, and the role of Son of Heaven was considered a fitting one for the *Roi Soleil* to adopt in his more light-hearted moments. Chinese art was seen as the product of a great empire, not simply as a decorative addition to the magnificent and fanciful sets constructed at Versailles to display the King of France.

Sound practical considerations rather than symbolic ones led to the demolition of the Trianon only 17 years after its construction. Change and decay (both spiritual and structural) led to its demise. Madame de Montespan had been superseded in the king's favours by the altogether more pious Madame de Maintenon, and it was likely that the Chambre des Amours of the pavilion with its decoration wholly *à la chinoise* seemed no longer appropriate. In addition, the faience roof-tiles were porous and proved to be quite unable to stand exposure to frost and cold. The whole edifice must have leaked like

a sieve and required constant, expensive maintenance and repair throughout its short life.

The gulf separating the Trianon's description as Chinese and its baroque reality might well explain the fact that although the king and his court collected chinoiserie passionately and the inventories of the period abound in references to textiles and furniture *à la chinoise* and *façon de la chine*, hardly a single example of these 'chinoiseries' appears to have survived. Surely revolution, accident and fashion's dictates could not account entirely for the complete eclipse of all these objects? Perhaps, as with the Trianon de Porcelaine, chinoiserie decoration was so restrained as to be unrecognized by all but the most acute of eyes. It may well be that the bizarre qualities of chinoiserie were repressed by the girdle of classicism imposed by the Louis XIV style.

A lone example of contemporary lacquer work survives. This is all that remains of an extremely popular fashion, used not just for furniture but to panel entire rooms. In the Musée Carnavalet in Paris is the black lacquer writing bureau of that redoubtable correspondent, Madame de Sevigné. Made and decorated in China in about 1680, the decoration is much more restrained and less extraordinary than the lacquer work that was imported into England. This tempering of excess was an integral part of *le bon goût*, and lacquer decoration may have been even further simplified by those Parisian *ébenistes* making furniture decorated with chinoiseries.

In 1684 the French court was able to enjoy the exotic appearance of an embassy from the Court of Siam, which arrived bearing gifts from their king. Their embassy to France did not result from a

AMBASSADEURS DE SIAM.

spontaneous desire to show Louis XIV their high regard. They were part of an elaborate ploy organized by a Greek adventurer, Constant Phaulkon – the real power in the Siam of the 1680s – who was seeking French support to help bolster his shaky position. Two years later another, grander, Siamese embassy was treated to a formal reception by Louis XIV in the newly decorated Galerie des Glaces at Versailles, where myriad candles illumined the gold and marble that outshone even the opulence of the ambassadors' gifts. There were cups and ewers of Japanese gold and lacquer, crates of K'ang Hsi porcelain and bales of embroidered silks which must have made the court's China connoisseurs quite faint with envy.

The Siamese Embassy. French seventeenth-century engraving. *In 1686 the singular appearance of an embassy from the Court of Siam to Louis XIV stimulated a popular craze in France for all things eastern.*

The two successive embassies proved so stimulating to the oriental cult that not even the news of the massacre in 1687 of all the Europeans in Bangkok dampened French enthusiasm for the East. Indeed this enthusiasm increased steadily, reaching a high point in 1700 when a Chinese fête was held at Versailles to proclaim the arrival of the Chinese century.

The Jesuits, who jealously preserved their special relationship with China, were at pains to point out that the gifts from the Siam embassy originated largely from China, and were not Siamese at all. The general population, however, was not concerned with such niceties. A new cloth called *siamoise* was produced in imitation of the ambassadors' robes. Almanacs were decorated with prints of their reception at Versailles, imaginative prints of the King and Queen of Siam astride elephants were widely circulated, and bibulous rural entertainments celebrated the embassy with masques and serenades.

As a counter-attraction to these remote and insignificant Siamese who were stealing the limelight, the Society of Jesus produced a Latin-speaking Chinese convert to Catholicism, a boy they called Mikelh Xin, for the king's inspection. Suitably attired in green satin and a dragon-embroidered cape, this prize was presented to the king who contemplated him as the boy ate with chopsticks and said his prayers in Chinese. Mikelh Xin went on to beguile the English royal family too, and Sir Godfrey Kneller painted his portrait clutching a crucifix and looking suitably pious.

The observation of the Duchesse d'Orléans that 'Germany not only imitates France but always does double what is done here', must be borne in mind when comparing the unparalleled enthusiasm for chinoiserie encountered north of the Rhine with the restrained Frenchification of the style that was the rule in Paris. Yet chinoiserie, destined to be of such importance in Germany's artistic development, arrived in the country as part of the fashionable baggage imported from France. France was already well established as the taste-setter in Europe when Germany was still making a slow recovery from the ravages of the Thirty Years War, which had finally ended in 1648. Although old-fashioned and boorish by French standards, many of the German princes had emerged from the war with increased power. As they picked themselves up, dusted themselves down and started to reassemble their shattered principalities, there was one – and only one – shining example to follow: France.

Augustus the Strong, King of Poland and Elector of Saxony, the leader of the Chinese cult in Germany, was to earn immortality in the history of taste by founding the Meissen porcelain factory. As shall be seen, he had a passion for porcelain and in the first decades of the eighteenth century created a Japanese palace to house his collection. His court architect, Matthaeus Poppelmann, converted a previous 'Dutch Palace' into a *Japanisches Palais* by the simple expedient of substituting baroque chinoiserie caryatids for the pilasters in the main courtyard and tinkering with the roofline. An earlier attempt at an oriental style for this Saxon Sinophile was the Indianisches Lustschloss at Pillnitz, a building that appears to the untutored eye more German than Indian, and more baroque than Chinese. However the double concave roofs and overhanging eaves of

Faience vase decorated with Chinese figures. Frankfurt c.1680. *While the secret of porcelain production remained unknown in Europe, faience* *production imitated Chinese shapes and was fashionably decorated in blue and white with a variety of chinoiserie subjects.*

the Lustschloss signify the Orient, a point reinforced by the Chinese scenes painted on the undersides of the eaves. It was easier to provide a Chinese interior than to design a building in the style, and many a *Chinesisches Zimmer* found in *schloss* and garden pavilion provides tantalizing glimpses of the charm their French originals must have possessed.

The first German attempts at chinoiserie interiors are only sporadically Chinese, and the overall effect is undoubtedly baroque, but this was common to the chinoiseries of this period, whether German, French or English. So the Chinese room of the Elector Franz von Schönborn, an early patron of chinoiserie, which was installed in his Neue Residenz in Bamberg in 1705, has its lacquered Chinese panels inserted into heavy baroque decoration, where they co-exist somewhat uneasily with the carved swags of fruit and an overbearing painted and stuccoed ceiling.

Chinoiserie interiors were considered sublimely appropriate to house and display the collections of oriental porcelain that every right-minded German princeling was amassing. A few such *porzellan zimmers* survived in Germany until the bombing of the Second World War. The earliest and most remarkable, at Schloss Charlottenburg outside Berlin, has been restored and the original K'ang Hsi porcelain it housed, all destroyed in 1943 when the palace was badly damaged, replaced. The room dates from about 1710 and bears the usual confusion of chinoiserie scenes on the dado and pagan gods lolling about on the ceiling. But the principal effect is created by the porcelain. Poised on a multitude of little brackets it covers the entire wall space from the dado, and rises in five tiers above the doors and

alcoves to meet the elaborately coved and painted ceiling. In what little space remains, mirror, gilding and carved Chinese figures proffering porcelain on oustretched palms allay any anxiety that the well of decoration may have run dry.

More obviously 'Chinese' was the small Pagodenburg – the name says it all – built between 1716 and 1719 for the Francophile Elector of Bavaria, Max Emmanuel. After an imprudent alliance with France had resulted in the defeat of the Bavarian army at Blenheim, Max Emmanuel passed an agreeable exile at Versailles. On his return to Germany in 1715 he built the Pagodenburg, the first in a collection of the most charming garden pavilions ever built and which stand in the park of his summer palace at Nymphenburg. In this small octagonal building blue-and-white Delft tiles are used to decorate the interior, and two rooms are furnished *à la façon de la chine*: one a small cabinet hung with Chinese paper, the other an octagonal drawing-room lacquered locally in black and red.

The earliest surviving example of a *lackcabinett* is found in Scandinavia, where German princes ruled in Sweden and in Denmark, united then with Norway. Their passion for China travelled with them, and sometime in the 1660s a room in the Rosenborg Castle in Copenhagen was decorated in green lacquer set in imitation tortoiseshell frames. The gold decoration picked out on the lacquer came from the most up-to-date source on Cathay, Nieuhoff's *Travels*. A more accomplished example is a room in Schloss Württemburg of about 1720. Tall oblong chinoiserie panels, exquisitely painted by Johan Jakob Saenger, rise above a shallow dado to the height of the ceiling, each panel separated by a fillet

bearing scrolled consol supports for porcelain vases while gilded late-baroque carvings enclose the panels and provide further opportunities for the display of porcelain trifles.

In England, grand houses like Burghley, Chatsworth and Hampton Court all had lacquer rooms before the century was out. And not only grand houses. In 1689 John Evelyn described the house of his neighbour, a certain Mr Bohun, as 'a cabinet of elegancies, especially Indian; in the hall are contrivances of japan screens, instead of wainscot … the landscape of the screens depicts the manner of living and country of the Chinese'.

In general, seventeenth-century interiors throughout Europe, even grand ones, were sparsely furnished. Furniture needed to make an impact, and lacquer – whether imported from the East, or 'japanned' locally – was highly favoured. Two of the finest japanners of the century worked for German masters, producing furniture and bibelots of outstandingly high quality. Gerard Dagly was employed as *Kammerkünstler* by the Elector of Brandenburg in 1687, and had his appointment confirmed by Frederick I of Prussia when he succeeded to the title a year later. His pupil, Maximilian Schnell,

Lacquer Room at Rosenborg Castle, Copenhagen, c.1660. *The rage for lacquer in seventeenth-century Europe extended to panelling entire rooms, either with true lacquer or with a local 'japanned' equivalent, as here. The green panels are bordered by imitation tortoiseshell and the scenes picked out in gold are taken from Nieuhoff's* Travels.

left Berlin in 1709 to return to his native city, Dresden, where his talents were put to ample use by Augustus the Strong.

Dagly was responsible for the lacquer room in Berlin, which did not survive the Second World War, and for cabinets, tables, *gueridons* and cases for keyboard instruments. His unique contribution was to vary the ground colour of his japanned pieces. Although he used black and gold, he would decorate on white in brilliant colours so that his furniture looked as though it were a huge piece of porcelain. One piece was actually decorated in blue on white. When Frederick I died in 1713, Dagly retired, but his brother, who had worked with him, moved to Paris where in a reversal of the usual order he breathed new life into the French *manufacture des ouvrages de la chine* which Marie de Médicis had installed in the Louvre a century before.

Dagly's birthplace, Spa – a famous resort in the Low Countries – was a magnet for rich hypochondriacs from all over Europe. Between taking the waters and frequenting the gaming tables they also found time to shop, especially for *bois de Spa* products, then the most famous japanned ware in Europe. A wide range of *bois de Spa* objects were thus dispersed over the Continent, ranging in size from large cupboards to snuffboxes, and usually decorated with gilt chinoiseries on a black background.

Dutch excellence in lacquer production arose as a direct consequence of their trade with the Orient. As principal importers of lacquer from Japan – generally reckoned to be of far higher quality than the Chinese lacquer – they were familiar with the best the East could produce. But however much was imported, the demand for it continued to grow, and from early in the seventeenth century Dutch 'japanners' found a ready market for their work. Dutch japanning was so skilled that late seventeenth-century and early eighteenth-century Dutch japan has often proved difficult to distinguish from Japanese export lacquer. The resemblance is close enough to suggest that the Dutch brought over Japanese lacquer workers to teach the local craftsmen. Certainly very few surviving specimens can be said with all confidence to be of Dutch origin.

Unlike the chinoiseries produced by the French, which were so discreet as to pass unobserved, or by the Dutch, which were of such high quality that they were easily mistaken for the real thing, English japanned work of the seventeenth century is not hard to recognize. The ground, now tarnished and dull, was even then neither as smooth nor as lustrous as in its eastern progenitor, and the bold pictorial decoration quite without an oriental approach to composition. The experimental character of early japanning in England shows in the decoration, which has panache but lacks the refinement of oriental lacquer.

According to the diarist John Evelyn, Charles II's bride, Catherine of Braganza, brought from Portugal as her dowry 'such Indian cabinets as had never before been seen here'. Imported lacquer was often confusingly called Indian work. Adding to the confusion the local lacquering process was known as japanning and, in typical fashion, the term was applied quite generally to all lacquer products, so that the 'japann cabinets' offered for sale in late seventeenth-century England could be either western or oriental. 'Indian' shops offered oriental lacquer for sale in London, available because the East India Company was shipping in large quantities the lacquer that formed the model for English japanners.

The screens, boards and panels that formed the bulk of the lacquer imports were of two kinds. One with incised decoration in different colours, known as Coromandel work, then referred to as Bantam

Harpsichord, *c*.1710. Schloss Charlottenburg, Berlin. *Elegant Orientals strolling in a landscape of spindly trees and exotic flowers ornament this keyboard instrument, probably decorated by the great German lacquermaster Gerard Dagly.*

Cabinet on a stand, *c*.1700. *A key piece of furniture of the period, this example – attributed to Gerard Dagly – is lacquered in gilt.*

The Lacquer Cabinet, Drayton House, *c*.1700. *(above)*
A Coromandel lacquer screen was cut up to provide the brilliantly coloured panelling of the Lacquer Cabinet at Drayton House, Northamptonshire.

Interior of a private house, late seventeenth century.
(left) The panelled walls of this small English room are filled with chinoiseries in painted or japanned leather.

Black lacquer cabinet on a stand. English, *c*.1695.
(opposite top) This is a combination piece, with Japanese lacquer drawer fronts and English 'japanned' decoration on the sides, the whole raised on an English stand.

Tripod table, English or Dutch, *c*.1700. *(opposite bottom) The oval-shaped top is decorated in the manner of Soho tapestries of the period, with colourful vignettes of chinoiserie figures disporting themselves.*

work (after the trading port on the west coast of Java) was more durable and very beautiful; the other had raised and gilt decoration on a monochrome ground, almost always black. Mirror frames, table-tops, stands and cabinet doors were constructed by cutting up the screens and panels; these strips were often used without regard to the sense of the scenes depicted, so horsemen would ride upside-down and sea creatures would be found in woods, attesting no doubt to the prevailing notion of Cathay as a topsy-turvy land.

Designs for lacquer furniture were sent out to the East to be manufactured, from where they were imported in some quantity. However, although the lacquer was admired, the furniture was criticized as being badly made and sometimes furniture fashioned by English joiners was sent out to the East for lacquering. Wherever the cabinets came from, florid baroque stands of carved and gilded wood heavy with putti and swags were constructed to display them. With such a demand to satisfy, English makers started to produce for themselves a creditable alternative to the 'Indian' process.

The English japanner had to use quite different materials from the lacquer worker in the East. In 1688 the method was minutely described in a *Treatise of Japanning and Varnishing* by John Stalker and George Parker, who probably gleaned their information from Dutch craftsmen. Size and whitening were applied in successive layers to a soft-wood carcass, usually deal. The resulting surface, perhaps as thick as a quarter-inch, was blackened or coloured, varnished and polished: the authors recommended that the process should continue until the surface 'glissen and reflects your face like a mirror'. The designs were then either

traced onto the surface in tinted gold or vermilion size, and coloured. The raised parts – such as trees, buildings, rocks and so forth – were made by dropping a paste of whitening mixed with gum arabic and sawdust onto the prepared ground. The descriptions were easily understood, the instruments needed clearly stated, and though it may sound complicated, it was an easy enough process for it to become a fashionable pastime which the ladies of the period took to with relish, japanning everything they could lay their hands on, even walnut furniture. The craze was so widespread that even children tried their hand at it. 'I find you have a desire to learn to japan, as you call it, and I approve', wrote Sir Ralph Verney to his ten-year-old daughter, Mary, in 1683.

Stalker and Parker considerately produced over a hundred engravings of designs for the amateur japanner to copy. Their *Patterns for Japan-work in imitation of the Indians for Tables, Stands, Frames, Cabinets etc.* were, the authors proclaimed, exact imitations of the oriental, but better: 'The artist has endeavoured to help the designs a little where they were lame and defective.'

In fact the designs are a haphazard medley of flocks of exotic birds, curving arrangements of large-petalled flowers growing out of rocks shaped like ostrich eggs, patterned pavilions with upswept roofs from which flutter strange wind-vanes and pennants. They often include a favourite motif of early English japanned work, a tree with buildings set in a strange, rocky landscape: in essence, the landscape of Cathay. In a few of his engravings the artist attempted a composition with figures. In one a curious trio are assembled: a seated, barefoot, hatted man is pouring water from a long-necked spouted flask onto the

head of a kneeling figure, while the third, seemingly clad in a dressing-gown and tea-cosy and bearing a sacred flame, looks on with approbation. The whole is labelled 'A Pagod Worhipp in ye Indies'.

In 1660 Thomas Allgood of Pontypool discovered a way of japanning on metal, which became known as Pontypool japan. A by-product of coal, capable of application under heat to the surface of metal, was used to varnish local wares made of thin rolled iron plate. The process was expensive – the numerous coats of varnish required firing at high temperature – but the results were lustrous and durable, which was not the case with japanning on wood. The first Pontypool japanning factory turned out all sorts of decorative objects, from trays to candlesticks, whose coloured grounds – tortoiseshell, brown or black – bore gilded decorations, always of

Two engravings from Stalker and Parker's *Treatise of Japanning and Varnishing* of 1688. *(opposite) These exuberant fantasies were designs intended for amateur japanners, the fashionable ladies of Stuart England.*

Two examples of Stuart lacquer work. *A rare Queen Anne cream lacquer cabinet and a seventeenth-century lacquer box from Ham House, Surrey. The delightful possibilities of lacquering small boxes, cases and containers stimulated the transformation of Chinese and Japanese pictorial elements into true chinoiserie.*

chinoiserie subjects. Its manufacture spread to
Birmingham and London, and continued into the
nineteenth century. In 1729 George II's cabinet
makers, the firm of Gumley and Turing, rendered
the king an account for 'japanning four fine large tin
receivers in Red with neat drawings in silver and
fixing them up with silver chains to the large double-
branched plate sconces'. One longs to know what the
neat drawings in silver depicted. Perhaps the royal
candles illumined dancing figures in Chinese robes
and Cathay and Pontypool were united in these
simple objects.

Dutch pre-eminence in japanned ware was also
strongly felt in the remarkable growth of the pottery
universally known as Delft, although it was also made
elsewhere. The town of Delft was once renowned for
its beer, but when the brewing industry collapsed in
1615 the disused breweries became the premises for
the new pottery factories, many of whom retained the
old brewery names – the Moor's Head, the Greek A,
and others. These potteries began by producing tin-
glazed earthenware that imitated the decoration on
the porcelain which was being imported in such large
quantities by the newly-formed Dutch East India
Company. Soon however they moved on, striving to
emulate the still mysterious body of the porcelain
itself. Cobalt was imported from Saxony and
specially fine clay from Tournai. The potting was
as thin as they could make it and given a final lead
glaze, *kwaart*, to reproduce the hard glitter of
true porcelain.

Delft potters created baroque forms – pagoda-
shaped towering tulip stands, lobed dishes and sets
of vases – and their sense of fantasy, freed from any
oriental conventions, produced not only quite new

shapes, but new decoration. They moved away from copying W'an-Li and K'ang Hsi designs to pure chinoiserie scenes, often taken from engravers' manuals or the illustrations in travel books such as Nieuhoff's *Embassy to the Great Cham* of 1665. All the same, while Indian, Japanese and Chinese inspirations may have combined to produce the monsters, weird birds, pot-bellied gods and luxuriant trees and flowers that embellish the Delft products of the late seventeenth century, their vitality and flourish remains essentially baroque.

Although porcelain was not produced in France until the eighteenth century, the production of faience (as tin-glazed earthenware was known there) was strongly encouraged by the king's Finance Minister, Colbert, who hoped it would prove an acceptable, cheap and home-made alternative to the porcelain of the East. As the king's vainglorious wars brought the country closer and closer to ruin and the chambers at Versailles were stripped of their silver furniture and plate, the entire aristocracy was prohibited from using silver at the table. Faience, particularly the Rouen wares, had to take its place.

Rouen was already known for its production of polychrome dishes decorated with chinoiserie subjects, but their later decoration, intended for the smart tables of the aristocracy, became extremely baroque, with forms derived from silverware designs, 'sunbursts', and borders of *lambrequin*, a kind of pointed scallop, very typical of the Louis XIV style. At Nevers, the faience factory was better able to resist the pervasive pressure of the Baroque. As far back as 1644 potters at Nevers were copying the shape, not simply the ornament, of Chinese vases, which they applied to both baroque and Chinese pieces, albeit

with an air of French orderliness completely lacking in the oriental. Blue-and-white production – which came about as a result of the Ming dynasty porcelain being imported into Europe – became increasingly popular as the century progressed, and in the 1670s the Nevers factory produced a variant, *bleu persan*, which reversed the colour scheme so that the ground is a deep blue and the decoration applied on it is white.

All seventeenth-century English pottery is firmly baroque in shape, and much of it is blue and white. English Delftware was manufactured in the 1680s at Lambeth and at Bristol, while at Fulham an ecclesiastical lawyer, John Dwight, was granted a patent in 1672 for the manufacture of 'transparent earthenware commonly known by the name of Porcelaine or China and Persian ware'. Despite the optimism engendered by the granting of the patent, he was no more successful at discovering the formula for porcelain than the other hopefuls before him. He had more success with his patent to produce

Decorative wall panel. Dutch Delftware, early eighteenth century. *(opposite)* **Faience bottle. Nevers, early seventeenth century.** *(right) The chinoiseries of European baroque faience are distinguished by a vitality and sense of fantasy freed from too close an adherence to any oriental conventions.*

A collection of English Delftware. *One hundred and thirty years divide the plate (top left) of 1630 from the teapot (bottom right) of 1760, but a typically English combination of robust design and whimsical subject matter is common to all these charming objects. Blue-and-white designs, popular in the seventeenth century, are seen in the Southwark plate and on the posset pot (top) whose extravagant shape is typically baroque. The plate's design, of a bird perched on a rock surrounded by highly stylized flowers, is inspired by the popular W'an-Li porcelain imported from China. The decoration of the later Delftware is a partial response to the eighteenth-century vogue for polychrome chinoiserie decoration, and for figure subjects more like the* famille verte *K'ang Hsi porcelain produced for export.*

English Delft tiles, eighteenth century. *Manufactured in Liverpool, 1760-80 (opposite top), and probably Bristol, 1725-50 (opposite bottom). London, Bristol and Liverpool, the three main centres producing English Delftware, closely followed Dutch styles.*

'the Misterie of the stoneware vulgarly called Cologne ware', manufacturing a red stoneware very like the Chinese Yi Hsing. Similar wares – tea pots and thin beakers – were made in Staffordshire by David and John Elers, who had previously worked at Fulham. These tiny Staffordshire teapots mimic the shape of their oriental prototypes and are similarly decorated in relief with sprays of flowers or chinoiserie birds.

Silver returned to popularity after the Restoration as noble households replaced the plate which had been sacrificed to finance the Civil War. At first, silver versions of a *garniture* of porcelain jars – display pieces of very thin metal which took their shape from the Chinese ginger-jar – were embossed with classical motifs in a typically baroque manner. Some time around 1670, however, chinoiserie motifs

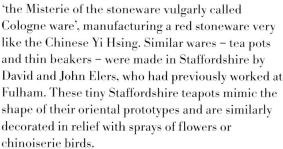

began to appear on the silver. They were to remain in vogue for about 15 years, reaching their height of popularity around 1683. In an aspect of the taste unknown in the rest of Europe, the baroque forms of porringers and tankards, pincushions and mirrors, caskets, brushes, trays and candlesticks were ornamented with flat-chased engraving of warriors on horseback, long-legged birds flying above rocky landscapes and thoughtful Orientals walking in groves of strange plants. It is believed that one workshop was responsible for the style, and it is uncertain where the designs originated. Perhaps the silversmith was inspired by the Chinese porcelain vases sent to him for silver mounts, perhaps by the lacquer cabinets of the period. Whatever the source we can be reasonably sure that the style was not directly inspired by oriental silver; apart from filigree, silver and gold were simply not imported from the East at the time.

Another possible explanation for the singular introduction of Chinese birds and the world of the Great Cham onto the silvered landscapes of Stuart plate may be in the gifts that Charles II received from the Sultan of Bantam. The king received an embassy from the Sultanate, a powerful Moslem state on the coast of Java, where the English East India Company had established a factory in 1603 and where it remained until driven out by the Dutch in 1682. He was delighted with the gifts brought by the ambassador which included a number of Bantam birds. King Charles kept the Bantams, and other tropical birds too, some of them in his dining-room. Perhaps it was this exotic aviary that was responsible for one of the most charming inventions of the chinoiserie style seen in the seventeenth century.

The domestic crafts of embroidery and needlepoint had rather more success at capturing the essential spirit of chinoiserie than appears to have been the case with the grander decorative arts. Embroidered panels that have survived show a series of discreet scenes where little figures, singly or in groups, are discovered being fanned while seated under baldaquins, crossing rickety bridges, or sitting at low tables drinking tea. These are the inhabitants of the rococo world that was to replace the mono-maniacal visions of Louis XIV, but their poses are stiffer and their preoccupations lack the high fantasy attained by their eighteenth-century descendants.

English needleworkers had succumbed to the Orient with the same passion as the amateur japanners. From the middle of the century imitative designs in the Chinese manner or 'after the Indian

Chinoiserie punchbowl or monteith by George Garthorne, 1688. *As an independent style, true chinoiserie did not imitate an eastern prototype. Punch is no Chinese drink, nor could these strutting warriors be seen as a serious attempt at verisimilitude.*

Detail of embroidered bedspread. Signed and dated Mary Thurston 1694. *The exquisitely coloured silks used in this delicate pattern show Stuart chinoiserie embroidery at its most enchanting.*

Silk petit-point and cross-stitch chair back. Early eighteenth century. *Now set in a giltwood firescreen surround, this unusual piece of embroidery is worked with a chinoiserie design of blue-and-white porcelain.*

Needlework hangings, Castle Ashby, Northamptonshire. Installed in 1772. *(opposite) Tapestry rooms were highly fashionable in Stuart households. These chinoiserie landscape needlework panels, the work of the aunts of the 8th Earl of Northampton, are set into tall panels typical of the Stuart interior.*

fashion' made their appearance on the counterpanes and curtains of the Stuart household. Expensive finery in the delicate manner of oriental silk meant patient hours dedicated to chain-stitch, satin-stitch and French or Peking knots. Prunus, peony, lotus flower and chrysanthemum, worked on white silk or satin, thus blossomed in a domestic chinoiserie of ravishing colour and charm. Jacobean embroiderers took the Indian Tree of Life pattern – where a single asymmetrical tree rises from hummocky ground and twists its way up the fabric – and made it their own, working the design in crewel wools in strong blues, greens and browns in imitation of the printed cotton brought from Masulipatnam by the East India Company.

The tall panels that lined the rooms of the Stuart period provided a challenge to the industrious needlewoman. At Wallington Hall, Northumberland, the Needlework Room displays the quality of work that the young wife of a rich and sociable land owner could produce. In 1716 Sir Walter Calverley confided to his diary: 'My wife finished the sewed work in the drawing room, it having been three and a half years in the doing. The greatest part has been done with her own hands. It consists of ten panels.' If this is the case, and not just a husband's proud boast, Lady Julia must have been a demon with the needle: each panel of floral canvas work is just under a yard wide and nine and a half feet long. The design is strong evidence that the Tree of Life pattern was still fashionable at this time; all the panels are filled with richly exotic blooms, and owe much to the painted Indian palampores.

Palampores were large painted calicos, and had been popular for decades. As early as 1663 Samuel

Pepys noted that he had bought his wife a 'chint, that is, a painted East India callico for to line her new study' and they became so enormously popular that English textile manufacturers brought pressure to bear on parliament to have their import banned. In 1700 parliament obliged, banning not only the importation, but even the wearing of Indian calicos and chintz, a move received with horror by the fashionable world whose thirst for these fabrics had now to be slaked by smuggling.

The influx of light printed fabrics from India revolutionized late seventeenth-century dress design, making the wearing of stiff embroidered brocades quite unfashionable. So successful were the imports of *toiles des Indes* to France that a measure of tariff protection was in place by 1684. The weavers of Europe responded to the threat posed by the importation of oriental silks – 'glorious vests wrought and embroidered on cloth of gold, but with such lively colours that for splendour and vividness we have nothing in Europe that approaches it', according to John Evelyn – by developing their own equivalents, the so-called bizarre silks. So profoundly oriental were the curious swaying and tropical-looking floral and foliage motifs that pattern these silks, that the fabrics were once erroneously thought to be Indian in origin. The Lyons silk factories, which had employed over 3000 master weavers in 1660, had benefited from silk manufacturing's new status as a protected industry to lead European taste, originating the fashion for bizarre silks which swept the Continent from about 1690 until the end of the second decade of the eighteenth century. In England the Huguenot immigrants of Spitalfields wove these beautiful silks too. But oriental fabrics dominated

fashion. When Pepys had his portrait painted he hired an Indian gown for the occasion.

As the wool trade declined and silk factories closed, so workers faced unemployment and starvation. In 1719 the weavers of Spitalfieds rioted and raced around the city splashing acid on the dresses of any calico-clad female who crossed their path. Those women imprudent enough to gather and mock the pilloried rioters had their gowns torn from their backs by the weavers still at liberty. These desperate actions made clear the degree of resistance to the importing of oriental cottons; the ban on eastern fabrics was extended to all cotton goods and from the 1720s they could only make their appearance discreetly, through the back door, as part of the smuggler's bounty.

***The Audience of the Emperor
of China.*** **Beauvais tapestry,
c.1690**. *One of a set of
Beauvais tapestries of* The
History of the Empire of China.
*Typical of French chinoiseries
of the Louis XIV period is the
manner in which*

*the sumptuous clothing of the
emperor, his magnificent if
wayward setting, the prostrate
courtiers and exotic animals,
birds and flowers, all testify
to the power and glory of the
sovereign, whether Emperor of
China or King of France.*

**Soho tapestry, seventeenth
century**. *(opposite) The style
of chinoiserie figures floating
against a dark background
may have been inspired by
oriental lacquer or Moghul
miniatures, but the sense of
gaiety is typically English.*

Tapestries, always fashionable, had begun to take account of the new interest in the East. In 1690 the Royal factory at Gobelins wove a series entitled *Les Tentures des Indes*. Completely European in their perspective and composition, they were 'Indian' only in so far as their subject matter depicted scenes of exotic luxuriance, such as an Indian king sitting under a Chinese umbrella while around him parade a menagerie of odd-looking beasts. A series of tapestries woven at Beauvais, depicting the well-loved Italian *commedia dell'arte* characters, took account of the new fashion by placing the figures under fantastic curtained canopies surrounded by a mixture of classical and chinoiserie motifs. Only one Beauvais tapestry of the period actually attempts to portray a Chinese landscape; here a pagoda is found, albeit a rather squat and stumpy example, and an exotic bird makes a lone appearance in the sky.

In England, a series of chinoiserie tapestries were woven at the Soho factory in about 1700, the first set for a rich nawab, named Elihu Yale, who had been the Governor of Madras for the East India Company before returning to England in 1699. Yale collected Mogul miniatures, and these may have served as inspiration for the designs. Each hanging has a dark blue background upon which exotically dressed Orientals, as much Mogul as they are Chinese, disport themselves. Yale's set of tapestries is now at the American university that bears his name. Others are scattered in country houses across England. These Soho tapestries have all the gaiety and *joie de vivre* of the early rococo. Typically, a broad and placid stream branches and meanders across the tapestry. On its banks a warrior prances on horseback, a long-robed mandarin displays his

cormorant's latest catch, two figures converse politely, a bearded nobleman fishes and a llama draws a basket chair topped by a domed umbrella, while an attendant fans the small seated figure within and others walk daintily in the flowering landscape.

Although chinoiserie objects of this period were often bizarre or naïve, they have become clearly recognizable. Even if they do not yet attain the dignity of a separate, acknowledged style, they remain distinct from Chinese export ware and its direct imitators. In the seventeenth century chinoiserie had been assimilated into the prevailing taste for the Baroque, but by the time the century drew to its close, the days of the Baroque were numbered. Tapestries and embroideries in both France and England give us premonitory glimpses of the role chinoiserie would play in the eighteenth century when it was to become a vital ingredient in the creation of the new taste: the Rococo.

Rococo chinoiserie in France

He who has not lived during the years around 1789 can not know what is meant by the pleasure of life.

Charles-Maurice de Talleyrand, 1814

The Chinese Garden by François Boucher, 1742. *Rococo chinoiseries no longer depict Cathay as grotesque or bizarre. Its inhabitants, undeniably exotic, are in all other respects recognizable as sophisticated, civilized, well-bred Parisians.*

Gilded ebony and lacquer bureau, 1784. *The taste for small-scale feminine furniture coincided with the emphasis on chinoiserie as a style of luxury and refinement. There could be no better synthesis than the beautiful workmanship of this piece made by Adam Weisweiller, from Marie Antoinette's apartments at the château of Saint Cloud.*

If chinoiserie had been adapted to fit the Baroque, it was tailor-made for the Rococo. While the Baroque accommodated chinoiserie into a general fascination by the exotic, the artists and designers of the new rococo style found, to their delight, that chinoiserie decoration expressed the essence of European Rococo completely. This easy assimilation of chinoiserie into the Rococo is as much dependent on qualities both styles eschew as on the attributes they possess in common. Both are far removed from classical notions of restraint and symmetry. In fact the Rococo is positively anti-classical, the first style to turn its back on such standard classical features as acanthus leaf and Vitruvian scroll, goats-hoof and ox-skull, and to look elsewhere for its decorative inspiration: to natural sources and to naturalistic – and thus asymmetric – movement. It is easy to see how chinoiserie would find its place in this scheme of things. The style's lack of pomposity, its clear and bright colours, its amusing and fantastic qualities, and perhaps above all else, its asymmetric wayward design and clearly non-classical provenance, were all employed to produce rococo designs that are at once frivolous, sophisticated and enchantingly pretty.

Asymmetry, a key element in rococo design, is unselfconsciously present in oriental taste. Irregular ornament had appeared a 'deformity' to the French Jesuit, Père Louis le Comte when he compared Chinese architecture to the 'true architecture' of Europe, but that was during the height of the Baroque. Things were different now; irregularity was one of the pivots upon which the Rococo turned. As taste changed, so the European collector of oriental porcelain turned away from the blue-and-white Ming dynasty porcelain whose free, robust decoration frequently covered the entire surface of the vessel, and coveted instead the sparse and distinctly asymmetrical designs of Japanese Kakiemon porcelain. It was this asymmetry, coupled with its delicate charm and refined elegance, that made Kakiemon ware immediately popular with devotees of the new rococo taste.

Not that the Rococo cultivated sparseness. On the contrary, ornament proliferates: painted and carved shells, water in waves and swirls, C scrolls and S scrolls, flowers singly or in bunches, monkeys behaving like fashionable Frenchmen, Chinamen strolling in painted landscapes. All of these elements, singly or combined, garland rococo rooms with decoration. Modelled in stucco or carved in wood, the ornament climbs the walls, invades the ceilings, entwines the mirrors that lighten, shimmer and reflect the delicate colours of white and gold, of blue, yellow, pale grey and silver.

The springboard of this new taste lay in a turning away from the Baroque and everything it stood for – state art and the glorification of the king, enshrined in the vanity and pomposity of the palace of Versailles. One would not expect the Crown to lead

Mid-eighteenth-century French fan. *(opposite) Fans and fan-sticks were among the earliest imports of the East India Companies. Refined and flirtatious, they perfectly expressed the rococo spirit.*

Louis XV Mennecy candelabra with ormolu mounts, c.1750. *The candelabra is elegantly modelled, in a restrained rococo style, in the fine quality soft-paste porcelain for which Mennecy is famous.*

the way in abandoning the Baroque and embracing the Rococo, and in fact the lead came from Paris and the newly-rich, the financiers and tax-farmers, rather than from Versailles and the king. Yet even Louis XIV was aware that the Baroque had become a bore, and in some sense approved of a change in emphasis. In 1699, in the dying years of his reign, Louis himself turned down the proposals for the decoration of the apartments at the Château de la Ménagerie for the young and high-spirited Duchess of Burgundy because the designs were not light-hearted enough. The king wrote: '*Il me paroit qu'il y a quelquechose à changer que les subjects sont trop serieux qu'il faut qu'il y ait de la jeunesse melée dans ce que l'on ferait … Il faut de l'enfance repandue partout.'* (It seems to me that something should be changed, that the subjects are too serious, that there should be youthfulness mixed with what we do … We need childhood spread throughout.)

However, a style which evolved to express one view of the world cannot easily be altered to express its opposite. Although the death of Louis XIV in 1715 and the Regency that followed it liberated the Baroque, and forms became lighter and less monumental, the first three decades of the eighteenth century show no absolute break with what had gone before. In the early eighteenth century the lacquer panels and porcelain designs of the East still formed an abiding source of chinoiserie inspiration. As the style developed, the chinoiseries were combined with purely European rococo motifs, often in the same work. So felicitous were the results, and so popular was this combination of East and West, that it became one of the Rococo's most notable features.

Lacquer rooms remained popular. During the Regency, when the court had moved to Paris, they were installed in the hotels of the newly fashionable city dwellers. Dating from the 1720s, these rooms still had their sections of Chinese lacquer confined within the wood panelling, rather than rioting around the walls as they were later to do. One Parisian who had such a room was Pierre Crozat, one of the new generation of art patrons. He owned a magnificent hotel in Paris and an astonishing art collection. Crozat's real interest was paintings, and he was a perceptive patron, for he was an early employer of

the undisputed inventive genius of the Rococo: Antoine Watteau.

Another friend and patron of Watteau, the art dealer Gersaint, commissioned the artist to paint a new sign for his shop at the Pont Notre-Dame. This exquisite painting, *L'Enseigne de Gersaint*, was completed in the summer of 1721, only months before Watteau's early death from consumption. The painting shows a group of the dealer's beautifully dressed and fashionable clientèle in his shop, surrounded by works of art, including chinoiseries. This new shop sign was commissioned to commemorate a change of name as Gersaint's shop, *Au Grand Monarque*, was transformed into *A la Pagode*. Chinoiserie had arrived at the centre of fashion.

Watteau did not paint or design many chinoiseries, but those he did produce were of such profound influence that they set the course for all later rococo chinoiseries throughout Europe. His inventive genius and delicate touch created an imaginative world far removed away from the rather leaden-footed fantasies of the seventeenth century, or the grotesque creatures of the early travel books. Unlike earlier chinoiseries which dwelt on the gaudy splendours of the mandarins' court and the curious creatures who inhabited it, Watteau's chinoiseries embody the spirit of his *fêtes galantes* paintings, depicting parties and gatherings in the open air where the participants seem to have achieved a perfect, effortless adjustment to their surroundings. Like the *fêtes galantes*, too, Watteau's chinoiseries reflected the values and desires of that most refined section of Parisian society for whom he worked. Although they were chinoiseries, what they conjured

up was not Cathay but the sophisticated and
beautiful inhabitants of a Parisian salon. There
the mysterious rites of Cathay were performed – in
French no doubt – by a group of devout worshippers,
obsequious courtiers, priests and pagods, beautiful
goddesses and mandarin-headed terms. Typical of
the style is an undated engraving of a chinoiserie
grotesque design, *Divinité chinoise*, which shows
how easily Watteau combines western motifs
with chinoiseries. Two C scrolls at the base of the

**Divinité Chinoise. Drawing
after Antoine Watteau,
probably by Gabriel Huquier,
1729-30.** *The delicate and
imaginative elegance of the few
chinoiseries produced by the
great genius of the French
Rococo, Antoine Watteau,
charted the course for all
European rococo chinoiseries.*

engraving provide arching supports for a tall flight of flimsy, zig-zag steps up which elegant devotees climb towards a cross-legged pagod who is seated on a dais in a woodland glade.

There were some more or less accurate Chinese models on which Watteau may have drawn in his creation of this sophisticated, if still-mysterious, society. A series of Chinese paintings presented to Louis XIV by one of the Jesuit missionaries to China could have been the source for a decorative scheme that Watteau completed around 1718 for the *Cabinet du Roi* in the Château de la Muette, where the

Idole de la Déesse Ki Mao Sao. Engraving by Aubert after the painting by Antoine Watteau of *c.*1729. *The original painting of this enchanted devotion was for the* Cabinet du Roi *in the Château de la Muette and may have been inspired by a series of Chinese paintings presented to Louis XIV.*

La Grande Singerie, Château de Chantilly. Panels painted by Christophe Huet, 1735. Lady being perfumed by monkeys. *(opposite left) Monkeys dressed as Chinamen formed an integral part of the motifs of rococo chinoiserie. This scene mimics Watteau's celebrated painting of the worship of the goddess Ki Mao Sao. Monkey holding a jester's rattle.* *(opposite right) The essential chracteristic of singeries is that the monkeys not only adopt human dress, but also human behaviour.*

Duchesse de Berry used to hold drunken orgies. The room has long perished – it was destroyed in 1750 – but engravings of the Chinese and Tartars that Watteau depicted have survived. Some of these figures were gods and goddesses who were given their correct Chinese appellations – Ki Mao Sao, or Thvo-Chvu, for instance. This fact supports the idea that Watteau may have modelled his designs on Chinese originals, but that is the limit of the resemblance between Watteau's view and that of the Chinese artist. Watteau's version of the worship of the goddess Ki Mao Sao, for example, presents a distinctly Gallic and frivolous view of the object of devotion, a goddess with the grace and confidence of a Parisian hostess, seated on a perfect rococo scroll made from the gnarled root of a tree and carrying in her outstretched arms the mysterious totems of a bamboo parasol and what could be a pineapple on a stick. The sycophantic poses of her two male worshippers would doubtless not have looked out of place in the salon, although their robes, pointed hats and drooping moustaches provide assurance of their Chinese origin.

Watteau's *Figures Chinoises et Tatares* from the Château de la Muette were engraved as twelve plates by François Boucher in 1731, and helped to promote the taste for rococo chinoiseries. The ironic tone struck in Watteau's depiction of Chinese worship was taken further by Christophe Huet when he introduced chinoiseries into the paintings of the *grande singerie* room at the château of Chantilly in 1735. The essential mark of *singeries* is that the monkeys depicted are not only dressed as human beings but act as if they were human too, and Huet produced a *singerie* of Watteau's scene, where the identical characters are parodied, the goddess appearing as a coquette, her idolaters as two kneeling monkeys.

By the mid-1730s chinoiseries and *singeries* were commonly fused, although it is hard to say why. Their story is something of a muddle. The genesis of *singeries* can be traced through the depiction of monkeys performing human tasks on the pages of medieval manuscripts, their occasional appearance on oriental imports, and their role in the pantheon of Hindu deities. In the late seventeenth century Jean Berain hit on the idea of replacing classical fauns with monkeys in his grotesque designs (a fanciful type of decoration deriving from Roman times, and popular in classical design since the Renaissance). This incorporation of simians into current western design was a new development. Claude Audran took the next step when he endowed his monkeys with human attributes, painting an 'arbour with monkeys seated at a table' for the Château de Marly in 1709. By the time Huet was working for the Prince de Condé at Chantilly in the 1730s the monkeys had doffed their French *couture* and taken to parading about the place dressed as Chinamen.

The rooms that Christophe Huet decorated at Chantilly – the *grande singerie* on the first floor, and a less famous *petite singerie* on the ground floor – are acknowledged masterpieces of their type. A series of large, gaily painted grotesque panels are framed in elaborate, gilded rococo *boiseries* (carved wood panelling). Each chinoiserie panel shows a separate activity in which the central characters are Chinese, and their attendants are monkeys. As the monkeys are also wearing the robes of the celestial court it

Salon Pillement, Château de Craôn, Haroué. Mid-eighteenth century. *Interior view and ceiling detail. A small, brightly coloured, circular chamber in a tower, this room typifies the work of the peripatetic French designer, Jean-Baptiste Pillement, who created delicate chinoiseries of all kinds in most of Europe's major cities.*

***L'Enseigne de Gersaint* by Antoine Watteau, 1720-21.** *(previous pages) Shop-sign commissioned to commemorate the renaming of the art dealer Gersaint's shop from* Au Grand Monarque *to* A La Pagode.

is quite easy to confuse monkey with mandarin, presumably the point of the joke. More monkeys scamper and caper on the panels of the door and around the stucco scrolls of the ceiling. Although Huet's work is more exuberant than Watteàu's, and untinged by the sense of melancholy that underpins all of the latter's work, the delicacy and sense of fantasy portrayed so clearly derive from Watteau that at one point the work was believed to be his.

Huet painted other rococo chinoiseries. In the Hôtel de Rohan in Paris the monkeys had to content themselves with rampaging round the upper sections of the walls while a *fête galante* filled the central panels of the room. He also worked for that ardent Sinophile, Madame de Pompadour, at the Château de Champs, one of a string of houses she bought and did up. Around 1748 Huet decorated the *salon chinois* and the boudoir with a delightful series of vignettes of Chinese and exotic birds. Unfortunately, in both rooms the decoration had to be contained within the simple panelling of the original decor – the château was built at the beginning of the eighteenth century – and this imposed restrictions on Huet's style and reduced the overall effect.

After Watteau's death, the new look to chinoiserie decoration was taken further by François Boucher, Madame de Pompadour's favourite artist. Boucher's highly individual chinoiserie style was infused with the sensuality that permeates all his work. His Chinese are less remote and superior than Watteau's and consequently more solid, more vital and more voluptuous. Boucher himself was clear-headed and hard-working, able to turn his hand to decorative work, designs, easel paintings, scenery and costumes, and engravings, where his expertise

A la Pagode. Trade card designed by François Boucher for the famous shop of the Parisian art dealer, Gersaint.

The Chinese Fishing Party by François Boucher, 1742. *An easel painting, a version of the same subject was used for a tapestry at Beauvais.*

earned him an early commission: to engrave a series of plates of Watteau's work soon after that artist's early death in 1721.

Chinoiserie designs were so popular that they were used to ornament everything. Engravings furnished most of the patterns, but an artist like Boucher would also design directly for a specific object. He produced all kinds of chinoiseries, from easel paintings to designs for fire-screens. Like Watteau, he executed a commission for Gersaint's shop *A la Pagode*: in Boucher's case, a trade card that shows a lacquer cabinet with all the treasures of the East heaped beneath it and an exotically-attired fat pagod perched on its top. For Madame de Pompadour's château at Bellevue he devised a Chinese boudoir and painted two *paysages chinois* for the drawing room. Boucher's painting, *The Chinese Fishing Party*, probably also intended for Bellevue, is close to one of the tapestries in the famous series he designed at Beauvais.

The fishing party was to become a favourite theme for chinoiserie designers. As Boucher's influence spread across Europe little Chinese figures fishing under a willow tree began to ornament pottery, wallpaper, fabrics and bibelots, a trend that continued throughout the eighteenth century and beyond. In about 1740 the first of many suites of Boucher's chinoiserie engravings was issued, *Diverses figures Chinoises*, nine plates of Chinese figures and Chinese props including umbrellas, tables and chairs. All of the designs were widely copied and adapted; they were used for statuettes in bronze and terracotta, gold and enamel snuff-boxes, overdoors and painted panels, and designs on porcelain in factories from Meissen to Lowestoft.

Boucher devoted much of his working life to producing paintings for tapestries, both at the Gobelins factory and at Beauvais, where he became director in 1755. Eastern subjects had invaded tapestry design at Gobelins in the late seventeenth century, but in the early years of the eighteenth century Beauvais responded to the interest in exotica in a much more original manner. The factory began to produce tapestries that reflected a new view of the Orient, positioned somewhere between the predictable late seventeenth-century vision of fabled luxury, and the fully-fledged rococo vision of a *fête champêtre* in Chinese robes.

In none of this early set of Beauvais tapestries dating from about 1700 is there any attempt to capture the actual appearance of Orientals. Indeed, all the Chinese are firmly western in feature and deportment. The tapestries, a set of ten *tentures chinoises* portraying the activities of the Emperor of China, were based on real descriptions, largely from

Johan Nieuhoff's book, and also from the accounts of the Jesuit priests, who provided such a valuable conduit of information between the courts of Louis XIV and the Chinese Emperor. In fact two Jesuit priests who were involved with the newly created observatory in Peking are portrayed in one of the tapestries, *The Astronomers*, both wearing long beards, dangling moustaches, Chinese robes and insignia of rank granted by the Emperor. Another tapestry in the suite depicts the harvesting of pineapples, a fruit Nieuhoff greeted with rapture, smacking his lips over its scent and taste, and describing it as the most rare and precious of nature's creations. (Small wonder that a painting at Ham House near London shows the first pineapple grown in Europe being presented to King Charles II in a suitably reverential manner by a gardener on his knees.)

One of the early Beauvais suite, *The Audience of the Emperor of China*, presents a clear example of the change in attitude towards chinoiserie that accompanied the shift in contemporary taste away from the Baroque and towards the Rococo. The subject matter, the power and glory of the monarchy, is typically baroque. The treatment hovers between faithfulness and fantasy. Classical allusions, which would have been relentlessly employed in pure baroque, are entirely absent. However extraordinary the Emperor's robes – which include a bonnet with a peacock feather and a collar of pearls – they are as described in Nieuhoff's *Travels* and therefore believed to be accurate. But the Emperor in the tapestry is sitting in a kind of loggia unknown in either East or West, whose flimsy roof, Moorish arches and slender colonettes decorated with

serpents and dragons conjure up the pastiche of
the Brighton Pavilion a century before its time. The
other appurtenances – prostrate figures, a roguish
elephant, exotic fruits, porcelain vessels, and endless
carpet – are the standard eastern trappings, and are
given no additional airs of droll self-consciousness.

With the second set of chinoiserie Beauvais
tapestries, designed by Boucher, we enter another
world, one of the artist's own invention. To Boucher
the East appeared neither mysterious nor awe-
inspiring, but rather charming and faintly erotic. His
Chinese are orientals in face and figure. They do not
look like Europeans at a fancy dress party, although
they certainly behave as though they were. The
Goncourt brothers, writing in the nineteenth century,
relished the wit of Boucher's vision of Cathay:
'*Approchez-vous! La Chinoise et le Seigneur qui
prennent le Thé, ce sont des Parisiens.*' Parisian
they may be, but in the manner of the Parisians
of Boucher's day, captive to the charms of country
pursuits. In Boucher's six designs for this second set
of *tentures chinoises* – *The Fishing Party, A Chinese
Wedding, The Fair, The Emperor's Audience, The
Royal Breakfast* and *The Toilet of the Sultane* –
the courtiers of Cathay follow their fully rococo
preoccupations. The only buildings in the dream-like
landscape are pagodas or kiosks with upswept roofs,
and the activities of its inhabitants involve nothing
more arduous than the playing of weird musical
instruments, carrying birds in bamboo cages, and
dallying among their fishing tackle or tea-trays.

The suite was a wild success and the tapestries
were woven many times between 1745 and 1775. In
one of those extraordinary cultural exchanges that
abound in the history of chinoiserie, a set was sent

by Louis XV to the Chinese emperor, Chi'en Lung.
Boucher's nonchalant mixture of exotic birds, bizarre
animals, hedonistic orientals, multicoloured flowers,
grottoes and palm trees, must have struck the
emperor as a delicious novelty, and the Jesuit priest
who presented the gift reported him as being deeply

***L'Embarquement de
l'Impératrice.* Beauvais
tapestry, early eighteenth
century**. *One from the first
suite of Chinese tapestries at
Beauvais, in which the Chinese
monarch behaves as royally
as any Bourbon. Here the
emperor, already seated in his
dragon-ornamented barque,
waits for his wife to board,
while a bare-chested attendant
shields him from the rays of
the sun.*

Le Thé de l'Impératrice.
**Beauvais tapestry, early
eighteenth century.** *An outdoor
breakfast that anticipates the
fêtes galantes of the rococo
style. Seated in a domed and
flowered garden pavilion, the
Empress of China toys with the
tea and fruit offered her by
attentive ladies of the court.*

**Panel of painted Lyons silk,
c.1750.** *(opposite) This light-
hearted design of a Chinaman
peering through a telescope is
typical of the chinoiseries of
Jean Pillement.*

appreciative. One drawback was where to hang them;
the emperor would have liked to use them to adorn
his temples, but thought that would upset the
sensibilities of the Jesuits who were perhaps more
reverential towards Confucianism than Chi'en Lung
himself. In the end Father Benoist, the Jesuit priest,
reported back to Louis XV that it had been decided
to build a special palace to house the tapestries.
It may or may not have been built. What is certain
is that one tapestry panel was still hanging in the
Imperial Palace in Peking when it was sacked by the
British in 1860.

The last great French designer of rococo
chinoiseries is also the most fun. Jean-Baptiste
Pillement was a peripatetic designer who worked
not only in France, the country of his birth, but in
practically every major city in Europe, from London
to Warsaw. The shadow of Watteau fell across
Pillement too. But whereas Boucher had emphasized
the corporeality of Watteau's vision, Pillement did
quite the opposite. He was interested in fantasy, and
his chinoiseries exaggerate the wispy, fragile qualities
of the style. It is as though the world was a fairyland
conjured out of gossamer and stalks of grass, and the
humans inhabiting it fanciful little creatures who
dance and tumble around, so effervescent and lively
that they seem more creatures of air than earth.

Like most designers of the period, Pillement was
happy to turn his hand to any kind of commission,
designing with equal facility and *joie de vivre* a
chinoiserie study for the King of Poland, a rococo
pavilion at Cintra in Portugal, floral designs for silks
and cottons, and designs for enchanting 'Chinese
ornaments' complete with bells, dragons, birds,
monkeys, shells and Chinamen wearing upside-down

flowers instead of hats. As is so often the nature of
things, much of this exquisite ephemera has long
vanished. However that arch-romantic, William
Beckford, who visited Portugal in 1787, has left us a
glimpse of Pillement's garden pavilion where he and
his host, the Marques de Marialva, 'loitered till it was
pitch dark'. 'It represents,' wrote Beckford, 'a bower
of fantastic trees mingling their branches, and
discovering between them peeps of a summer sky.
From the mouth of a dragon depends a magnificent
lustre with fifty branches hung with festoons of
brilliant cut-glass that twinkle like strings of
diamonds.' Take note of the dragon: he is a
peripatetic reptile who will reappear throughout the

Eighteenth-century carved
and painted chinoiserie panels
in the style of Jean Pillement.
Originally in the Hôtel de la
Lariboisière, Paris. *Chinoiserie
rooms enjoyed great popularity
during the reign of Louis XV.
The frivolous pursuits of the*
*inhabitants of Cathay,
captured in a rococo cartouche
of twining stems and wispy
pavilions, must have been
a perfect backdrop to the
sophisticated and insouciant
gatherings of an eighteenth-
century Parisian salon.*

French eighteenth-century needle-case. *Made from papiermâché with lilac lacquer, and decorated with a spiralling chinoiserie hunting scene.*

Vignettes by Jean Pillement from *The Ladies Amusement*. *(opposite) This rich compendium of rococo designs was published in 1762.*

history of chinoiserie, from Portugal to Brighton, from Brighton to Buckingham Palace and even the 5th Avenue Cinema in Seattle.

An exquisite draughtsman, Pillement's easy inventiveness created hundreds of chinoiseries whose charm survived their engraved translation into fields as various as marquetry, textiles, tiles, wallpapers and room decoration. Between 1755 and 1760 Pillement prints were published in London as well as in Paris, and up to 1774 he continued to produce prints of ornaments in large numbers, nearly all of rococo chinoiseries. He died in poverty in Lyons, his birthplace, in 1808.

Although the origins of the Rococo had lain outside the walls of Versailles, both the king and queen, and most importantly the king's mistress Madame de Pompadour, were unwavering supporters of the style, and especially of the chinoiserie elements it incorporated. During the long reign of Louis XV – from 1715 to 1774 – the number of Chinese and chinoiserie objects in the French royal collection grew so large that the *Intendant du Garde Meuble*, which recorded all the furnishings possessed by the Crown, found it necessary to have a special section of the royal inventory expressly to catalogue these *Divers ouvrages de la Chine*. The *petits appartements*, the king's private apartments at Versailles, were full of lacquer furniture, both Far Eastern and French in origin. The brilliance of the local version resembled that of oriental lacquer, and the two are often easy to confuse. Certainly the inventories of the period do not discriminate.

The crown was not alone in its passion for chinoiserie. Parisian dealers in furniture and bibelots were able to supply the wants of the fashionable world. Known as *marchands-merciers*, these men were not manufacturers themselves, and certainly did not work with their hands. Market-makers, as they would be known today, their role was to present their clients with new objects that they would want to buy. Lazare Duvaux, a leading dealer, patronized by the king and all the most up-to-date members of the court, kept an inventory of sales that provides a very clear indication of what was fashionable. His *livre-journal* of 1748-9 shows that over half of the wares sold from his shop were chinoiseries of one sort or another. Among these, the most popular items were porcelain objects of various kinds, which had been given rococo mounts of ormolu. Thus it turns out that the combination of oriental and western arts, so typical of the Rococo, was of major importance in the promotion of the style by the *marchands-merciers*.

The attitudes that lay behind the Rococo were not weighty; the style might even be thought morally irresponsible. Perhaps this was why the fashion persisted at court well into the reign of Louis XVI. But the Chinese cult did enjoy intellectual approval quite removed from its entanglement with the Rococo.

The attitude of the Jesuit priesthood towards the writings of Confucius was only one of the manifestations of an admiration of Chinese philosophy that extended well beyond Jesuit circles. According to Voltaire, his play *Orphelin de la Chine* was written as a 'dramatization of the morals of Confucius' in an attempt to rebut the ideas of Rousseau. The entire play was set in China, the actors wore full Chinese costume, and the sets were chinoiserie too. Voltaire's approval of the Chinese taste extended as far as having the room in which he wrote – whether at Citrey or at Ferney – embellished with Chinese and chinoiserie decoration.

The Chinese empire was used as an example to buttress the economic theories of another writer, François Quesnay, who originated an economic doctrine that land is the source of all wealth and that it alone should be taxed. Quesnay was a friend of Madame de Pompadour, who persuaded Louis XV to

follow the example set by the Emperor of China and guide the plough at the spring tilling. The circle was complete when a book, *Reflexions sur la formation et la distribution de la richesse*, based in part on Quesnay's view of Chinese government, was a farewell gift to two young Chinese who had been visiting France.

Madame de Pompadour remained faithful to chinoiserie all her life. Although the somewhat mousy character of the queen, Marie Lesczynska, was scarcely able to compete with that of la Pompadour, she too favoured Chinese taste. As late as May 1761 her *petit cabinet* at Versailles was being altered to receive painted chinoiserie garden scenes, the queen's own work, doubtless the product of many hours of a largely uneventful life. Painted chinoiserie rooms seem to have remained fashionable up to the 1770s. In Paris the Duc d'Orléans was reported to have a salon '*fait à la chinoise*' and the Duchesse de Chartres a dining-room '*boisée en jaune avec de petits tableaux chinois enchaussés*'. Alas such tantalizing snippets of information have to suffice. Like so much else the dancing figures of these mandarin courts have long passed from our vision.

Fabrics imported from the East, satins and embroideries from India and painted silks – *pekins* and *bazins* – from China were also used to decorate chinoiserie rooms. The fabrics were treated rather like wallpaper, as panels to decorate small rooms or to line an alcove. They were costly, but very popular with those that could afford them. A less expensive way of achieving a fine Chinese room was to use wallpaper or *toile de Jouy*, a cotton fabric decorated with engraved copperplates of little vignetted scenes, often chinoiseries in the style of Pillement. Only one

colour was used for the decoration; it could be a rich purple, a red, sepia, or indigo blue, and was guaranteed not to fade. Although both Ireland and England had perfected the process 20 years earlier, manufacture began in France only in the 1770s, when a factory was set up at Jouy. The fashion was at its most popular in France in the latter part of the eighteenth century, when there were few homes, even among the grandest, that did not have one room – a cabinet, a bedroom, or even a drawing-room – hung with *toile de Jouy*, which was also used to cover chairs and beds. Very few of these rooms have survived, although there are examples of the fabrics preserved in the textile collections of all the major

'Chinois dits à la Brouette'. Toile de Jouy, c.1760-64. *(opposite) The discovery of a new process for plate printing in blue on white cotton made the products of the factory at Jouy an immediate success, and was particularly apposite for charming chinoiseries such as this example.*

Louis XV black lacquer chest with ormolu mounts. *Both European and Japanese lacquers ornament this commode, one of a pair made for Queen Marie Lesczynska's bedchamber at Fontainebleau.*

museums, and textile companies today have reissued document prints of eighteenth-century *toile de Jouy* designs. Typically the pattern consists of a repeated motif of four or five cameos, each little scene floating alongside the next: separate islets where two sages converse in a tea-house, a page squats balancing a tea-tray on his head, a trio of elegant mothers watch while their children play, a mandarin descends a trellis-lined and vertiginous stairway, all in an airy landscape of curving trees, jagged rocks and fragile buildings.

Wallpapers filled any gap caused by the huge demand for printed cottons. The account books of Lazare-Duvaux are filled with references to supplying painted papers, both oriental and European. Like the textiles, the papers were fixed to the wall by mounting them on wooden frames, which made them easy to take down. The brightly-coloured, painted Chinese export wallpapers naturally influenced the design of French papers, and by mid-century boldly-drawn and brightly-coloured papers had become generally fashionable, many of them of chinoiserie subjects. The separate panels used to line a room were not required to be of the same design. One might be a Chinese wearing a tiered and pointed hat, long moustachios and a billowing robe and stroking a peacock, in another a similarly garbed mandarin, standing next to a table of markedly up-to-date French design.

Rococo decoration was always extremely colourful, and the lacquer used at this time reflected the prevailing taste for pure colours. Red and polychrome lacquers were generally preferred to black, which Louis XV is known to have disliked. But Japanese lacquer, generally regarded as the finest of

the Far Eastern lacquers, was almost invariably black. Doubtless this explains the pair of black lacquer chests of drawers made for Queen Marie Lesczynska's bedchamber at the château of Fontainebleau. Both European and Japanese lacquers are combined in these pieces, a not uncommon practice at this period, and one which was to persist into the reign of Louis XVI. However the lacquer, of whichever type, is quite secondary, subservient to the glorious ormolu mounts that in true rococo fashion trail and twine

Toile de Jouy, c.1785. *A typically spirited design in the style of Jean Pillement. Against a backdrop of huge blooms and rococo scrolls, an elegantly-dressed Chinaman, shaded by a parasol carried by a young boy, mounts a vertiginous stairway to a straw-roofed pagoda.*

Embroidered satin brocade. Lyons, c.1735. *Boatmen propel their fragile barques through a flowery landscape where tiny islets float among the clouds.*

over the front of the cabinets, almost masking the lacquer's exquisite quality. In pieces such as these cabinets the lacquer becomes part of the background, valued as would be any other precious material for its opulence and rarity, rather than for its specifically oriental qualities. However in other pieces, in which its quality is supremely outstanding, the lacquer would be the chief attraction and the mounts, even in the rococo period, would retreat to the sides. With a commode entirely constructed from Coromandel lacquer of the highest quality – polychrome scenes with large-scale, boldly executed figures – assertiveness of both shape and mounts would be avoided in order not to diminish the lacquer's decorative impact.

The chinoiserie decoration on French mid-eighteenth century lacquer is mostly restrained, when it is present at all. The decoration is generally in light relief in gold with charmingly delicate, small-scale vignettes of people, boats and pavilions. Relatively sparse, and with superb rococo mounts, it is of high quality and infused with a Gallic feeling for

propriety. This is a region of Cathay familiar with the rules that govern polite behaviour.

Vernis Martin, a French version of lacquer, was produced in response to the growing taste for colour in furniture and decoration. The lacquer, which takes its name from the surname of the four brothers who perfected its production, is no mere copy of oriental lacquer; it is the development of a special type of coloured varnish once known as 'chipolin', a reference to the use of garlic in its composition. *Vernis Martin* was not seen as an alternative to oriental lacquer, but as a material in its own right. It was not used exclusively for furniture with chinoiserie designs, which in any case, as we have seen, were not particularly common. Applying the varnish to a piece of furniture was a laborious process (over forty coats could be necessary, and each one had to be rubbed down and polished before the next could be applied) but the range of colours was large and their lustre and depth unrivalled. *Vernis Martin* was available in all the favoured rococo colours, from pearl grey to lilac, jonquil yellow and

Prussian blue *vernis Martin* writing desk. Made for Madame de Pompadour's château at Bellevue, eighteenth century. *Even when the chinoiserie cult was at its height in France, decoration would be applied with a sense of restraint and order as on this exquisite small piece so typical of the Louis XV style.*

Chinoiserie fabrics, eighteenth century. *Favourite subjects for eighteenth-century textile designers ranged from the fantasies of Jean Pillement – here, in a rococo adaptation of the Tree of Life, gigantic flowers scroll up the design and butterflies soar above diminutive Chinamen – to the more accurate renderings of flowers and vases that derived from Chinese originals (top right).*

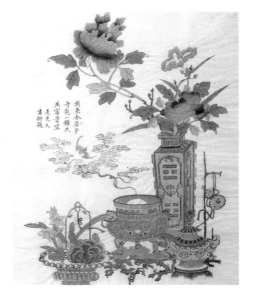

pale green, including a deep blue and a strong, bright green. Colours strongly associated with China – like the blue and white inspired by Chinese porcelain – could be employed to lend a chinoiserie air to *vernis Martin* furniture decorated in a quite un-Chinese way. One mid-eighteenth century room in the Château de Choisy, destroyed during the revolution, had an entirely blue-and-white colour scheme. Evidently the Rococo had not entirely swept aside this earlier taste. The Martin brothers produced the blue-and-white furniture for the room. The decorative motifs on one of the pieces, a corner cupboard, where the white of the original background colour has turned a deep yellow, show the favourite pastime of the aristocracy, hunting, combined with the vogue for chinoiserie. Its delicate, deep-blue decoration of waterfowl and a prancing dog includes a sinuous bough of exotic flowers among which butterflies browse and birds flutter.

The Martins were regularly patronized by the crown, and by Madame de Pompadour who paid them 58,000 livres for work they did for her at Bellevue. A small writing-desk from Bellevue, lacquered in Prussian blue *vernis Martin*, is similar in feel to the furniture the brothers made for Choisy. Once again chinoiserie and French rococo motifs are used as if there were no contradiction between the two styles. The front of the desk shows an entirely asymmetric chinoiserie scene executed in gold: on the shores of a lake two Chinese converse with a dog under the shade cast by a gnarled tree, and two others show mild interest in a lion-like creature one of them has on a lead. But the drawer beneath shows a purely western rococo motif, a tendril of flowers executed in Chinese colours, not blue and white on

this occasion, but red and gold. The sides of the desk revert to Cathay in the subject-matter of swaying palms and female Chinese figures.

High rococo fashion was relatively short-lived. By the 1760s the return to the Antique had led to a less seductive, more severe neo-classical style, which grew in fashion during the reign of Louis XVI. Despite this, the court still clung to its devotion to the East. Marie Antoinette was a passionate collector of extremely expensive furniture made with Japanese lacquer, the type favoured above all others as colours grew more restrained and black and gold returned to fashion. The imported lacquer panels would either be used symmetrically, in a quite un-eastern fashion, or were set rather like a huge precious stone into the piece of furniture and then surrounded by the jewel-like swags and festoons of flowers formed by ormolu mounts. In the last years of the *ancien régime*, in 1785, the *Mesdames* of France, the two spinster daughters of Louis XV who had taken up residence

Louis XVI secretaire, *c*.1775.
The severe outline of this upright secretaire is tempered by marquetry decoration of the highest quality. The drop front features a Chinese pavilion executed in marquetry. (detail, opposite)

at the château of Bellevue, took delivery of a suite of exquisite Japanese black lacquered furniture made for them by Martin Carlin in the severely rectilinear Louis XVI style.

A greatly increased range of woods – not far short of a hundred varieties – gave pictorial wood marquetry a chance to emulate the colour, sheen and sumptuousness of furniture made from lacquer. Sometimes chinoiseries were used to ornament these pieces. Roger van der Cruze Lacroix produced a number of pieces with marquetry of Chinese subjects. Such was his technique that he used Boucher prints as the subjects for his marquetry pictures. A commode of 1775 has not one but five scenes of '*différents amusements chinois*', all taken from engravings of Boucher prints. The wizardry of David Roentgen's marquetry is of the same high order. Here, preserved in wood, we find the citizens of Cathay, the bird-sellers, mandarins and parasol-carrying pageboys, that recall the rococo world of Boucher and Watteau at the end of the century which saw their birth.

Chinoiserie in Europe in the eighteenth century

I was surprised suddenly to see a real fairy-land, for His Majesty had ordered a Chinese pavilion to be built, the most beautiful ever to be seen.

Letter from Queen Louisa Ulrika of Sweden to her mother describing her birthday present from the king, July 1753

Sans Souci, Potsdam. The Chinese tea-house designed for Frederick the Great, 1754-7. *Frederick's numerous brothers and sisters were scattered all over northern Europe. Inspired by the example of his Chinese tea-house, chinoiserie pavilions arose in parklands from Bayreuth to Sweden.*

Fan showing chinoiserie scene. Possibly Dutch, c.1770. *The pastoral chinoiseries that ornament this fan are enclosed in irregular shapes similar to the fragments of mirror that some devoted Sinophiles believed used to decorate the palaces of the Ming emperors.*

Two things give German rococo chinoiserie its distinctive character: a lack of restraint, and a network of family connections. China-mania ran in families, and in Germany it ran wild. But this was not necessarily to chinoiserie's detriment. The decorative elements of chinoiserie can easily extend to absorb almost any whim or flight of fancy, and these additional layers of *esprit* do not inevitably debase the style as might occur with a more disciplined taste.

The existence of many separate German courts led to variations in style and taste, a greatly enhanced role for individual patrons, and a chance for them to extend their influence by marrying one another. Augustus the Strong in Saxony, and Frederick the Great in Prussia, were the most important arbiters of taste in the north of the country, while in the south, the Elector of Bavaria made Munich a notable artistic centre. Between them these princes were responsible for some of the most enchanting chinoiserie fantasies created in Europe, and extensive family connections ensured that their influence spread across the Continent from Naples – where the queen, being the daughter of Augustus, naturally started a porcelain factory – to St Petersburg, where the German Czarinas, Catherine I and Catherine II, harboured a passion for China among other, more notorious tastes.

And there were so many German aristocrats. Augustus the Strong was reputed to have fathered well over three hundred children; even the more temperate rulers had large families. Frederick the Great was one of twelve children. His favourite sister, Wilhelmina, married the Margrave of Bayreuth; another sister, the King of Sweden. Both built and furnished *à la chinoise*. In Bavaria, Max Emmanuel built the Pagodenburg. His son, Clemens August, the Prince Bishop of Cologne, was so devout in his adherence to chinoiserie that he was borne about his diocese seated on a palanquin, like a mandarin. Both he and his elder brother, the Elector Karl Albrecht, built chinoiserie follies that outdid their father's Pagodenburg.

Karl Albrecht was responsible for the Amalienburg Pavilion at Nymphenburg, where his court architect, François Cuvilliés, designed the most exquisite of Germany's rococo buildings. There were chinoiserie scenes in blue and white in three of its rooms, the *Hundekammer*, the *Retirade* and the kitchen. Clemens August rebuilt Schloss Bruhl to contain an *Indianisches lakcabinett* whose walls were lined with cream-coloured japan panels on which bunches of flowers and chinoiserie scenes were picked out in bright reds and blues. A hunting bishop, he employed Cuvilliés to provide a retreat at his hunting lodge, Falkenlust, where after a hard day in the saddle he could relax in a room decorated with black japan panels, gaily painted chinoiserie scenes, gilded dragons and scrolls of rococo woodwork. And in the 1750s Clemens August built an entire *chinesches haus* at Bruhl. This building had a two-storey centre block with two smaller linked pavilions covered by bell-hung pagoda roofs. A mandarin fountain is all that survives.

Pair of lacquer coach door panels. South Germany or Italy, second half of the eighteenth century. *Within floral and foliate borders, a Chinese woman holds a parasol and a Chinese musician beats a drum.*

All the German rulers bowed down before the preponderant power in Europe: France. The French might have considered them less civilized, but the German princes were willing to learn. They spoke French, read French, took mistresses, squeezed money out of their subjects to build palaces, pavilions, orangeries, follies and opera houses modelled on Versailles. The Protestant princes welcomed the French Huguenots, and those who considered themselves intellectually up to it corresponded with Voltaire. When the great man visited Sans Souci his host, Frederick the Great, gave him newly-decorated rooms next door to his own. Voltaire, whose devotion to China was well known, could converse with the king under the gaze of carved hoopoe birds and busy monkeys.

Frederick's chinoiserie tastes may have been spurred by a boyhood visit to Dresden when he saw Augustus's 16 palaces. His most notable essay in architectural chinoiserie, the Chinese Tea House at Potsdam of 1757, was French-inspired. Stanislas Leszcynski, King of Poland, was in the fortunate position of being father-in-law to the King of France and able to lead a pleasant life as Duc de Lorraine on his estate in France at Luneville. There he erected a Chinese building called *le Trèfle*, built in the shape of a three-leaved clover. He obligingly sent the plans to Frederick, and Frederick supplied his architect, Johan Gottfied Buring, with a highly original, not to say fantastic, design based on the same three-leaved clover. While le Trèfle no longer stands, the Potsdam tea-house has survived to delight us still. Its steeply-angled main roof is separated from the shallow cupola, which forms a second roof, by a six-windowed drum which lights the interior. The cupola

is topped by a gilded Chinese figure holding an umbrella, a lone lookout for an entire Chinese community on the ground floor, sheltering under the gilded palms that form the columnar supports for the deep eaves of the main roof. These life-size statues of gilded sandstone sit in lively groups, chatting or playing instruments, while others, of more solitary disposition, stand nonchalantly in the shadows.

There were however certain of Frederick's contemporaries who proved unreceptive to the bizarre charms of his tea-house. One critic solemnly

Details of gilded sandstone figures of musicians. Sans Souci, Potsdam. *Animated groups of life-size Chinese figures, including these musicians, amuse themselves under the shade of carved palm trees in the Chinese tea-house erected by Frederick the Great in 1757.*

Kina, the Chinese pavilion at Drottningholm, Sweden. Detail of overdoor decoration. *(left)* **Exterior view.** *(right) One of the most northerly outposts of Cathay is this perfectly preserved pavilion, designed by the court architect, Carl Frederick Adelcrantz, and partly influenced by the Potsdam tea-house.*

denounced the entire idea as un-Chinese. He pointed out that although the Chinese might put pagods in their temples they did not put statues on their roofs. With heavy Prussian sarcasm he added:

> *Still less do they place images of themselves drinking tea or smoking pipes of tobacco in company in front of their houses, and whether they planted palm-trees at regular intervals, in order later on, when they were sufficiently grown, to build roofs on their green stems and to erect dwelling-houses under them, is extremely doubtful.*

He continues at length in the same vein.

In 1753 a sister of Frederick's, Louisa Ulrika, the wife of the King of Sweden, was given an entire Chinese pavilion as a thirty-fourth birthday present. In an elaborate ceremony which included Chinese drill – described by one of the participants as 'rather ridiculous' – as well as Chinese salutes by the entire court (all dressed as Chinamen), the keys were handed to the queen by her mandarin-robed eldest son, a child of seven. The memorable birthday concluded with a Chinese ballet.

In a letter to her mother detailing the day's events the queen described the pavilion:

> *There was a main room decorated in exquisite Indian style with four big porcelain vases, one in each corner. In the other rooms there were old Japanese lacquer cabinets and sofas covered with Indian fabrics, all in the finest taste. There was a bedchamber with Indian fabrics on the walls and bed, and the walls were decorated with the finest porcelain, pagodas, vases and birds.*

The queen's account is tantalizingly incomplete, almost as baffling as her insouciant references to Chinese drill, salutes and, most remarkably, ballet. We shall never know what the 'exquisite Indian style' or pagoda-decorated walls were really like because the wooden pavilion was replaced in 1763 by Kina (China), a brick pavilion designed by the court architect, Carl Frederick Adelcrantz. Perfectly preserved, this rococo chinoiserie gem, more delicate and refined than any of its German equivalents, stands on the site of Queen Louisa's fairy-tale birthday present, which had proved unable to withstand the Swedish winters.

There are four pavilions and an aviary at Kina, but the main building is a two-storied, small, symmetrical, semi-circular pavilion that filled the same role for the Swedish Royal family as the Petit Trianon did for the court of Versailles. In the charming phrase of the time, it was a *solitude*, a place where the family could be themselves. Daily, if the weather allowed, the royal family would drive the six miles from their palace to Kina where, a contemporary recorded, 'the King worked with his lathe, the Queen listened to her reader, the Prince drew, the Princesses made lace, Prince Carl sailed his frigate, Prince Frederick ran about on the grass and the guards smoked their pipes'.

The queen sent her architect's designs for Kina to a fellow enthusiast, her brother Frederick, the creator of the *Chinesisches Teehaus* in Potsdam.

The Green Salon, Kina, Drottningholm. Interior view and detail. *While the life-size standing figures, dressed in Chinese costume, recall the decoration of the Potsdam tea-house devised by Frederick the Great, the details of the decoration in the Green Salon are evidence of the pre-eminence of France's vision of Cathay among the princely Sinophiles in the rest of Europe. The walls of this Swedish rococo chinoiserie gem are painted green and gold with chinoiserie designs after Boucher and Pillement.*

There are similarities in the elevation of Kina and Frederick's pavilion, and the influence of the tea-house is particularly apparent in the use of English sash-windows, common to both buildings, which allow greater penetration of the northern light into the Kina's exquisite interiors. These reflect a mixture of European chinoiserie designers. The French are represented by Boucher and Watteau, the English by Halfpenny and Chambers, and the whole balanced by an architect who was neither too biased towards the rather over-exquisite taste of the French, nor towards the tendency to caricature of the English draughtsmen.

The plan as carried out consists of a central hexagonal entrance hall leading into an oval saloon, and flanked on either side by a red drawing-room and a pink drawing-room. These rooms in turn open into galleries, green to the west and yellow to the east, whose curved wings terminate in apartments, a green saloon in the east wing, a blue in the west. These two rooms, brilliant in colour and extravagantly mirrored, are decorated relatively inexpensively with wall paintings deriving from Boucher's engravings. Here in the icy north stand the mandarins and concubines of the land of Cathay. Inoffensive and contented, they idle away their time, not working at a lathe or making lace but in the immemorial pursuits of that enchanted land, fishing, arranging flowers in porcelain vases, and playing stringed instruments.

While Boucher's ladies dream under parasols on the over-door paintings of the yellow gallery, its walls are panelled with lacquer leaves of a Chinese screen split lengthways so as to allow both sides to be used. Engravings of costumes from Sir William Chambers'

recent publication *Designs of Chinese Buildings, Furniture, Dresses, etc.* provide the prototypes for the figures that swagger and posture on the red frieze below. The belief that Chambers depicted a realistic view of China was widely held. An engraving he published of the interior of a Cantonese house inspired the decoration of Kina's red room, with its black-and-gold lacquer panels, coral silk upholstered stools and red-painted woodwork.

The upper floor of Kina was a retreat where the queen could satisfy her intellectual interests. There was a library, and the set of rooms was exquisitely if less elaborately decorated, the walls covered with Chinese wallpaper or lined with painted taffeta. The library was left undecorated, although filled with porcelain treasures.

Not to be outdone, Frederick's favourite sister, Wilhelmina, the Margravine of Bayreuth, built a summer palace, Schloss Eremitage, which was bursting with chinoiserie. There was a Chinese kiosk in the garden; drawing-rooms decorated with a full complement of *singeries*, butterflies, Chinamen and flowers; and the *pièce de résistance*, a mirror-room. Here the eighteenth-century yellow wooden panels that line the walls are bewilderingly broken up, first by a series of seemingly randomly-dispersed, horizontal and vertical rectangular frames that enclose raised chinoiseries. These in turn are surrounded by pieces of looking-glass, unevenly shaped fragments which provide a kaleidoscopic series of fragmented images. For some reason this was supposed to be remarkably Chinese; it was believed that such patterns of fragmented mirror were found in the Ming palaces. Wilhelmina was so pleased with her mirror room that she had an almost exact copy built for her at Schloss Favorite, her villa near Baden-Baden. A contemporary engraving, now alas destroyed, depicted a Chinese Feast at Schloss Favorite with all the revellers wearing Chinese costume, but somehow its prevailing tone was more Hun than Han.

Much of Germany's chinoiseries came to the country second hand, but in one field Germany led and the rest of Europe followed. It was on German soil that the first true porcelain was produced in Europe, at the factory set up by Augustus the Strong at Meissen, a small town near his court at Dresden.

Engraving of a Chinese Feast held at Schloss Favorite, Baden-Baden, in 1729. *The Margravine of Bayreuth – sister of Frederick the Great and owner of Schloss Favorite – was infected with the family's dementia for all things Chinese.*

Stromsholm Palace, Sweden. Late eighteenth century. *(opposite) Detail of decorative painting by Lars Bolander in the Chinese Salon, a late example of the delicate chinoiseries favoured by the Swedish aristocracy.*

Augustus was a determined, not to say deranged, collector of oriental porcelain. He would pay any price for a piece that he wanted. His fellow prince, Frederick William of Prussia, displayed a similar sort of enthusiasm, though in his case its object was giants, whom he went about Europe kidnapping. As he also had a fine collection of porcelain, he and Augustus were able to indulge their respective penchants: in a logical – if lunatic – deal, Augustus swapped an entire regiment of Saxon dragoons for 48 vases. Augustus' obsession was draining the state's finances. 'China has become the bleeding-bowl of Saxony', shuddered Ehrenfried Walther von Tschirnhausen, the minister of finance at Augustus' court, and an amateur chemist. The only salvation for the Saxon treasury seemed to von Tschirnhausen to lie in the Saxons discovering how to produce porcelain for themselves. To aid him in the task the minister linked up with an alchemist, Johan Friedrich Böttger, who had been forced to leave Prussia rather precipitately when he had disappointed Frederick William (the giant stealer) by his failure to turn base metals into gold.

The ominous appearance of a military escort sent to accompany him to Dresden must have alarmed Böttger. But once there, after a short time spent at his old and fruitless quest for the philosopher's stone, Böttger and von Tschirnhausen settled down to crack the unsolved problem of the manufacture of hard-paste porcelain. The essential ingredients are china clay (kaolin) and china stone (petunze), which provides the translucence, but these are only part of the recipe. Success depends on their fusion at high temperature. Von Tschirnhausen had been experimenting with these techniques for

almost a decade, without results. The alchemists'
joint efforts at the vitrification of clay and rocks –
alabaster was used instead of petunze until 1719 –
first produced a hard, red, stoneware: rather like that
on Yi Hsing ware. A year later, in 1709, the year of
Tschirnhausen's death, Böttger produced the first
piece of white hard-paste porcelain manufactured
on European soil. Despite the rather grumpy sign
he had erected over his workshop, which read:

Gott unser Schopfer hat gemacht

aus einem Goldmacher einen Topfer

(God our creator has turned a gold-maker into
a potter), he must have felt a sense of triumph.

Interestingly, these first pieces of German
porcelain were not copies of Chinese porcelain at all.
They were firmly European, taking their forms from
the baroque silver of the day and their decoration,
which was applied not painted – and for which a

silversmith was responsible – from the standard
classical repertoire of acanthus leaves, masks and
rich mouldings. However unoriental it was, the
Elector was sufficiently pleased with Böttger's
work to to establish the Royal Saxon Porcelain
Manufactory at Meissen in 1710. A true white body
was achieved by 1715 and before Böttger's death in
1719 he had succeeded in producing a wide range of
enamel colours with which to decorate the porcelain.
Of course the secret of manufacture leaked out,
although it was considered so precious that workers
at the factory were threatened with death if they
breathed a word of it to anyone. Porcelain factories
began to spring up all over the place: one of the first
deserters from Meissen, Christoph Konrad Hunger,
busied himself from Vienna (1719) to Venice (1720),
and was to be found in Denmark a decade later and
in St Petersburg by 1743.

Meissen held on to its monopoly until 1747. But every German princeling wanted a porcelain factory, and most of them got one. It became, as the founder of the Ludwigsberg factory, Carl Eugen von Württemburg, candidly confessed, 'a necessary attribute to the glory and dignity of a prince'. In 1747 the *arcanum* was winkled out of the daughter of the owner of the Vienna factory, Claude Du Paquier; its lucky new possessor was off like a rocket and over the next decade or so eight porcelain factories were established on German soil in competition with the factory at Meissen.

Despite the establishment of other factories, Meissen's dominance continued. Its ascendancy was helped because one of the defecting employees of 1719, a man called Samuel Stötzel, returned from his traitorous excursion to Vienna after a year, bringing with him one of the most versatile enamellers

A selection of Meissen porcelain tableware, dating from 1720 to 1735. *The tankard and tea caddy are the work of the pioneer of chinoiserie decoration at Meissen, the renowned engraver and enameller Johann Gregor Horoldt.*

and engravers to work in the field of porcelain decoration, Johann Gregor Horoldt. Under Horoldt's direction a muffle-kiln was introduced to fire the painting on Meissen vessels and a faultless glaze and luminous range of colours began to appear. It was Horoldt who started the use of delightful chinoiserie decoration, both in bright polychrome enamels and in gold-leaf, a vein of pure fantasy that partly derived from the engravings of Watteau and Claude Gillot, and in some way anticipated the master of chinoiserie fantasy, Jean-Baptiste Pillement. Horoldt depicts all the common pursuits of Cathay: butterfly-hunting, tea-drinking, pipe smoking, fishing and umbrella-carrying; its diminutive citzens, always neatly dressed, wear a kind of fancy dress that combines traditional Chinese robes with the costumes of the *commedia dell'arte*.

Horoldt's decoration remains within the recognized chinoiserie tradition. Another decorator at Meissen in the 1720s and 1730s, A.F. von Lowenfinck, drew more unusually on the sparse beauty of Japanese Kakiemon designs for his inspiration. Nevertheless, the Prunus blossom, lithe tigers, quails and lozenge-shaped diapered patterns derived from silks, were all given a purely western twist of frivolity and fantasy.

Most of Meissen's useful ware was decorated with the so-called *Indianische blumen*, emphatically-coloured, fancifully-drawn flowers deriving from the paeonies and chrysanthemums first seen on the *famille verte* and *famille rose* wares that started to arrive in Europe at the beginning of the century. The painting of *Indianische blumen* on dinner services at Meissen gave way after about 1740 to more naturalistic European flowers, the so-called *Deutsche blumen*, but exotic flowers remained popular at porcelain factories elsewhere in Europe throughout the eighteenth century, and in some cases well into the nineteenth century.

One particular attribute of German hard-paste porcelain is its *kleinplastiek*, its sculptural quality. Meissen's lasting fame rested on its figures. Apart from the suitability of the material for modellers, there are three good reasons for this: tradition, fashion and divine intervention. First, Germany had an artistic heritage of carving, and was well known for its small boxwood sculptures, many of which are of outstanding quality. Second, there was a vogue at court for decorating the dining-table with ephemeral figures of sugar or wax, which were placed down the length of the table and modelled to be seen in the round, not only from the front. Third, Johann Joachim Kandler was appointed *modellmeister* at Meissen in 1731.

Augustus the Strong had constantly pressed for colossal birds and beasts to be created out of porcelain, which he intended to display at his Japanese palace. Porcelain is not the medium for large-scale sculpture, and although Kandler obliged the Elector with some of these creations, his real genius lay in modelling a world of tiny figures – some say over a thousand – which invaded the drawing rooms, china cabinets, boudoirs and tables of countless fortunate owners all over the world. Never conceived merely as shrunken versions of monumental figures, these diminutive objects were perfectly attuned to their size. Kandler became recognized as the master of the material. The production of porcelain statuettes received the status of an art from the moment of its appearance.

Unfortunately chinoiseries played only a rather minor part in Kandler's production, although he did model numbers of monkey musicians, so adding a chapter to the strange story of *singeries*. Perhaps his greatest contribution to chinoiserie is a tea-set where the teapot takes the appropriate form of a Chinese woman riding a cockerel, and a pair of embracing Chinese lovers provide a convenient vessel for the sugar.

After the death of Augustus the Strong in 1733, the Meissen factory came under the direction of Count Brühl. By 1750 the factory employed nearly seven hundred hands and was Saxony's greatest source of income, but the manufacture of chinoiseries had declined and output had turned more to purely western sources of inspiration.

Of the many porcelain factories set up to rival Meissen, Nymphenburg, in Bavaria, was most perfectly in tune with German rococo taste. The factory was set up in 1747 by the Bavarian Elector, Prince Maximilian Joseph III, who was married to yet another granddaughter of Augustus the Strong, and whose earlier eighteenth-century forebears had produced the great rococo chinoiserie follies of the Pagodenburg and the Amalienburg. The Nymphenburg factory produced some attractive pieces in what was by now an established tradition, but then had the good luck in 1754 to employ a genius, Franz Anton Bustelli, as its chief modeller. Bustelli produced porcelain figures that combined a feeling for form, perhaps bequeathed him by his Italian ancestry, with delicacy, elegance and wit. They are among the masterpieces of the rococo style. Some chinoiserie figures form part of this charmed output: they include musicians, pagods and priests,

but perhaps the most enchanting are the figures of Chinese children in which spontaneity of pose and sweetness of expression are captured for all time in the most beautiful hard-paste produced in Europe.

Figure groups, sometimes of two figures sometimes of more, formed part of all German porcelain factories' output, and chinoiseries made up some of the group subjects, as they did individual figures. At Nymphenburg, a Bustelli group shows a Chinese teacher and his small pupil who clutches his head as he battles with the Chinese equivalent of irregular verbs. A rather grander note is struck by an anonymous modeller at Höchst, known only as the *Chinesenmeister*, who produced a pair of large groups, the Emperor and Empress of China, where the couple are flanked by elegant courtiers and a Pekinese dog makes an appropriate appearance.

If the colour and plasticity of German porcelain did not produce enough dazzle, its glamour and opulence could be augmented by adding ormolu mounts, and on occasion soft-paste Vincennes flowers too. Mounting porcelain in ormolu was a taste particularly favoured by the French, perhaps because their own soft-paste porcelain objects were so fragile and the oriental pieces so precious, but the practice was not restricted to oriental porcelain or the products of French factories.

Although hard-paste porcelain production had finally come to Europe, it would be wrong to think that the French gave up production of their exquisite soft-paste porcelain without a struggle. Soft-paste porcelain is more difficult to model, more expensive to produce, more inclined to break, and generally less practical, less white, and less durable than true hard-paste porcelain. But it is aesthetically superior,

Statuette of a seated Chinaman, the god of longevity. Chantilly, c.1725-50. *Soft-paste porcelain was notoriously difficult to model and figures are rare. The painted decoration on the robes of this charming example copy the style of Meissen rather than China, demonstrating the spread of chinoiserie as an independent style.*

Faience fish-plate, Luneville, c.1760. *(opposite) The plate is appropriately decorated in polychrome enamels with diminutive Chinese fishermen.*

a medium of such exquisite quality that one can understand the reluctance to abandon it. The soft paste is so soft that the pigment is absorbed into the body and the decoration thus becomes inseparable from the glaze; it is not painted on, it is part of the piece.

Until about 1740 French soft-paste porcelain factories were not really influenced by the great events taking place at Meissen. They had developed along their own lines with their own methods of production and their own styles, in which chinoiseries predominated. St Cloud specialized in *blanc-de-chine* wares, which were inspired by Chinese examples and decorated with the application of sprigs of flowering Prunus or an unusual pattern of overlapping scales, sometimes known as *fleurs d'artichaut*. Chinese and Japanese figures were produced, sometimes decorated in enamel, but more often left white. The soft paste was extremely difficult to model, and the figures lack the plasticity of those produced at Meissen, but they make up for it with an appeal and charm that is entirely Gallic.

Polychrome decoration, in a range of bright enamel colours, was introduced some time after 1730 for Kakiemon-style decorations. These were extremely varied: landscapes, elongated ladies, birds and flowers. The Duc d'Orléans, who was a great protector of the St Cloud factory, lent its workers examples of oriental china from his own important collection. This was a fairly common practice. Augustus did the same at Meissen, and the Prince de Condé, who had a superb collection, allowed his modellers at Chantilly to become familiar with his own Japanese and Chinese porcelain pieces before attempting a French translation.

The most famous French porcelain factory of them all, Sèvres, was protected and financed by the Crown. Founded at Vincennes in 1738, and transferred to Sèvres in 1756, it was granted a 20-year monopoly in 1753 – the year it was styled the 'Manufacture Royale de Porcelaine' – to make porcelain in the *façon de Saxe*, that is with figures and gilding. For good measure not only was porcelain production anywhere else in France prohibited but faience decorated like porcelain was banned too. After the factory's moved to Sèvres, its privileges continued. Even after the privileges were relaxed in 1766, no other French factories were allowed to produce porcelain with coloured grounds or with gilding. Paradoxically this embargo led to the production of chinoiseries of greater delicacy than those of Sèvres. This was particularly marked at Chantilly, where the Kakiemon palette of brick red, clear blue, pale yellow and turquoise-green were perfectly fused into the soft white glaze, and the figures were discreetly outlined in black.

At Sèvres the simplest piece of porcelain passed through the hands of eight different specialist craftsmen, and on special pieces no flaw, no matter how slight, was permitted. If a single black speck, the size of a pin-head, marred the glaze, the piece would be rejected, condemned to the ranks of 'seconds', to be sold at a discount to someone prepared to put up with less than perfection. The factory did not begin to abandon its notoriously difficult soft-paste for the more practical advantages of hard-paste production until the end of 1769. And even after the discovery of kaolin on French soil, soft-paste continued to be made at Sèvres. It was not abandoned finally until the nineteenth century.

Chinoiserie products at Sèvres are of three kinds. In the early, less opulent Vincennes period, the first chinoiseries were not much different from those of other factories. They included *blanc-de-chine* wares, chinoiseries sometimes with applied decoration, sometimes with delicate gilding or blue enamel decoration, and an exquisitely realized Kakiemon-style design, possibly inspired by Meissen. The porcellanous material however was already extraordinary, so beautiful that a member of the Academy of Sciences, Jean Hellot, could write: *'l'art imite parfaitement en Europe ce que fait la nature en Chine'.*

Once Madame de Pompadour and the king became interested in the factory, decoration grew more elaborate, and chinoiseries were often combined with the brilliant ground colours that were to distinguish Sèvres products. In this second stage of Sèvres chinoiseries figures were seldom modelled, because of the difficulties of working the soft paste. When they were, as in a rare example of two Chinese figures, a young woman and a young man, they possess all the well-bred charm and allure of a Boucher canvas. Some mid-eighteenth century Sèvres porcelain is decorated with entire Boucher canvasses, miniaturized and painted on the

Ice-bucket, Sèvres factory. Mid-eighteenth century. *Chinese fishing was a favourite motif of the period. This splendid example of the grande-luxe style of Sèvres soft-paste porcelain is painted like a tiny canvas with a version of* The Chinese Fishing Party *by Boucher.*

Vincennes soft-paste porcelain group, c.1750. *(opposite) French artists and craftsmen tended to integrate chinoiserie subjects into the overall taste of the time. Here, purely rococo motifs are mixed with a pair of exquisitely attired Chinese.*

Sèvres double-gourd vase, c.1789-92. *(opposite right) Enamelled black in imitation of lacquer. The chinoiserie decoration in the style of Pillement is applied in two tones of gold and in platinum. Chinoiserie designs lingered on at Sèvres, their frivolous subject matter often co-existing some-what uneasily with the moral severity of neo-classicism.*

porcelain. An ice-bucket, for example, bears an exquisite rendering of *The Chinese Fishing Party*, one of the scenes created by Boucher for the Beauvais tapestry factory, here transposed to another medium with consummate success. The handles of the bucket resemble bent twigs, a form also found in Chinese porcelain. This kind of naturalism is tailor-made for the rococo style. It is also a perfect foil for the qualities of the porcelain.

Chinoiserie subjects continue to decorate the hard-paste body developed in the third phase, although now more often found on severely neo-classical forms such as urns or egg-shaped vases with covers. Here the lighthearted painting of Chinese figures under parasols seems rather at odds with the shape of pieces that recall the grandeur that was Rome rather than the land of Cathay. Some of the unapologetically rococo forms and chinoiserie scenes found in the late eighteenth-century designs of

Sèvres must be reckoned rather old-fashioned. Perhaps they seem so because of the prevalence of the neo-classical taste, whose monumental and grave style of design and decoration is quite alien to the plastic properties and frivolous charm of porcelain. But also, the court, the chief purchaser of Sèvres, was attached to the Rococo. Court style was less austere in general than the prevailing neo-classicism, and the queen, Marie Antoinette, was as keen on exoticism as her predecessors. These factors may account for the Sèvres factory's persistence well into the late eighteenth century with chinoiserie subjects that recall Boucher's designs for the *tentures chinoises* dating from 1742, or playful scenes of *singeries* or see-sawing Chinamen which are reminiscent of the designs of Jean Pillement.

In Russia, the fretwork, bells and dragons of Cathay made an early appearance. Monplaisir, Peter the Great's summer palace in the grounds of Peterhof

Palace (and rather confusingly known as the Dutch House) had a scarlet lacquer cabinet, since restored, whose gilt chinoiserie scenes and brackets holding porcelain would have done credit to any European dreams of oriental pleasure. The grounds of Oranienbaum, the summer palace of the Czars on the Gulf of Finland, are littered with palaces, large and small, manifestations of the rather murky pleasures of Russia's rulers. Catherine the Great's architect, Antonio Rinaldi, designed Katalnaya Gorka, a small palace in the grounds that was intended for nothing more taxing than a day's amusement. This little plaything has a porcelain monkey-room where brackets – several in the form of monkeys, others of ho-ho birds with brackets perched on their heads or outstretched wings – support frivolous porcelain trifles manufactured at the Meissen factory in the eighteenth century.

　　In 1762, shortly after her successful coup against her husband, Catherine the Great

commissioned Rinaldi to build a Chinese Palace at Oranienbaum. This was erected as far away as possible from the Great Palace and the Palace of Peter III. Like Peter the Great's palace it began life as the Dutch House, an entirely unjustified description, although perhaps no more so than calling Chinese the pink-and-white exterior of the single-storied palace. It was also referred to as 'the Empress's Own House' or 'the Solitude', as was its contemporary, Kina, its neighbour in snowy Sweden.

Inside, the enfilade of state rooms does contain a number of interiors decorated with rococo chinoiseries. One, the Glass Bead Room, is unique in the history of chinoiserie taste. Three of its walls are

ornamented with decorative panels designed by the master of chinoiserie fantasy, Jean Pillement. Here his long-tailed birds inhabit a dreamy, moonlit world of giant flowers and delicate trees embroidered in thick silks on a background of two million glass beads, faintly coloured in blue, mauve and pink. The embroidery was done in France, the beaded background possibly in Russia. Presumably Rinaldi was responsible for the concept, while his team of Italian craftsmen carved the gilded palm trees that divide the panels, and the delicate, white, stuccoed tendrils that climb the wall above the mantel.

In other rooms the chinoiserie decoration is more conventional, with painted Chinese silks on

Chinese Palace, Oranienbaum. Interior showing the enfilade of state rooms. *(left) While guests could stroll through a sequence of chinoiserie interiors, they did not tarry long. In a reign of 34 years, Catherine the Great is reported to have visited her chinoiserie summer palace no more than once or twice a year.*

Exterior *(above)* **and detail.** *(right) Catherine the Great's Chinese palace was one of a number of palaces set in the extensive grounds of woods and lakes at Oranienbaum on the Gulf of Finland. She commissioned an Italian architect to design her palace, and an Englishman to lay out the gardens.*

Chinese Palace, Oranienbaum. *Designed by Antonio Rinaldi in 1762-8. In common with much eighteenth-century architecture that purports to be Chinese, the exterior of the palace is innocent of any trace of chinoiserie. It was widely accepted, however, that a relatively sober exterior could conceal a mandarin-infested interior.*

Detail of porcelain Chinese family from the Royal Palace at Portici, 1757. *From one of the most exquisite and elaborate of all the eighteenth century's chinoiserie follies: the Porcelain Room at Portici, the palace of the King and Queen of Naples.*

the walls and Chinese dragons flexing their wings on the ceiling. The Large Chinese Room, the final room in the enfilade, has its walls decorated with inlaid wooden panels of Chinese landscapes, finely realized in Karelian birch, rosewood, Persian oak, amaranth and boxwood. Overhead a Chinese wedding is celebrated on the painted ceiling. Incongruously, the room houses nothing more exotic than a richly carved English billiard table.

Italy, the home of classicism, had no aversion to chinoiserie. The cult flourished there as elsewhere in Europe, and received a particularly Mediterranean twist by being absorbed into the Italian gusto for pageantry. When Augustus the Strong visited Venice in 1716, the traditional regatta staged in his welcome featured a junk bulging with bells in addition to the normal complement of gondolas. On board were an

exotic cargo of Chinese singers, dancers and musicians, and the whole crazy craft was propelled down the Grand Canal by coolie gondoliers. More than half a century later, a chinoiserie entertainment was still considered the height of fashion. When the marriage of the Duke of Parma to the daughter of Empress Maria Theresa was celebrated, the guests were invited to a Chinese fair, where troupes of entertainers dressed as Chinese performed in a specially built piazza which housed Chinese shops. The high point was the arrival of a series of eastern caravans, each carrying musicians who, according to a contemporary description, 'discoursed singular music'. Next, a scene drawn from the most extreme imaginings of the porcelain decorators suddenly sprang into life: 'All at once, the puppets acted and danced, the players on musical glasses performed

Engraving after Ennemont Pettitot, 1769. *A chubby Chinese baby shielded by a bell-hung parasol is flanked by two classical amorini in this engraving published in a folio celebrating the marriage of the Duke of Parma to a daughter of the Empress Maria Theresa.*

Yellow lacquer door decorated with chinoiserie figures. From the Palazzo Rezzonico, Venice, mid-eighteenth century. *In 1754 there were 25 lacquer masters in Venice, all with thriving workshops.*

their tunes, and the children jumped over their cassolettes or walked on tightropes while at the same time sounding their bells above their heads.'

Venice had been open to the East since the days of Marco Polo, and Venetian lacquer was known and admired in the seventeenth century, although no known examples have survived. Its production reached its apogee in the eighteenth century, and it is still produced today. The charm of Venetian lacquer lies in its pretty colours and the exuberance of its decoration. Unhappily the carpentry was often of a very poor standard. This was furniture intended for show, furniture made to cut a *bella figura* against the glitter and gilding of the piano nobile, not meant for use in the simpler, more comfortable family rooms above and below the first floor. Thus bureaux and swelling high-bosomed commodes became prime targets for lacquer-makers.

Early eighteenth-century lacquer designs were directly inspired by the Far East. The red or black ground colours were decorated in gold with an assortment of exotic subjects: mandarins, women shaded by umbrellas, opium smokers, Mongol servants, elephants, camels, parrots and huge flowers. This cast was assembled and arranged, often with more vitality than skill. Little by little the style grew freer, more western, with children and goddesses surrounded by flowers and *rocailles*. Sometimes the japanned decoration was executed in the studios of well-known artists, not above a little humble work.

Lacquer painting was practised not only in Venice but throughout Italy, and for those unable to afford the style there was a cheap and cheerful alternative. *lacca contrafatta*. These were little paper cut-outs that could be stuck onto furniture, chiefly used on display pieces like console tables or commodes. Local wood was given a cover of stucco or plaster, the decorations were painted in tempera and then the whole surface lacquered or varnished. The designs were principally supplied by Remondini, a firm in Bassano who published a series of engravings suitable for the purpose. They are similar to those of Pillement, with Chinamen in whimsical pursuits surrounded by large flowers and gigantic insects.

Green-and-gold lacquered chest of drawers. Venetian, mid-eighteenth century.
The opulence and vibrancy of colour of the rich decoration are typically Venetian, while the combination of chinoiserie figures with European sprays of flowers is characteristic of the rococo style.

The Earl of Cork, doing the Grand Tour in 1754, declared approvingly of the Palazzo Reale in Turin: 'Amidst all the exotic decoration not one effeminate toy, not one *Chinese* dragon, nor Indian motif is to be seen.' How he missed the lacquer room is mysterious. Sixty pieces of oriental lacquer, augmented by others japanned locally in Turin, all depicting birds, flowers, and Chinese scenes in blue, red and gold on a black background, were set in rococo scrolls and placed on the vermilion walls of the room. Piedmont in the north of Italy was more subject to French influence, and lacquer rooms were not uncommon. In other parts of the country where the native style of fresco decoration flourished, its subject matter was extended to include chinoiseries.

Decoration in Palazzo Reale, Turin, 1735. *(opposite) Turin ranked second only to Venice in the production of lacquer in Italy, and one of the most impressive lacquer rooms of the early eighteenth century is in its royal palace. Some of these shaped lacquer panels are of oriental lacquer, others are local copies.*

Red lacquer room from Piedmont, eighteenth century. *(above) Brilliantly coloured lacquer panels set in ornate gilded borders make the decoration of this small room opulent without being overwhelming.*

Detail of decoration in private theatre in the Italian Embassy, Paris. *(above left) The decoration incorporates pieces from an eighteenth-century lacquer room in Palermo.*

The Villa la Barbariga at Stra has one room with specifically Chinese motifs: little figures in pagoda hats, spindly trees, canopies, idly wandering mandarins. At the Villa Valmarana at Vicenza, decorated by Gian Domenico Tiepolo (the son of the great Venetian rococo artist, who painted very much in the same style and worked with his father on numerous projects) an entire series of frescoed rooms has survived. One room, the Foresteria, is frescoed with large Chinese scenes given a particularly Venetian quality of richness and lightness.

The most extraordinary examples of chinoiserie in Italy lie far further south, beyond Rome, in Naples and in Sicily. Here, within shouting distance of the greatest excavations of classical remains at Pompeii and Herculaneum – which had then been recently revealed – the King and Queen of Naples created a porcelain room at their royal palace at Portici, later removed to the Museo di Capodimonte in Naples. The room was completely lined with around three thousand pieces of Capodimonte porcelain, mostly in a pure, glistening white. They fitted together like a jigsaw and had their interstices covered by festoons of flowers, bunches of ribbons and trophies of musical instruments. Between the windows and above the doors stand groups of brightly enamelled porcelain Chinamen in high relief, reflected in the grey glass of tall mirrors placed between the windows. The ceiling is stuccoed with fantastic birds and butterflies perched on rococo scrolls, and from its centre a monkey, crouched among the feathery plumes of a pineapple, dangles a sparkling chandelier from his paw.

The whole concept may appear a little overwrought to more puritan northern tastes, but

Fresco in Villa Reale, Stupinigi. *A suitably inscrutable fresco decoration of a Chinese cobbler, his pipe-smoking companion, a mother with bound feet and their plump children, ornaments the Salotto Cinese of the Villa Reale, a splendid royal hunting-lodge outside Turin.*

Villa Valmarana, Vicenza. Fresco decoration by G. D. Tiepolo, 1757. *A mandarin, Venetian in all but name, rustles in his silken robes while a diminutive pig-tailed jester carries a bell-hung cane.*

the king was so delighted with it that when he succeeded to the throne of Spain in 1759, two years after the completion of this porcelain *parfait*, he took its guiding spirits with him and set about recreating the room in his palace at Aranjuez. Here the Capodimonte workers produced similar decoration, but at Aranjuez the large-scale porcelain relief figures of Chinamen are so markedly superior that we must look elsewhere for their design. They bear close affinities both in detail and in general composition to Tiepolo's frescoes at the Villa Valmarana. G. D. Tiepolo was in Madrid in the early 1760s. Along with his three brothers he was helping his father in his labours at the Royal Palace in Madrid where, over a four year period, huge expanses of ceiling were decorated. It seems likely that this son had a hand in designing the porcelain reliefs at Aranjuez.

In the way that a passion for chinoiserie seems to be transmitted among family members, Carlo III of Spain – the owner of the porcelain rooms – had a son, the grandly-titled Ferdinando IV, King of the Two Sicilies. Ferdinando built just outside Palermo what is undoubtedly the most elaborate and complete specimen of late eighteenth-century Italian chinoiserie, a building that is unique in the history of the style: the villa La Favorita. Also known as the *Palazzina Cinese*, it has been closed to the public for over 20 years while undergoing restoration.

This Chinese palazzo owes its existence to the fortunes of war. As Napoleon's armies pressed ever closer, so King Ferdinando rapidly transferred his court from Naples to Sicily, arriving at Palermo in December 1798 somewhat ingloriously, on board Nelson's flagship *Vanguard*. Safe and sound, and rather bored, the king and queen amused themselves with the construction of a summer palace, where they entertained their saviour Nelson at a banquet in May 1799, shortly before he departed for Naples to inflict a crushing defeat on the Parthenopean Republic that had displaced the king. After fireworks and fêtes to celebrate their deliverance, Ferdinando returned to Naples, but quite soon found himself back in exile at La Favorita. There from 1805 he whiled away the time, living at La Favorita, cooking and making ice-cream, until the victory of Waterloo deposited him back on the throne of Naples.

The author of this architectural frivolity was a neo-classical architect, Giuseppe Patricola. He designed a square four-storeyed villa, originally stuccoed in a warm yellow with *trompe l'œil* architectural ornaments of pointed canopies and curving brackets picked out in brick red. The entrances to the two main façades are the same, colonnaded semi-circular porticoes whose classical appearance is subdued by architraves emblazoned with Chinese characters and upswept polygonal canopies. The roof has an octagonal belvedere crowned with a rather dumpy pagoda roof of two bell-like cones, and is flanked by large loggias surrounded by iron fretwork railings. The same Chinese railings are found on all the balconies that run around the façade like open galleries on both of its principal floors.

The first guidebook to mention the house, the *Guida Italiana per Palermo e Dintorni* of 1816, informs its readers that 'the pavilion is built in the Chinese taste and wholly conforms to the usage of that nation. On the façade hang numerous little bells

Porcelain Room, Palacio Real, Aranjuez. *(opposite) A recreation of the porcelain room at Naples was one of the first acts of King Carlo III when he succeeded to the Spanish throne in 1759. The large-scale reliefs of Chinese figures closely resemble the frescoed figures of the Villa Valmarana.*

Villa Favorita, Palermo, Sicily. *Chinese motifs bedeck the gates of the Palazzo Cinese.*

Villa Favorita, Palermo, built in 1799 to the design of Giuseppe Patricola. Exterior view. *Neo-classicism and chinoiserie combine to embellish the façade of La Favorita. A semi-circular portico whose architrave is lettered in Chinese characters rises beneath a squat, pagoda-roofed tower. The yellow of the traditionally stuccoed walls is decorated with* trompe l'œil *architectural ornaments picked out in red.*

Fresco decoration in the Sala da Giuoco or card-room. *A series of frieze-like panels framed within an elaborate Chinese trellised surround, portrays groups of Chinamen showing off their rich robes under a cloudless Sicilian sky.*

that tinkle in the breeze … In the rooms there is
nothing that is not of great worth, the most exquisite
workmanship and variety of materials having vied to
adorn them.' The interior certainly employs various
styles, but this being Italy painted decoration
prevails, and fresco decoration is predominant.
The villa contains one of the prettiest conceits of
the eighteenth century, a ground floor apartment –
reputedly where the king used to conduct business
with his ministers – painted in *trompe l'œil* to
resemble a ruined Pompeian villa, its roof decayed
and open to the sky and large patches of damp on the
walls. There is also a Pompeian boudoir with painted
decoration said to be of Lady Hamilton in her
'attitudes'. If 'Pompeian' can be stretched this
far then it is hardly surprising to find a kind of
Pompeian chinoiserie decoration present too.

All the chinoiserie interiors are to be found in
the king's first-floor apartments. There is a supper-
room, where Ferdinando's guests could appreciate
his culinary prowess, a gaming room to which they
could later repair, and the king's bedroom, separated
from the other rooms by a long saloon. The dining-
room is painted to resemble a leafy arbour – a well-
known Italian device – but the trellises through
which the branches twine are painted to look like
Chinese frets and are capped with pagoda roofs from
which stiff little pennants flutter. The landscapes
painted on the flanking walls depict pastoral scenes
where Chinese coolies are hard at work in the
rice paddies.

The painter of this delightful room, Giuseppe
Patania, may also have been responsible for the
decoration of the king's bedroom, where the Tree of
Life motif found on the walls is quite eclipsed by the
painting of the double-coved ceiling. Here an array of
Chinese notables stand behind the fretted railings of
a balcony and gaze down on the king. The little *sala
del giuoco* – the games room – has a similar cast of
Chinese onlookers, who line the walls with an air of
solid self-assurance that marks them as the product
of the classical world. As in the central saloon, the
ceiling is painted in a style best described as
Pompeian chinoiserie: richly attired mandarins and
pagoda-roofed fretted pavilions replace the Roman
temples and classical maidens of the Pompeian style.
It is no surprise to learn that the Palermo-born artist,
Giuseppe Velasco, was normally to be found
depicting the chaste heroes of the neo-classical
pantheon. The octagonal belvedere at the top of the
house is again embellished in the Chinese taste, but
this time the room is hung with Chinese wallpaper,
rather oddly offset by English prints. The queen's
apartments on the second floor are a mix of
Pompeian and other styles, and include an exquisite
'Turkish' boudoir, all light green, turquoise, gold
and white.

The eclectic mixture of styles found in the Villa
Favorita tells us that we are trembling on the brink
of the nineteenth century, and the exoticism of the
Brighton Pavilion. But the wit and assurance with
which a group of local Sicilians combined to make
this chinoiserie fantasy for a Bourbon king is
essentially Italianate; it grew out of the artistic
traditions of the country. This moulding of the style
to fit the nation's taste is seen in France, in Germany,
in Scandinavia, in Russia and in Italy. And in
England, as shall be seen, chinoiserie decoration also
draws on existing traditions, to add another highly
individual flavour to the style.

Rococo chinoiserie in English interiors

Thus it is happened … we must all seek the barbarous gaudy *goût* of the Chinese; and fat-headed Pagods and shaking Mandarins bear the prize from the greatest works of antiquity; and Apollo and Venus must give way to a fat idol with a sconce on his head.

Letter from Mrs Montagu, 1749

Plate-printed Irish linen. Late eighteenth century. *A process of decorating fabrics using engraved copper plates was pioneered in Ireland. Designs were obtained from a wide range of sources; here, among the blossoming branches and asymmetrical lines derived from the Tree of Life pattern, are the familiar long-tailed birds and flimsy pavilions of Cathay.*

Sheet iron lacquer kettle with gilt fittings. English, c.1760. *An English invention, lacquering on tin-plated sheet iron is popularly known as Pontypool japan, after the town in Monmouthshire that was the source of much of the best eighteenth-century tin-plated japanned ware.*

English taste always lagged behind French. France set the pace in Europe, and in France rococo taste was already old hat when its novelty was creating shock waves across the channel. Its late arrival in England, around the middle of the eighteenth century, challenged the Rule of Taste, the dictates of Lord Burlington and the domination of the Palladian style he had so ardently espoused. The world had grown tired of the predictability of the great Whig palaces, the grand and masculine façades, the vast scale, the cold and splendid manner of it all. People were ready for something new.

The long reign of classicism was drawing to a close, and the Rococo appeared to be its somewhat unlikely-looking heir. It might have helped Rococo's cause that for once England and France were at peace. But the allure of French fashion led to wide copying, whatever the state of relations between the two countries. Nevertheless, a French provenance did not necessarily assure commendation. In 1738 the fashionable magazine *The World* cautioned its readers against any such slavishness: 'The ridiculous imitation of the French taste has now become the Epidemical distemper of our Kingdom, our cloathes, our furniture, nay our food too, all is to come from France.'

Among those who were not readers of *The World*, the artisans and craftsmen, the opinion of France was distinctly negative. Since the end of the seventeenth century, immigrant French craftsmen had provided England with a much-needed infusion of intellectual talent and design skills, but this had not made them welcome. Any move by parliament to better their status met with a barrage of shrill dissent. 'No French Bottle-Makers! No Lowering of Wages of Labouring Men to 4d a Day and Garlick!' was the chant of a Bristol mob in 1754. Cordiality towards the new French taste had somehow to be reconciled with disaffection towards France. It was not only labouring men who opposed the Frenchification of English taste. Astonishingly, many of the artists and patrons of the new Rococo movement were also members of the Antigallican Society, which was founded around 1745 expressly 'to oppose the insidious Arts of the French Nation'. And of course the Whig party was patriotically committed to Palladian classicism.

By and large the new French taste found its early adherents among those on the fringes of power, and those least committed to Whig taste: Tories and Catholics anathematized by the Whigs, and the fashionable world beyond Whig politics. But not all Whigs were xenophobic 'mountains of roast beef', as Horace Walpole had quiveringly described them. Much as they disliked the politics of France, these Whigs admired and emulated its cultural and artistic primacy, accepting France as being, in Voltaire's phrase, 'the whipped cream of Europe'. French Rococo, or 'the modern style' as it was often called, did become accepted in certain quarters in England. In 1747 Lord Chesterfield, as smart as paint and Whig to the marrow – if out of office – decorated the drawing-room of his house in South Audley Street in a completely Frenchified rococo style. The example was not greatly followed, for the style depended on the use of *boiseries* – decorative panelling – a fashion not easily adopted in English houses, where the rooms lacked the proportions of the French salons, and the owners wanted to keep the walls free of decoration in order to display the paintings they had acquired on the Grand Tour.

Variety was part of the charm of the Rococo, and years of an unchanging diet of Palladianism had sharpened an appetite for it. If the purely French aspects of the rococo style were not in favour, there were other ways to be *à la mode*. Two other styles rose with the Rococo: the Gothic and chinoiserie. Eighteenth-century Gothic taste could easily be accommodated within the Rococo; the desire for irregularity of outline and ornament was naturally present in both, and eighteenth-century 'Gothick' was gay and colourful, qualities it shared with the Rococo. Nor did the Gothic's admirers feel the need for stylistic purity. Indeed both Gothic and chinoiserie ornament could be combined on a single piece of English rococo furniture. This kind of admixture would not have been tolerated in France. Even in England it raised eyebrows. 'It has not escaped your notice,' a contributor to *The World* wrote ironically, 'how much of late we are improved by architecture; not merely by the adoption of what we call Chinese, nor by the restoration of what we call Gothic; but by a happy mixture of both. From Hyde Park to Shoreditch scarce a chandler's shop or an oyster-stall but has embellishments of this kind.'

Chinoiserie, largely suppressed by the emphatic and narrow dictates of the Burlington school, was liberated by the rise of the Rococo, and was about to enjoy unparalleled success. But its success in England differed from its success in France, where it had been seamlessly absorbed into the body of the rococo style. In England chinoiserie was a quite independent element, a wild and frivolous changeling of the parent style. Its eccentricity and complete lack of seriousness may have been due to the insouciant view of China already present in the

English decorative tradition: the exotic scenery and well-known wayward behaviour of Cathay had a natural claim to represent any element of fun in the taste of the day. But there was another key difference: patronage. Unlike France and the rest of Europe, rococo chinoiserie in England was not the exclusive plaything of the rich and well-born. Here, there was no royal patron, no formal mentor, no powerful champion to sanction the style with his imprimatur as Horace Walpole did the Gothic.

On the contrary, chinoiserie attracted the attentions of the compilers of pattern-books and of carvers, occupations not pursued, at least in England, by men of greatly educated taste. Yet it was these men who were responsible for chinoiserie's vitality and for the craze for all things Chinese that swept through the decoration of the period, reaching its height in

Toilet mirror, c.1720. *The sober outline of this Queen Anne green lacquer mirror is decorated with sprightly red-and-gold chinoiseries.*

the 1750s. And the style that they produced did not rest on French chinoiserie taste at all. It was Horace Walpole himself who spotted this trend while it was still in its infancy. Writing anonymously in *The World* in 1751 this great enunciator of taste produced the barbed observation: 'Our Chinese ornaments are not only of our own manufacture, like our French silks … but, what has seldom been attributed to the English, of our own invention.'

By 1765 the craze was on the wane, although the new style, neo-classicism, did not eclipse it entirely. Ten years later, in 1775, the Duke of Argyll's mansion at Twickenham could still be described as 'highly Oriental in its furnishing'. Both of the neo-classical masters, Robert Adam and Sir William Chambers, produced refined chinoiserie designs or used the style for interiors, the latter doing so at the same time as expressly deprecating the 'extravagant fancies that daily appear under the name of Chinese'. Chambers issued these strictures in 1757, in *Designs of Chinese Buildings, Furniture, Dresses, etc.*, the last of the pattern-books of chinoiserie designs that had appeared so thick and fast in the 1750s.

These books presented patrons and craftsmen with engraved plates of designs. They offered a choice of style to a society interested in fashion and design, one that had some money and was eager to spend it. The first pattern-book explicitly devoted to chinoiserie designs was *New Designs for Chinese Temples, Triumphal Arches, Garden Seats, Palings etc.* by William Halfpenny, sixty plates of entertaining designs all in the Chinese taste. Garden ornamentation was an abiding preoccupation of rococo chinoiserie designers. For just as rococo design indoors commonly used decorative motifs derived from nature – not only rocks and shells but flowers, branches and woodland creatures – so the ideas of the drawing-room began to invade the garden. Landscape gardening was by now well underway and parklands had begun to change their character, undergoing reconstruction as outdoor drawing-rooms, dotted with architectural additions of gazebos, follies, grottoes, gates and temples. And oddity of oddities, these were often Chinese – for reasons that will be more closely examined in the following chapter.

Engravings from Sir William Chambers, *Designs of Chinese Buildings, Furniture, Dresses, etc.*, 1757. *Bamboo makes its appearance in western design (left) with these chairs and table illustrated in Chambers' compendious publication. His meticulous draughtsmanship introduced a more scholarly note to the previously unfettered chinoiserie fantasies of eighteenth-century Europe. Plate II (top right) is described by the author as 'almost an exact copy of the Cochin-China Pagoda'. Plate IX (right) shows a Chinese merchant's house.*

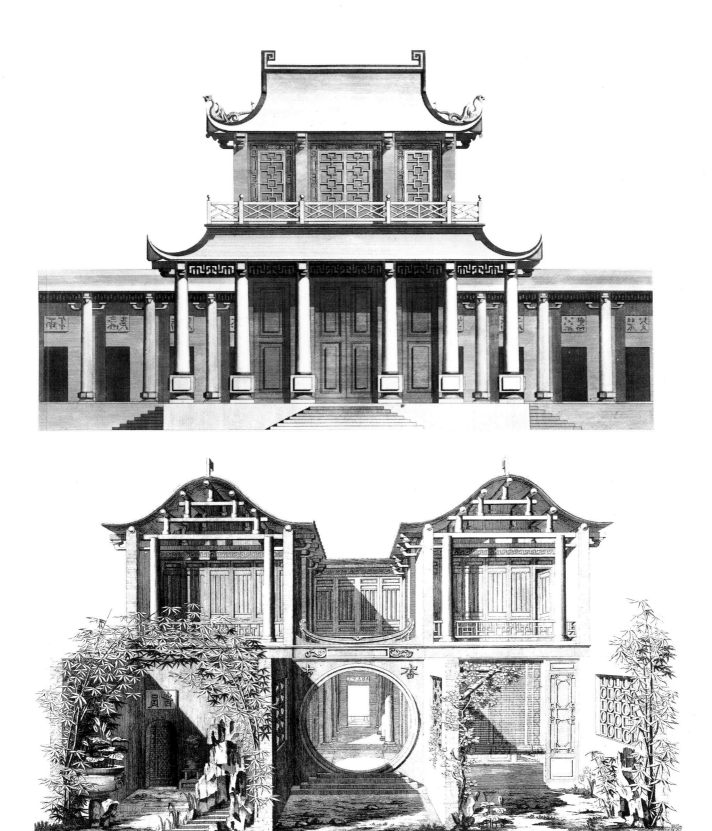

Engraving from William Halfpenny's *New Designs for Chinese Temples*, 1750. *English rococo taste abjured any kind of stylistic purity, and a mix of Gothick and chinoiserie designs was common.*

Illustration for a design for a mirror. *(opposite) From the first book of English chinoiserie designs for interiors,* A New Book of Ornaments in the Chinese Taste *(1752), by Lock and Copland. English rococo chinoiserie design was favoured by carvers anxious to demonstrate their versatility, but fantastic designs like this would have taxed the most skilled among them.*

Pl.54.

The Elevation of a Temple partly in the Chinese Taste.

10 9 8 7 6 5 4 3 2 1   10 fe.

William Halfpenny quickly followed his *New Designs* with *Rural Architecture in the Chinese Taste* (1752) and lest he be supposed biased, brought out a companion volume, *Rural Architecture in the Gothick Taste*. The year 1752 also saw the first pattern-book devoted to chinoiserie designs for interiors, Mathias Lock and Henry Copland's *A New Book of Ornaments in the Chinese Taste*, a set of twelve designs for mirrors, console tables, wall lights, a candle-stand and a chimney piece. Lock's earlier essays in the French taste, published in the 1740s, had presented those carvers intrepid enough to attempt his designs with engravings for furniture crammed with birds, winged dragons and leaping hounds, all entwined in frothing waves and carved cascades. Such exuberance of design promised something quite hair-raising when attached to the accepted idea that Chinese ornament was intrinsically wayward. Lock's imagination, which must already have been severely taxed by the previous publications, did not let him down. His new designs in the Chinese taste added Chinamen and pagodas, canopies and ho-ho birds, lattice work fences, stairs, gates and masses of bells to the basic elements of foaming water and hyper-active animals.

Lock and Copland's designs were followed by *A New Book of Chinese Designs Calculated to Improve the Present Taste* by Mathias Darly and George Edwards. Here were designs for furniture, chimney furniture, vases and stands, as well as illustrations of landscapes and ornaments useful for japanners, porcelain painters and embroiderers. These designs appeared on printed cotton and on Bow porcelain, and some were reprinted in 1762 in *The Ladies Amusement, or the whole art of Japanning*

made easy by Robert Sayer. Sayer disarmingly advised his readers of the 'liberties [that] may be taken' with Chinese or Indian designs, 'for in these is often seen a Butterfly supporting an Elephant, or things equally absurd'. Darly's and Edwards' designs were also appropriated in *Chinese Architecture*, a publication by Paul Decker of 1769.

The best known pattern-book of the period was Thomas Chippendale's *Gentleman and Cabinet-Maker's Director*, first published in 1754, reprinted a year later and reissued in 1762. Its subtitle was 'a large collection of the most Elegant and Useful Designs of Household Furniture in the Gothic, Chinese and Modern Taste'. Although the publication was firmly linked with the name of Chippendale,

it appears more than likely that many of its designs were not by Chippendale at all but by Lock and Copland, then in Chippendale's employ. Among the 160 plates were designs for chairs, china cabinets, tables and chests of drawers in the Chinese taste. These mark the first occasion when the passion for chinoiserie ceased to be merely ornamental, and entered the realm of form. 'Chinese Chippendale' furniture not only has fret and lattice work, and other decidedly 'Chinese' ornamentation such as pagoda cresting or pierced and fretted galleries. Its shape is different. The outline is square and angular and the legs are straight, not curved. Of course these designs were purely imaginative and not copied from anything actually Chinese. Indeed when William

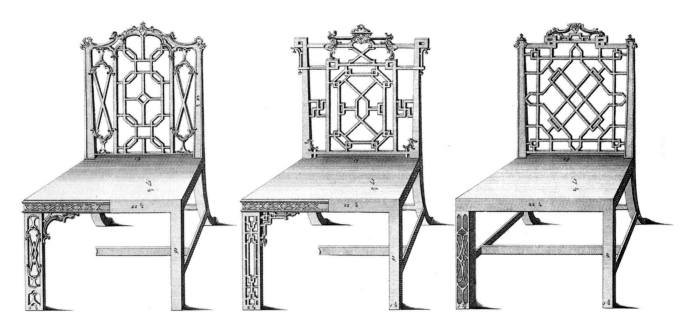

Chinoiserie trinkets illustrated in *A New Book of Chinese Designs* by Mathias Darly and George Edwards, 1754. *(opposite) The public's passion for chinoiserie designs seemed inexhaustible. Publications offered a wide choice, from carvers' pieces destined to daunt all but the most ambitious, to squat and grinning Chinamen whose simple outline could be traced by an army of dedicated amateur japanners.*

Designs for Chinese Chairs, from Thomas Chippendale's *The Gentleman and Cabinet Maker's Director*, 1762. *(above) Three designs in the Chinese taste from the master of English furniture. Mahogany was particularly suitable for the finely carved detail and pierced frets of 'Chinese Chippendale'.*

Lacquered mahogany china cabinet, c.1755. *The cabinet is probably the work of Thomas Chippendale, whose great contribution to chinoiserie was to produce designs which did not simply graft chinoiserie motifs on to established forms but altered the shape of the piece of furniture.*

Chambers reproduced two drawings of chairs actually seen in China in his *Designs of Chinese Buildings* and noted that rosewood, ebony and bamboo were the woods chiefly used for furniture in that country, his authoritative patterns were blithely disregarded.

Chippendale's *Director* showed several plates of chairs in the Chinese taste and noted these as being 'very proper for a Lady's Dressing-Room;

Designs for chinoiserie fireplaces and mirrors.
The treatment of a wall as a continuous unit with chimney piece and mirror above gave the designers a great chance to excite the imagination. From Thomas Johnson's Collection of Designs, *1758 (left), and Ince and Mayhew's* Universal System of Household Furniture, *1762. (right)*

Chinoiserie wallpaper, *c.*1770.
This hand-coloured etching of a typically whimsical English chinoiserie design shows a flowery landscape where a small man on a large camel is talking to an equally lopsided pair, a child with a greyhound on a leash.

especially if it is hung with India Paper'. By the middle of the century there was a craze for Chinese bedrooms and dressing-rooms, and a mandarin-infested room lay behind the pedimented door of many a sober Palladian exterior. Indeed, as the writer of *Letters on the English Nation* dolefully observed: 'Every chair in an apartment, the frames of tables and glasses must be Chinese: the walls cover'd with Chinese papers fill'd with figures which resemble nothing in God's creation.' Even Mrs Montagu, whose gloomy musings on the passing of Antique taste were widely known, boasted of a 'Chinese room' in her house in Hill Street, decorated 'like the Temple of an Indian god'. And this was only a year after her declared opposition to that 'barbarous gaudy *goût*'.

By the early eighteenth century Chinese wallpapers of high quality were being imported into England. Generally referred to as Indian papers, they were made expressly for the European market. Their high cost encouraged the production of locally-made versions, and their designs served as the inspiration for patterns that continue to be produced today. Papers were imported as separate sheets, not in rolls, each one painted using the same techniques of brush and paint as those employed for decorating scrolls and screens in China. A preliminary outline was filled in with colour washes, onto which highlights of metal were painted. Sets of sheets were stuck together to provide a pattern which would go across an entire room.

Often English paper-stainers were expert at imitation, though the manner in which the motifs were copied and the pattern of their arrangement was substantially less oriental than the originals. Du Halde's encyclopaedic compendium of Chinese customs referred to the Chinese using paper on their walls, but the papers fashionable in Georgian England were like nothing ever seen on the walls of Chinese houses, which were usually papered in a plain white. Typically, the patterns were lively and bold. They might have been deemed suitable for ladies' bed-chambers, but there was nothing 'ladylike' about them. Indeed to the modern eye, accustomed to pale stripes or demure flowers, these patterned papers seem positively overbearing.

Fragment of early eighteenth-century chinoiserie wallpaper. *The exotic blooms that so captivated the imagination of the West are delicately evoked in this hand-painted design.*

Two panels of Chinese wallpaper mounted in bamboo frames, c.1760. *Separate sheets of wallpaper, hand-coloured and boldly illustrated, were produced in China specifically for export to the Orient-bewitched Europe of the eighteenth century.*

Favourite subjects included hunting scenes or vignettes of everyday life showing the various stages of tea cultivation or the making of porcelain. The most popular pattern was of brightly coloured, botanically implausible plants and trees with weird birds roosting in them.

Most rococo Chinese rooms had their walls lined either with printed linen or wallpaper. Sales of wallpaper shot up as demand increased. In 1713 197,000 yards of wallpaper were sold in England. By 1785 the figure had grown tenfold, to over two million yards. There are country houses in England that still have rooms hung with 'Indian paper' of the mid-eighteenth century, for where the family was conservative, or financially down on its luck, the paper could outlast the fashion for it. At Saltram House in Devon, a small dressing-room is hung with an early eighteenth-century paper of a kind known as 'Long Eliza' – a corruption of the Dutch *lange eleizen*. Here mandarins brooding among their moustachios are surrounded by willowy ladies standing stiffly and discreetly in twos and threes against a background of curving slender trees. It is the scale that surprises: the figures are large and emphatically drawn. In the same house there is a Chinese bedroom, where a non-repetitive pattern, drawn either on silk or cotton, rises above a white dado. Little Orientals tirelessly grow, cure and pack tea, transport it on rafts piled high with jars, and deliver it to merchants sitting in straw pavilions. Another papered room at Saltram displays more aristocratic pursuits. Against a background of cloud-capped mountains, twisted trees and rocks stand the zig-zag bridges, tea houses and pagodas of Cathay. Among them the adult citizens chat in pavilions, go

Plate-printed linen and cotton, c.1766. *Most rococo Chinese rooms had their walls lined with wallpaper or printed linen. The newly erected pagoda at Kew Gardens was a highly fashionable motif.*

Detail from an early eighteenth-century 'Long Eliza' wallpaper. *From the Chinese dressing-room at Saltram House, Devon. According to Mrs Libbe Powys, a tireless visitor to country houses, Chinese bedrooms were expected to be 'excessively pretty and droll', and while the large-scale, boldly drawn figures on this paper would certainly never appear in the bedrooms of China, they perfectly fitted the eighteenth century's image of Cathay.*

boating, and charge about on tiny piebald horses, while their children fish or gravely dance.

Chinese mirror paintings were considered ideally suited to hang on the walls of Chinese bedrooms, where they would add to the confusing multiplicity of images of Cathay. Often they were set in elaborate, beautifully carved and gilded English rococo frames. The vogue for these painted mirrors seems to have developed relatively late – certainly later than the passion for Coromandel screens, porcelain, and embroidered silks; later even than the taste for mango atchar or chutney, the unlikely gift despatched by the governor of Madras to his neighbour, Mrs Edisbury of Erddig, in North Wales. Among the earliest arrivals of mirror paintings were those brought back by Commodore Anson to his family house, Shugborough Hall in Staffordshire, after his world circumnavigation in 1747 during which he had spent a considerable time in Canton. Once home, these charming objects were suitably displayed in a brand-new setting, a Chinese summer house.

Most of the furniture made in the Chinese taste was of mahogany, a wood that took carved decoration extremely well, although its dark colour was perhaps more sober than continental taste demanded. 'It must be said,' wrote Monsieur Roquet, a French observer of the English scene, 'that in spite of its extreme seemliness, English furniture always looks a little gloomy to eyes unaccustomed to it.' Mahogany's sway did not extend to the large frames of looking-glasses that were generally of soft wood, mostly gilded, occasionally japanned. They bristled with carved decoration, often wilfully fantastic, rather rustic and extremely charming. Looking-glass was so

expensive that there seemed little point in counting pennies on the cost of the frame, with the result that they could, and did, provide a skilled carver with the chance of a lifetime. Any description that omits the size of these carver's pieces will mislead. These mirrors could be huge, well over eight foot tall and around five foot across. They were crowded with birds, buildings, fronds, scrolls and bent stems, while the silhouette could be composed of gnarled and wavy branches, its crested top pierced with watery forms and its base dripping with stalactites. Japanned steps invade the glass to climb to a bracket separating the panes, above which rise slender japanned columns supporting a pierced canopy upon which perch some agitated birds and a Chinaman.

A mirror of this type is known to have had a place in the most famous Chinese bedroom of the period, which was decorated around 1753 at Badminton House in Avon for the 4th Duke of Beaufort. The furniture was sold in 1921; some of it is now in the Victoria and Albert Museum, set against a Chinese wallpaper of bold design, with stems of bright pink flowers and long-tailed birds against

Mahogany dressing-table, c.1760. *Chinese bedrooms were commonly furnished with 'Chinese Chippendale' mahogany furniture, carved on this example with a combination of Gothic tracery on the front and sides and Chinese frets on the frieze and legs.*

Design for a japanned beechwood armchair. John Linnell, c.1753. *(opposite) The armchair was designed for the*

Chinese bedroom at Badminton House, in its day the grandest example of the China-mania that swept through the boudoirs of mid-eighteenth-century England.

a bright blue ground. The Badminton bedroom furniture – long supposed to be by Chippendale but now recognized as the work of John Linnell – is japanned, and of the highest quality. The room is thought to have contained eight chairs, two knee-hole dressing tables, probably two mirrors, a commode and two pairs of standing shelves, in addition to its glory: the bed. Square in shape, japanned in scarlet, canopied by a black-and-gold pagoda roof, hung with bells and ornamented with dragons, this spectacular bed has a latticed head-board as high as the top of its posts.

The glamour of a Chinese bedroom could surface in the most unlikely places, as Dr Johnson discovered. In 1773 he allowed himself to be dragged off to the Hebrides with Boswell where he noted:

> *We were driven once, by missing a passage,*
> *to the hut [i.e. a dwelling of one storey] of*
> *a gentleman, where, after a very liberal supper,*
> *when I was conducted to my chamber, I found*
> *a very elegant bed of Indian cotton, spread with*
> *fine sheets. The accommodation was flattering;*
> *I undressed myself, and felt my feet in the mire.*
> *The bed stood upon bare earth, which a long*
> *course of rain had softened to a puddle.*

Although Palladianism had held aloof from the frivolous and non-classical chinoiserie taste, japanning had not declined in favour in early Georgian England. 'Everybody is mad about japan work,' wrote Mrs Delany to her sister in 1731, adding 'I hope to be a dab at it by the time I see you.' The reign of classicism had some effect on the motifs employed by these dab-handed ladies. Previously-fashionable bold designs derived from oriental prototypes declined in favour, and more western flowers and foliage took their place. The shapes of the japanned furniture conformed to the walnut furniture of the early eighteenth century, although the carcass of the piece was of a less expensive wood: deal, oak or beech.

The passion among English women for japanning seemed insatiable. *The Ladies Amusement or Whole Art of Japanning Made Easy* had 1500 plates. It provided little technical instruction, and from about 1755 japanned decoration began more and more to resemble simple ornamental painting. This trend was not confined to the amateur efforts of

the ladies. The japanned furniture of great cabinet-makers such as Chippendale is often merely painted and varnished. In a suite of green-and-buff painted bedroom furniture made by Chippendale for the actor David Garrick, the chinoioserie panels of the wardrobe are all japanned in the new style. This set of furniture freely mixes chinoiserie and neo-classical motifs. The chinoiserie motifs on the japanned wardrobe – vignette scenes of palms, pagodas, flying birds, a junk with a sailor rocking on the billows, a squat peasant tilling the hummocky ground – are bordered by *rinceaux* and paterae, and a guilloche pattern divides its two stages. The suite includes a number of rush-seated fake bamboo chairs – another new chinoiserie form – and a four poster bed with painted classical ornament, hung with East India Company chintzes with a Tree of Life pattern.

The Garrick bed-hangings had a chequered history. The importation of Indian chintzes was prohibited, and the material highly prized. When Mrs Garrick was lucky enough to receive a bale of Indian palampores – a gift sent by the merchants of Calcutta – the Chinese bedroom, and all its Chippendale furniture, was conceived purely as a setting in which to display what Garrick called 'this favourite token of East India gratitude'. In 1775, four years after the arrival of the chintz in the country, the Customs swooped down on Chippendale's workshop, where the offending fabric was being made up into curtains and bed-hangings, and impounded the lot. Years passed. Mrs Garrick remained without her hangings. Bitterly she cursed everything in sight, including the 'unfortunate furniture which my evel stars made me deliver up into your [Chippendale's] hands'. Only after David Garrick's death in 1779 were

the controversial chintzes cleared by the authorities and finally returned to his widow.

The actor was a devotee of chinoiserie. Not even a spectacular financial loss on an entertainment called *The Chinese Festival* (which, despite the presence of the king, was booed off the stage on its first night with xenophobic shrieks of 'No French dancers') could dampen Garrick's enthusiasm for the land of Cathay. His Adam house in the Adelphi in London had a papered drawing room decorated by Pillement, the wittiest exponent of rococo chinoiseries in France. Pillement had been in London in the 1750s and had published there *A New Book of Chinese Ornaments* as well as contributing to *The Ladies Amusement*. Twenty years later his chinoiseries were still fashionable enough for Garrick, who lived 'rather as a *prince* than as an actor', as a contemporary rather snidely remarked, to employ them in the decoration and furnishing of his new house. So vain a man was unlikely to employ a style that would invite ridicule. Chinoiserie must still have been considered smart, although the taste of the times did allow for a variety of styles, even in the same room. Thus we find that in the drawing room at the Adelphi the chinoiserie wallpaper acted as the backdrop for a sofa and chairs painted green and yellow – no dreary mahogany for Garrick – and inlaid tables and commodes in the neo-classical Adam style.

In one of Adam's most celebrated commissions, the architectural reconstruction of Nostell Priory in Yorkshire, the 5th baronet Sir Rowland Winn called in Chippendale to decorate a suite of state rooms – the state bedroom and dressing-room, and two adjoining closets – in the chinoiserie style. Winn was

State bedchamber at Nostell Priory, Yorkshire. Decorated by Thomas Chippendale, 1769. *The well-bred exoticism of the later part of the eighteenth century exiles the ho-ho bird and grinning pagod and turns instead to restraint and finesse, as demonstrated here in one of the loveliest rooms in the chinoiserie taste.*

**Pair of Bow porcelain vases,
c.1755**. *The vases are decorated
with the long-tailed birds,
spindly trees and sprays of
flowers typical of the Kakiemon
palette that originated in
Japan and was first seen in
European porcelain at Meissen.*

Chippendale's greatest patron. His faith in the latter's ability as a decorator rather than as a simple cabinet-maker was well-founded. Chippendale not only provided the marvellous 'Indian paper' for these state rooms at Nostell, but the chintz curtains of painted Chinese cotton, the blinds, the green-and-gold border that edges the wallpaper, and the wallpaper itself, eighteen sheets of brilliantly coloured birds roosting on twisting branches. Above all he supplied the green-and-gold japanned chinoiserie furniture:

eight armchairs, a clothes press, a dressing table and stool, a sofa at the foot of the bed, an easy chair for by the fire, a 'very neat commode for the pier' – the commode was a Frenchified piece of furniture and very much a speciality of Chippendale's – and a pier glass to go above it, with a 'very large border'd Chinese frame Richly Carv'd and finish'd'. All this, perhaps the most brilliant ensemble of chinoiserie japanned furniture in existence, is still today in the state bedroom at Nostell Priory, each piece occupying the position for which it was designed, presenting an unrivalled chance to appreciate how luxurious and ravishingly pretty chinoiserie could be. Only the bed is an addition, made at a later stage to match Chippendale's designs. The state dressing-room contains a Chippendale bed, japanned in green and gold, which had been made for the room in 1771, along with the rest of the furniture, which includes six more superb armchairs with Chinese fret arms and straight neo-classical legs.

Naturally there was a place for porcelain among the carved mirrors, the wallpapers, the hangings of painted silk or Indian chintz, the laquered commodes and Chinese Chippendale that reproduced the charms of the East in the home counties of England. Chinese porcelain was still collected with fervour. Often it was made especially for European Sinophiles, and featured birds and animals. Cranes were very popular, as were parrots, especially in France.

Taste began to alter with the rise of the European porcelain industry. At one time the Germans had painstakingly copied Japanese and Chinese porcelain birds. Now models, originally made by Kändler at Meissen in the 1740s, were reproduced in China and exported to the West.

Worcester porcelain, c.1755.
*Ebullient Chinese children
tumble and bound on this
sparsely decorated vase (left),
typifying the unsophisticated
charm of much English
chinoiserie porcelain design.
The mid-eighteenth-century*

*Worcester porcelain teapot
(above left), and salt-glazed
stoneware Staffordshire
punchpot of the same period
(above right), also demonstrate
the captivating quality of the
artless chinoiseries of English
porcelain factories.*

As a striking example of how influence passed
backwards and forwards, from East to West and back
again, consider the role of the pug dog. The pug had
never been modelled in porcelain by the Chinese,
although the breed was native to China. The animal
was considered adorable in Germany: a *mops* was
the fashionable accessory in Dresden in the 1740s.
Porcelain pugs were modelled by Kändler, the
greatest porcelain master at Meissen. The Meissen
mops was imported to China, and then copied by
the Chinese – for export only of course. Their own
interiors were far too chaste to support such triviality.

Although the charm and freshness of the
English porcelain factories makes their products
extremely attractive, they were unable to rival the
sophistication of China, or of their continental
competitors like Meissen or Sèvres. Of course there
was some influence from the Continent. Chelsea
copied the ground colours and gilding of Sèvres;

Worcester copied Chelsea; the others were more modest in their ambitions. As for patterns – Meissen Kakiemon designs, chinoiserie *blanc-de-chine*, the colours of the *famille rose* and *verte* palettes, underglaze blue-and-white patterns – all were seen on the porcelain production of the different factories. With the possible exception of Chelsea, which attracted a patron of taste and a manager of genius, these were commercial enterprises interested in markets and money. Small wonder that by the middle of the eighteenth century England produced the first bone china, a strong, cheap and reliable material, if much less beautiful than the soft-pastes then used by many of the English factories. Around the same time, it was an English factory that first used the infinitely less laborious method of creating decoration by transfer printing.

The charming, lively and fanciful qualities found in English chinoiserie in general are naturally present in the porcelain of the period. At its best, a kind of delicate vitality is coupled with a straightforwardness that gives the porcelain an almost rustic air, while the delightful nature of the decoration quite overcomes any reserve about the quality of the material or its modelling. Many of the porcelain factories were situated in the provinces, Derby, Bristol, Lowestoft, Liverpool, Worcester, Caughley – where the willow-pattern was invented – but even when they were based in London, like the Bow factory, the porcelain produced was artless, simplified, a kind of peasant porcelain with bright colours and pattern applied without rules. It was fortunate that so much of the decoration was of chinoiseries, where it was considered quite in order to suspend any rules of gravity or seemliness. In

the enchanted world depicted on such tableware, Orientals stroll under umbrellas, stand contemplatively in their gardens, wander through the countryside, do handstands, fish and fan themselves with branches.

The English factories also produced chinoiserie figures. Some were grotesque, such as a rare and early Chelsea figure of a squatting chinaman, who in fact forms a teapot, his coolie hat acting as the lid and a squawking parrot he clutches by its wings the spout. Other Chelsea Chinese figures include a charming red anchor period group of Chinese musicians of 1755. Four large figures are modelled in the round; a woman in yellow and pink, gold earrings ornamenting her turned head, holds a flute. Another, turbanned in a white dress flecked with gold flowers and a flowered jacket with turned-back sleeves spotted to look like fur, shakes a tambourine aloft. A little boy clutches a bell in one pudgy hand, and a Chinaman, in flowered jacket and boots, his pigtail stretching down his back, completes this delightful quartet.

By the middle of the century chinoiseries on silver had undergone a fashionable revival. The new rococo chinoiseries however quite eclipsed the rather naïve engraved or flat-chased chinoiserie scenes found on silver of the seventeenth century. Highly sophisticated cast and chased ornament became fashionable, often freely interpreting the designs found on Chinese export porcelain; these were considered highly suitable to ornament the equipment attached to the new national habit of tea-drinking. Caddies – tea was so expensive it was kept under lock and key – teapots and kettles, epergnes and cake baskets now feigned wicker-work, sprouted

A group of Chinese Musicians. Chelsea soft-paste porcelain, c.1755. *Statuettes and groups such as this probably derived from Meissen prototypes, but their charm and freshness is particular to the English vision of Cathay.*

bell-hung canopies, palm trees, mandarins and coolies, or were topped with a pineapple, the Chinese symbol of hospitality.

As with many chinoiseries of the period, oriental and western rococo motifs were mixed. A celebrated set of two silver-gilt tea caddies and sugar box by the greatest of the rococo silversmiths, Paul de Lamerie, combines rococo scrolls, bat-wings, Chinese masks and teaplant finials with embossed and chased decoration of pavilions, palm trees and Chinese peasants. These caddies fall into the most flamboyant period of the style. It is this aspect of the taste, the wilder, more extravagant and inventive path of English chinoiserie rococo, that distinguishes it from its continental counterparts. And Claydon House in Buckinghamshire, where the greatest chinoiserie interiors of the period are to be found, best exemplifies this particularly English quality of the style.

Seen from the outside Claydon appears a relatively stock product of the Palladian school. But step within and some of the most extraordinary decoration in England is revealed, the work of a carver of genius, one Luke Lightfoot – the very name is the stuff of Richardson or Sheridan. How Lord Verney, the extravagant and pleasure-loving owner of Claydon House, came to know and employ Lightfoot is uncertain. What is known is that in 1768 Verney commissioned Sir Thomas Robinson – a Yorkshire squire and business associate, who had turned architect in middle-age – to prepare a grandiose scheme to double the size of the house. Robinson was preoccupied with other schemes, and seldom on site. Lightfoot consequently had a free hand for almost a year.

Tea caddy, 1747, by Paul de Lamerie. *Rampant chinoiserie fantasies provide the embossed and chased ornament on this tea caddy by the great rococo silversmith.*

Detail of the Tea Party in the Chinese room at Claydon House. *It is the work of Luke Lightfoot, 'a knave with no small spice of madness in his composition', the unsung genius of English rococo chinoiserie.*

No single source for Lightfoot's fantastic compositions has come to light, and it seems safe to guess that he raided the pattern-books quite impartially. In the North Hall of Claydon House, which was once the Great Eating-Room, a classically correct cornice bears portrait medallions of Roman worthies who gaze across in stupefaction at the great

ho-ho birds perched on scrolling foliage that stand on the cresting of the classical doorcases. These may be influenced by the engravings of Thomas Johnson, although they are disturbingly life-like, as if they have flown in for a breather on the long flight from Cathay. The four wall niches are surrounded by carved foliage on which fabulous cranes roost, and wyverns – a kind of winged dragon – swish their barbed tails. Perhaps Lock and Copland's pattern-book designs for mirrors provided the impetus for these.

In 1769 Sir Thomas Robinson saw what had been created while his back was turned. Appalled, he beseeched Lord Verney to undo it all. Verney

Detail of hand-printed wallpaper in the Chinese bedroom at Blickling Hall, Norfolk. *The Chinese paper is contemporary with the room's contruction in the 1760s. Its pastoral scenes and calm pursuits are edged by a hand-painted border whose elaborate pattern and intricate design is European.*

White japanned wardrobe with chinoiserie designs in green. *(opposite) Very similar to one of the pieces of furniture made by Thomas Chippendale for the actor David Garrick's villa at Hampton, this wardrobe comes from the Chinese bedroom at Blickling Hall.*

declined, and Lightfoot, bitterly described by Robinson as 'fierce as an eastern Monarch … a knave with no small spice of madness in his composition', went on to produce woodcarving of the most extraordinary quality until he was dismissed in 1770.

There is more, much more of Lightfoot's fantasy world in the north hall. There a distinctly exotic confection of carved wood ornaments the overmantel, and a curious assortment of rococo and classical motifs bedeck the red-and-white marble chimneypiece. But all this is a mere foretaste, an appetiser for the *pièce de résistance* which lies above: the so-called Chinese room on the first floor.

This is not a Chinese bedroom with wallpaper and mahogany furniture of Chinese Chippendale. Here the walls are painted a brilliant blue, and the furniture matters not at all. The entire room is an

excuse for Lightfoot's carving genie to create an extravaganza in wood. The dado is patterned with a complicated fret design. The doorcases are crowned with pagoda crestings, hung with bells – nine to a door – fenced with fretted palings and supported by door jambs of solemn mandarin term figures. The carving is both intricate and delicate, rather like the ivories being imported from the Far East. The two chimney-pieces are orientalized versions of one or more of the untamed fantasies of Lock and Copland's designs of 1752, which had recently been re-issued. The entire wall facing the windows is devoted to an astonishing tea-alcove, a three-dimensional realization of the airy fancies seen on porcelain or lacquer, a kind of pagoda-pavilion carved in wood and painted a glistening white. Porcelain Chinese standing on spindly bamboo tables inhabit the elaborately carved niches that flank the alcove, and among the bursting flowers, shells, scrolls, bells and diaper-work that decorate it, a miniature Chinese family sits round a tea-table, each raising an arm in stiff salute, while on the table the meticulously carved tea equipage waits.

Fantasy on this scale is the stuff of *Alice in Wonderland*, but it is also a real room, a distillation of the English vision of Cathay and their gallant attempts to capture its magical and playful qualities. If Luke Lightfoot read poetry, he would surely have nodded approval of the description of a room in James Cawthorn's mid-eighteenth century poem *Of Taste*:

> *On ev'ry shelf a Joss divinely stares,*
> *Nymphs laid on chintzes sprawl upon our chairs;*
> *While o'er our cabinets Confucius nods,*
> *Midst porcelain elephants and China gods.*

The *jardin anglo-chinois* in the eighteenth century

Tout le monde sait que les jardins anglais ne sont qu'une imitation de ceux de la Chine.

George Louis Le Rouge, *Détails des nouveaux jardins à la mode*, 1774-89

The French have of late years adopted our style in gardens, but, choosing to be fundamentally obliged to more remote rivals, they deny us half the merit or rather the originality of the invention, by ascribing the discovery to the Chinese, and calling our taste in gardening *'le goût anglo-chinois'*.

Horace Walpole, 1771

View of the Alhambra and Pagoda at Kew Gardens. Aquatint, 1789. *The best known chinoiserie structure in Europe, Sir William Chambers' pagoda was modelled on the Porcelain Pagoda at Nanking.*

View from the pagoda at Chanteloup near Amboise.

In the eighteenth century England invented a new form of artistic enterprise: landscape gardening. The gardens of Europe had been developed as a kind of outdoor architecture: a series of courtyards where symmetrical beds were laid with sand, marble or coloured stones and edged with box, linked by long alleys punctuated with statues, colonnades and fountains, and extended by terraces terminated by great walls of clipped hedges. These traditional, formal gardens, where no plant dared to grow out of line, were a demonstration of man's mastery over nature. They had their most brilliant expression in André Le Nôtre's great scheme for the gardens at Versailles, and spread from there to the rest of Europe. Formal gardens had been adopted in England too, although there discontent with the style had been simmering for a number of years. As the eighteenth century dawned, discontent intensified into outright attack. Formal gardens, stigmatized as wicked, tyrannical – and French – were condemned. Lord Shaftesbury referred cuttingly to 'the mockery of princely gardens'. Alexander Pope urged that an 'artful wilderness' should replace the symmetrical paths and groves, and Joseph Addison inveighed against topiary.

These great Augustan rationalists discovered a host of classical theorists to buttress and support their endeavours, for it was their conviction that Republican Rome, their model of wise and beneficent rule, had gloried in the pleasures of natural gardens. 'The taste of the ancients,' declared Pope, 'favoured the amiable simplicity of unadorned nature'. A tougher age, more accustomed to empirical evidence, might wonder how he knew. The answer is through classical literature and contemporary landscape painting in which painters like Salvator Rosa, Nicolas Poussin and above all Claude Lorraine brought the pastoral delights of Horace, Pindar and Virgil to life. Pope claimed that 'all gardening is landscape painting', and English artists departed for Italy to paint the classical landscapes that were to hang in English houses and form the model for the gardens in which they stood.

But China was to make a surprising contribution to the argument that raged over formal gardens. Lord Shaftesbury, whose abomination of China was only equalled by his hatred of absolutism and popery, never alluded to the gardening principles of that flowery realm, but Joseph Addison did. Writing in *The Spectator* in 1712, he expressed his dissatisfaction with formal gardens by calling in the Chinese to support his case: 'Writers who have given us an account of China, tell us the inhabitants of that country laugh at the plantations of Europeans, which are laid out by the rule of line; because, they say, any one may place trees in equal rows and uniform figures.'

Here Addison was referring to Sir William Temple, one-time English ambassador to The Hague, who had retired to cultivate his garden at Sheen near London, and who published in 1685 an essay *Upon the Gardens of Epicurus*, which praised Chinese gardens. Naturally Sir William had never been to China, but he had read as many travellers tales as the next man. Moreover, he may have met Johan Nieuhoff when that intrepid diplomat returned from his colossal snubbing by the Chinese Emperor. Nieuhoff's *Travels* is determinedly elusive on the subject of the Emperor's gardens: 'If I should relate of all the other Artificial Ornaments, as of Gardens,

The Chinese Pavilion at Laxenbourg, Vienna. Late eighteenth century. *In the eighteenth century the* jardin anglo-chinois *extended its sway across Europe, and Chinese pavilions raised their pinnacled heads in gardens and parklands from the Gulf of Finland to Sicily.*

Wildernesses, Pools, and other particulars which adorn this court, I should far exceed the bounds of what I intend, and perhaps to some of belief.'

This seemed to be enough to fire Sir William's enthusiasm. Although his own views on gardens were not unconventional, what Temple proclaimed to be the Chinese view of them was startling. The Chinese, he wrote, scorn proportion, symmetry or uniformity:

> *Their greatest Reach of Imagination is employed in contriving Figures, where the Beauty shall be great, and strike the Eye, but without any Orders or Disposition of Parts, that shall be commonly or easily observ'd. And though we have hardly any Notion of this Sort of Beauty, yet they have a particular Word to express it; and, where they find it hit their Eye at first Sight, they say the*

> *Sharawadgi is fine or admirable, or any such Expression of Esteem. Any whoever observes the Work upon the best Indian Gowns, or the Painting upon their best Skreens or Purcellans, will find their Beauty is all of this Kind (that is) without Order.*

The notion that a conscious theory of beauty could have as its essence a contrived irregularity was quite new. The Rococo was decades away, and European aesthetic theory was based on strictly classical notions. As there was no term available in the West to describe this new concept, Temple coined one – *sharawadgi* – a word of his own invention that corresponds to no known Chinese word.

A further imaginative leap was taken by Joseph Addison, who simply assumed that Chinese gardens were typically of the same size as English parkland. 'Why may not a whole estate be thrown into a kind of garden by frequent plantations?' he asked, claiming that the Chinese showed a 'Genius in works of this nature'. The belief that Chinese gardens were normally as large an Englishman's country estate persisted for centuries. It was not until the gates of China were forced in the nineteenth century that the dreadful truth leaked out: the scale of the gardens of the mandarins compared to their equivalents in England rather as the bonsai does to the beech.

As yet there were no illustrations of Chinese gardens, and very few of their plants had been brought to Europe, so Addison can be forgiven for imagining the Imperial Gardens as being great woodlands thick with oaks and elms. Soon however an obliging Jesuit appeared on the scene to provide some evidence of grand Chinese gardens. Father Matteo Ripa, who had engraved 36 views of the

Emperor K'ang Hsi's summer palace and gardens at Jehol, arrived in London in 1724 and received the rapt attention of the leading lights of the day. He had two audiences of three hours with the king, and the prime enunciator of the Rule of Taste, the 3rd Earl of Burlington, obtained a set of Ripa's engravings of the gardens at Jehol for his library at Chiswick.

Perhaps the advocates of *sharawadgi*, browsing among the engravings, may have perceived in them a kind of oriental *campagna*. If so, it was a tribute to the power of their imaginations. Certainly these views of the imperial gardens at Jehol looked nothing like the English home counties. Ripa depicted a forbidding landscape of bare, hump-backed hills, sparsely clad with a few dejected and stunted trees, rising on either side of immense lakes or fast-flowing streams. The views are boundless, undomestic, but the land they depict is obviously inhabited, for perched on islets or standing by the lake-shore are

The Imperial Gardens at Jehol, c.1713. *Engraving by Matteo Ripa, an Italian Jesuit priest who frequented the Imperial Court at Peking, and was responsible for a series of views of the emperor's summer gardens and palace at Jehol.*

the familiar pavilions and pagodas of Cathay. Matteo Ripa explained that these numerous, unthreatening garden buildings were 'small pleasure houses … which are reached by means of boats or bridges'. He added: 'To these houses, when fatigued by fishing, the Emperor retires, accompanied by his ladies', a quintessentially chinoiserie explanation of their function.

It was to landscape gardening that Lord Burlington had first turned in 1715, when he returned to England from his Grand Tour and started to improve the grounds of Chiswick House, his country house near London. Helped by Alexander Pope, he planned a garden which would be a carefully organized Elysium abounding in columns, temples and funerary urns, free from the distortions of topiary figures and redolent of literary references. It was all still fairly formal, with straight avenues, terminals to vistas and regularly interspersed paths. But it was early days, before the genius of Burlington's life-long collaborator, William Kent, had been released, like a genie from a bottle.

'Kent leaped the fence and saw that all nature was a garden' was Walpole's description of the process. Kent's fence-leaping took advantage of a simple technical device, the ha-ha. It was a French idea, a ditch with one sloping and one straight side, which acted as a sunken fence and was so surprising to encounter that one exclaimed, according to taste, 'Hah! Hah!' or 'Aha! Aha!'. The ha-ha freed the house from its formal surroundings by doing away with the barriers of walls and boundaries. By shaping and cutting the woodland and planting trees in clumps, not rows, Kent brought the park beyond the ha-ha into harmony with the lawn that lay within.

Then he set the garden free to harmonize with the parkland that lay beyond, so that polished park and natural garden could lie uninterrupted side by side.

Geometry went out of fashion as trim paths cutting straight lines between pleached hedges gave way to walks that wound their way through bosky dells and groves of trees. What happened on land had its counterpart on water, where serpentine streams supplanted the formal canal. At Chiswick, Kent and Burlington did away with the regular, symmetrical sheets of water that now seemed intolerably old-fashioned; instead they turned the canal into a stream flowing from a cascade concealed in a grotto and then wiggling sedately through the garden before ending up as a pool with an island in the middle.

The style caught on so successfully that by 1736 the Earl of Leicester was complaining to Burlington of the 'cold insipid straight walks' of the old 'unpitoresk' garden. Chinese authority was not called to testify in favour of the change. Instead the alteration in landscape gardening introduced by Kent and Burlington was sanctioned by classical precedent, the classical gardens described in Robert Castell's *Villas of the Ancients*, a publication brought out at Burlington's expense in 1728.

Meanwhile, in China, it seemed that the emperor was up to something similar:

> One wanders from one vale to another, not as in Europe, by straight avenues, but by zig-zag winding paths … the canal sometimes widens, sometimes becomes narrower, there it winds, and there it describes a curve, as if actually deflected by the hills and rocks … the paths, too, follow a winding course, sometimes following the canals, sometimes leading away from them.

This is not Chiswick, but the great gardens of Yuan-ming-yuan near Peking, described in 1749 by a Jesuit lay brother, Father Jean Attiret, who was a portrait painter at the Chinese court. Yuan-ming-yuan – meaning round, bright garden – was established by the Emperor K'ang Hsi around 1700, but its development dates largely from 1735, during the reign of Chi'en Lung, making it an exact contemporary of the great English landscape parks of Stourhead or Stowe. The fame of Yuan-ming-yuan spread throughout Europe as paintings and woodcuts commissioned by the emperor, and descriptions of its beauty furnished by missionaries and travellers, made it a talking-point in the salons of the West.

Attiret's letter, published in France in 1749 as *A Particular Account of the Emperor of China's Garden near Pekin*, was soon translated into English, and proved so popular that it had been reprinted four times by the early 1760s. The account it gives of a landscape of 'beautiful disorder' included authoritative descriptions of lakes, grottoes, flowering trees, menageries, bridges and pleasure pavilions. The pavilions were meant to be occupied not only (in the words of Marco Polo) as 'shady recesses where men might indulge themselves all day in the company of their women', but for the more cerebral pursuits of study, music, chess or poetry composition. Attiret relates how they were placed very carefully in order to harmonize and enhance the view, both from within and without, and were frequently situated on or near water. To western sensibilities this garden architecture was undoubtedly less threatening than the untamed Chinese landscape. Moreover it could be reproduced in Europe. The pavilions with curving roofs, light bridges, covered walkways and lakeside belvederes marked the next advance of chinoiserie and were meat and drink to gardening Sinophiles.

European landscape gardeners had already placed a value on garden buildings, using them as 'eye-catchers', to close a view or provide a focal point for a stroll in the grounds. By the 1740s the classical temples ornamenting the English landscape garden found themselves with more light-hearted neighbours as Chinese and Gothic garden pavilions became acceptable alternatives. 'Chinese houses' – pagoda-roofed eye-catchers as gaily bizarre as their owners desired – began to appear as a chinoiserie vignette in the distinctly un-Chinese grounds of large estates. These were far less substantial than the garden buildings previously seen, even those that had been styled Chinese, like the tea-house at Potsdam, or Kina in Drottningholm. The new vogue was for a folly, as delightfully Chinese as dragons, bells, fretwork, papier-mâché and paint could make it, the living embodiment of the pavilions on the Coromandel screen or porcelain plate.

Chinese garden pavilion, Wrest Park, Bedfordshire. *Like their progenitors in China, the chinoiserie garden buildings of Europe were often situated near water.*

Design for a Chinese Temple by G. Landi, c.1810. *(opposite) Brightly coloured and light-hearted as any eighteenth-century garden folly, this little building would be equally at home on a porcelain trinket or silken bedspread.*

The pavilions of China were not built to last, and in this respect at least their chinoiserie relations in Europe were faithful to their progenitors. Elegant, amusing, brightly coloured and delicately enriched, these garden structures proved far less durable than their classical counterparts, which were solidly built of stone or brick. The appearance of pagoda and pavilion met with universal approval, providing what Horace Walpole called 'a whimsical air of novelty that is very pleasing'.

The first of these 'summer houses' was standing in the grounds of Stowe by 1738, and has survived an adventurous existence, being finally refurbished prior to its reinstatement at Stowe. More solid than its Chinese equivalent, this gay little building has diagonally-latticed windows, projecting eaves and painted chinoiserie vignettes, protected by a covering of canvas on its outside walls. At Stowe it originally stood on stilts in a pond that offered the additional diversion of two models of Chinese birds bobbing on its surface, and was connected to the land by a bridge adorned with vases. The first report of it, after describing 'a house built on piles, after the manner of the Chinese, odd & Pretty enough' goes on to add the interesting information that 'as the form of their Building is so well known from Prints and other Descriptions, there is no Occasion to say more of it'.

Possibly the anonymous commentator is referring to the publication of Père Du Halde's encyclopaedic compendium of Chinese lore, published in Paris in 1735 and serialized in *The Gentleman's Magazine* from 1737. But it is more

likely that its form was 'known' from its depiction on the imported lacquer and porcelain that had formed the basis of the chinoiserie style. In fact, Du Halde's account of Chinese views on gardens provides a disagreeably utilitarian alternative to the dreamy vision favoured in the West, where moustachioed mandarins and sway-hipped concubines dally idly in lakeside pavilions.

Du Halde states quite firmly that:

... the Chinese are far from preferring the Agreeable to the Useful: for they seldom make use of their land for superfluous things, such as making fine gardens, cultivating flowers, or making Alleys, believing it more for the public Good, and what is still nearer, their private Benefit, that every Place should be sown to produce useful things.

The Chinese House, Stowe, Buckinghamshire. Interior detail of the west wall, and exterior view. *The first chinoiserie summer house in England, this gaily painted little building was erected in the grounds of Stowe in 1738.*

Garden seats in the Chinese taste. *Plate from William Halfpenny's publication of 1752,* Rural Architecture in the Chinese Taste. *(opposite top) A contemporary garden bench, Chatsworth House, Derbyshire. (opposite bottom)*

These unpalatable sentiments, so inimical to the spirit of chinoiserie, were simply suppressed in later English compilations of Du Halde's voluminous *General History of China*, providing proof again, if it were needed, of chinoiserie's existence in the West as an independent style.

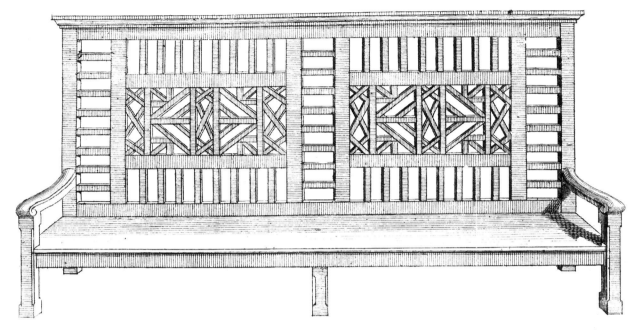

An early example of a European Chinese garden building that attempted authenticity was to be found in Yorkshire. Obviously inspired by Matteo Ripa's engravings in Lord Burlington's possession, John Aislabie, a close friend of Lord Burlington, built a circular one-storied pavilion with a conical roof and upward curling eaves (rather resembling an Edwardian park bandstand) in the grounds of his estate at Studley Royal. Gaily painted in red and blue with gilt enrichments, the pavilion was situated on the brink of as precipitous a gorge as could be found in those parts, which possessed the additional verisimilitude of a narrow river running at its base. Despite the owner's pains, the building – which stood for a century and a half – was criticized as being

'in very bad taste and not at all like their [Chinese] architecture', although a French visitor was able to admire its setting as *'une vallée enchantée'*.

A Chinese pavilion still standing, which was widely regarded as authentically Chinese when it was built, is found at Shugborough Park in Staffordshire. It was probably erected in 1747, and is the fruit of the collaborative effort of two brothers, Thomas and George Anson. Thomas inherited the land, and was a founder member of the Society of Dilettanti, and thus by declaration a man of taste. His brother George had spent several months in Canton in the course of a naval expedition round the world and could claim therefore to be an authority on China. A contemporary hailed the Shugborough summer house as 'a true pattern of the architecture of that nation, not a mongrel invention of British carpenters'. Square, with a concave roof and wide-spread eaves, the building stood originally on an island in the river Sow, and was decorated on the outside with a fret pattern in pale green on a pink

ground. Its interior was a medley of chinoiserie delights with a rococo stucco ceiling and gilded *singeries* above a red lacquer alcove; the whole was furnished with Chinese pictures and painted mirrors in delicate gilded pagoda-topped frames. A wooden hexagonal six-storied pagoda, alas no longer standing, was an additional chinoiserie adornment to the gardens of Shugborough.

By the 1750s the vogue for chinoiserie follies was sufficiently established to attract the attentions of the pattern-book publishers, and a multitude of designs for garden buildings, terminary seats, bridges and banqueting houses 'in the Chinese taste' began to appear. Bridges were particularly popular, and streams were created to give these latticed creations something to span. They have survived in larger numbers than the summer houses. At Painshill in Surrey a Chinese bridge dating from the 1740s still stands. There was even one across the Thames at Hampton Court, consisting of seven arches with concave-roofed kiosks; this has disappeared, but proof of its existence outside an opium-inspired dream is preserved in the British Museum in Canaletto's drawing of it, executed in 1754.

Even Stourhead, the *ne plus ultra* of classical gardens, had a Chinese pavilion, a Chinese bridge, a Chinese parasol and a Turkish tent dotted about among its temples and shrines. Gardens were now crowded with diversions, so many that one indolent visitor longed for the old days, 'when the price of a haunch of venison with a country friend was only half-an-hour's walk on a hot terrass; a descent to two square fish-ponds overgrown with frog-spawn; a peep into the hog-sty, or a visit to the pigeon house. How reasonable was this, when compared with the

William Halfpenny's design for 'A Double truss'd bridge in the Chinese Taste', 1752. *(opposite) Fretted bridges were a relatively cheap and popular way of adding a chinoiserie eye-catcher to garden and parkland.*

Wash drawing by Antonio Canaletto of a bridge over the river Thames at Hampton Court, 1754. *Although the quality and craftsmanship of Chinese bridges enjoyed a great reputation in the West, their chinoiserie equivalents often proved less durable. That built across the Thames from Hampton Court in 1753 was soon demolished or washed away.*

attention now expected from you to the number of temples, pagodas, pyramids, grottos, bridges, hermitages, caves, towers &c.'

In the 1750s the only informal gardens to be seen in Europe were in England, but the days of the formal garden were numbered, even in France. By and large the French were disdainful of English parkland – too few fountains and too much lawn – and were slow to respond to the changes in garden design emerging from the other side of the channel. Moreover, they steadfastly adhered to the belief that China, not England, was the true home of the landscape garden. It was a view nourished by the information flowing from the largely French contingent of Jesuit missionaries to China, and fortified by chauvinism.

The truth was that an informal and irregular garden was better suited to the rococo world of *fêtes galantes* and *fermes ornées* that was captivating increasing numbers of ultra-refined, sophisticated and predominantly urban French men and women. So charming an environment – so clearly complementary to the paintings of Watteau, Boucher and Fragonard – could hardly be credited as the invention of hard-drinking Englishmen with uncouth manners and mud on their boots. The Chinese seemed altogether more likely a source.

Despite such prejudice, the theories propounded by English landscape garden philosophers and practitioners gained currency in French intellectual circles. An expression of the new view of nature is found in Jean Jacques Rousseau's *La Nouvelle Héloïse*, published in 1761, the first book to endorse a natural scheme for garden design; it is interesting to note that the garden in the book is owned by an Englishman. Although Rousseau condemned the Chinese approach to gardens as artful and contrived, it had been commended earlier by Marc-Antoine Laugier, who wrote an influential *Essai sur l'architecture* in the 1750s. He praised the account of Chinese gardening provided by the Jesuit father Jean Attiret, and professed the hope that France might adopt '*un ingénieux mélange des idées chinoises*'. But the ingenious *mélange* was to appear from quite another quarter, the neo-classical English architect William Chambers. It was his ideas that the French took up, ideas that were to transform the English garden into *le jardin anglo-chinois*.

Chambers had actually been to China, albeit only as supercargo on a trading vessel, from whose deck he had managed to see enough to turn him into an authority on that country when he returned to England. In 1757 he published *Designs of Chinese Buildings, Furniture, Dresses, Machines and Utensils*, a weighty portfolio intended to confer a degree of academic respectability on Chinese architecture, and which carried the added sonority of a dedication to Augusta, the Princess Dowager of Wales. The mix of illustrations in the book ranged from the cross-section of a merchant's house to various pots and cups. All were completely devoid of the uninhibited whimsy of the chinoiserie designers. Far from the amusing parodies derided by Chambers as 'toys in architecture', here was an attempt to introduce a touch of realism into the fantasies of chinoiserie design. But while the engravings all provide beautifully and scrupulously drawn oriental detail, these are organized according to classical principles of design, and are no more authentic than the rococo chinoiserie designs Chambers sought to replace. Nevertheless, Chambers' designs were taken

seriously enough to become the primary source of architectural chinoiserie in France.

Soon after the publication of his *Designs*, Chambers was invited to radically remodel the royal gardens at Kew near London by introducing a series of exotic buildings into the park created by Kent in the 1730s. Kew already possessed a playful chinoiserie pavilion built in 1749, the year of Kent's death, and known as the House of Confucius. Despite his stern views on 'toys', Chambers did not destroy the House of Confucius but relocated it. He also built a 'menagerie pavilion', a kind of aviary, in the conventional chinoiserie idiom. In 1763 Chambers published a lavishly-illustrated portfolio of his designs for Kew. This comprised an impartial assortment of fancies providing diversions to suit all tastes, and epitomized the mid-century vogue for variety.

There was an 'Alambra', a Gothic cathedral, a cattle bridge like a ruined arch, a Turkish mosque, and the most celebrated structure of all: the Great Pagoda. This was based on that old war-horse of chinoiserie inspiration, the porcelain tower at Nanking. Built of grey brick and rising 160 feet, the pagoda still stands among the lawns and flowerbeds of what is now a public garden, although the 80 winged and coloured dragons that used to adorn the points of each roof on its ten diminishing stories are no longer there to provide the 'dazzling reflection' Chambers intended.

This was the most scholarly pagoda yet seen in Europe, and it perched uneasily among the brilliantly coloured and exquisitely pretty nonsense of the period. It was at once too solemn – and too big – and not accurate enough. However it won general

popularity, being reproduced not only in paintings and prints, but also appearing as a motif on the chinoiserie chintzes of the day.

An even more severe pagoda, so classical in its mien that a mandarin would have been hard put to recognize it as one at all, stands aloofly in a meadow in France, in the Loire valley, at Chanteloup near Amboise. Built in 1775 for the Duc de Choiseul, then in exile from the court, this tall stone tower was to commemorate the loyalty of some three hundred of his closest friends, whose names are inscribed on tablets within and may have been the centrepiece for a projected *jardin anglo-chinois*. Its majestic proportions and seven stories – simply placed one atop the other like a gigantic wedding-cake – mark out the pagoda as an architectural oddity in the chinoiserie tradition. It certainly owes nothing to the dictates of William Chambers or his pagoda at Kew.

But Chambers' achievements at Kew were enormously admired on the Continent, where he was regarded as the pre-eminent authority on oriental building. He had not yet uttered his last word on China, however. In 1772 Chambers produced a

View of the buildings designed by William Chambers for the royal gardens at Kew, c.1760. *Showing the mosque, the Alhambra and the first few tiers of the pagoda. The newly fashionable 'garden of incident' made for gardens crowded with a variety of buildings, providing a series of eye-catchers and the destination for a stroll in the grounds.*

sequel to his successful publication on Chinese architecture, entitled *A Dissertation on Oriental Gardening*. Abandoning academic pretensions – he had seen no more of Chinese gardens than the next man – Chambers used the book as an excuse to mount a savage attack on the doyen of the English landscape garden, Capability Brown, who had recently pipped him to a valuable commission, a country house for Lord Clive. With a deft rewriting of the history of ideas behind the English landscape garden, Chambers dismissed Brown's natural landscaping as too slavish an imitation of nature, while praising Chinese gardens for their artifice.

Indeed variety and artifice, according to Chambers, were the key elements of Chinese gardens. He divided Chinese garden scenery into three types: the pleasing, the horrid, and the enchanted. All were highly contrived, none sounded remotely restful. Among the miscellany of essential elements, cataracts, caverns and artificial mountains ranked high. Sumptuous-sounding Tartarean maidens in diaphanous robes were also a recommended feature. As a way of enlivening the duller reaches of the English countryside, Chambers recommended a dramatic Chinese-style eye-catcher: 'Bats, owls, vultures, and every bird of prey flutter in the grove; wolves, tigers and jackalls howl in the forests; half-famished animals wander upon the plains; gibbets, crosses, wheels, and the whole apparatus of torture, are seen from the roads.'

Such effects, he warned, should not be attempted by 'persons of narrow intellects', surely an invitation for their rapid emulation. Not surprisingly readers were nonplussed; perhaps it was really all one long jape, although the tirade against Capability Brown was real enough. One response was a parody of Chambers' views, *An Heroic Epistle to Sir William Chambers, Knight*, by Horace Walpole's friend William Mason, of which Walpole said, 'I laughed till I cried and the oftener I read it the better I liked it'. The parody had the unintended effect of increasing sales of the object of its satire sufficiently to allow publication of a second edition in 1773.

The spirit of the French *jardin anglo-chinois* was extremely receptive to the more macabre aspects of Chambers' *Dissertation*, and the publication was frequently consulted as scenes of terror, drama and contrast were rapidly embodied in the new garden schemes. Tombs were particularly popular. The park at Monceau had a Wood of Tombs, the famous gardens of Bagatelle an island of them, while the Princess of Monaco trumped everyone by giving them an entire valley. Adaptations of Chambers'

Design for a Chinese pigeon-house, *c.*1784. *This delightful folly has a lei-wen spiral roof topped by a flying dragon rising above the tree tops.*

The Philosopher's Hut at Bagatelle. Engraving from J. C. Krafft, *Recueil d'architecture civile*, 1812.

designs were frequently used for pavilions and pagodas. The Marquis de Marigny building a Chinese belvedere on his estate lamented not having Chambers' designs at hand. A pavilion at Cassan, near L'Isle Adam, north of Paris, was executed to designs by Chambers, principally that of his 'menagerie pavilion' at Kew. Recently restored, this is the sole survivor of the ephemeral chinoiserie

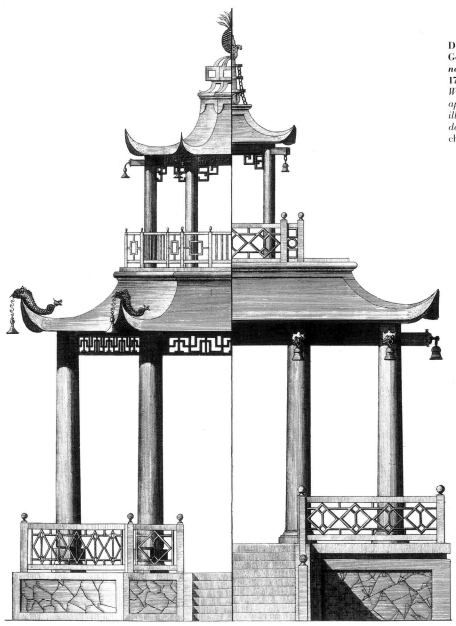

Design for a T'ing. From Georges Le Rouge, *Détails des nouveaux jardins à la mode,* **1774-89.** *The influence of William Chambers is clearly apparent in this French illustration of alternative designs for a kiosk or pavillon chinois,* called a T'ing.

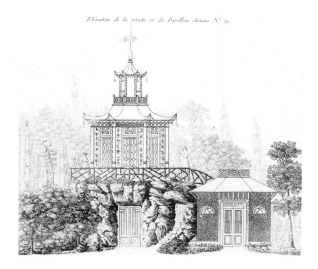

Elévation de la Grotte et du Pavillon chinois N.º 19

creations that had adorned the Anglo-Chinese gardens of France.

French garden designers were highly receptive to the ideas of artifice and variety recommended by Chambers as quintessentially Chinese. They took the garden of incident to its most theatrical extremes. The designer Louis Carrogis laid out the Parc Monceau in the 1770s for the Duc d'Orléans. Then situated on the outskirts of Paris (near to where the Arc de Triomphe now stands) its 48 acres were crammed with features, rather like a modern-day amusement park. Louis Carrogis, who was also an author and artist known as Carmontelle, was quite explicit about his intentions:

> At Monceau we have not tried to create an English garden … it is a fantasy pure and simple … and not an imitation of a nation which, in laying out natural gardens, runs a roller over every lawn and ruins nature by applying to it the art of a gardener bereft of imagination.

The pure and simple fantasies at Monceau naturally included those deemed to be Chinese. The pick of

the bunch was a *jeu de bague* or roundabout with four seats, conveniently topped by a parasol to shade the fair skins of its occupants. Two of the seats were in the form of cushions held by Chinese figures, two were dragons, and the whole was powered by three attendants dressed in Chinese costume. Roundabouts were very popular. There was even one in the gardens of the Petit Trianon at Versailles where the men rode dragons and the women peacocks.

To judge from the contemporary engravings and printed descriptions compiled in the late eighteenth century and early nineteenth century by Georges Le Rouge and J.C. Krafft (which, with few exceptions, represent all that remains of oriental buildings in pre-revolutionary France) most of the French chinoiserie garden pavilions erected were like those found in the English parks of the period. They were whimsical, ephemeral, octagonal kiosks with upturned roofs, liberally adorned with dragons, bells, exotic birds and flowers, and the ubiquitous monkey. In France, as in England, the most popular choice was relatively inexpensive, a bridge with gaily-painted, criss-cross balustrades. Generally these chinoiserie ornaments stood in the landscaped surroundings of the *jardin anglo-chinois*. Once they ascended to the roof of Charles Marin de la Haye's hotel in Paris, where a notable essay in gardening *anglo-chinois* style was to be found. But the two most spectacular Anglo-Chinese gardens were those at Bagatelle and at Saint-James, both in the Bois de Boulogne.

Bagatelle resulted from a bet entered into between Marie Antoinette and her brother-in-law, the Comte d'Artois. He wagered 10,000 francs that he would entertain the queen in a *palais de fée* (fairy palace) built within three months of the court's

sojourn at Fontainebleau. The comte eschewed a
magic wand for the more reliable expedients of a
huge workforce and the commandeering of building
supplies destined for other ends, and had won his bet
by November 1777. Next he transformed the gardens,
predominantly to a Chinese style. Among the
writhing paths and thundering cascades could be
found latticed bridges which spanned crags and
cliffs, the Great Chinese Tent, a Chinese pavilion and
a Philosopher's Hut balanced on an artificial rockery
and accessible only by a spiral staircase. Neither the
Palais de Fée nor its Chinese garden survive.

Close to Bagatelle, in the Bois de Boulogne, was
an estate bought in 1772 by the treasurer general of
the Navy, Claude Baudard de Saint-James. On his
new land he created an opulent landscape garden,
through which the waters of the Seine were pumped
to feed a waterfall, a lake and two rivers. Two Chinese
pavilions, one standing on stilts in the lake, and a
gaudy junk for cruising on the water, were among
its architectural features.

The Desert of Retz, an extraordinary creation of
the 1770s by a rich eccentric, the Baron de Monville,
was conveniently situated in the forest of Marly,
20 miles from Paris. Here its owner established a
magnificent *jardin anglo-chinois* and built for his
own residence a *maison chinoise*. This elegant
three-storied building with upswept roofs was built
in teak on a stone base with an exterior enriched by
simulated bamboo columns and intricate lattice
work. Its chimneys resembled incense burners, and
Chinese figures holding lanterns and umbrellas
were posted at its corners, while a robed and hatted
mandarin leaned against the little fretwork balcony
that crowned the lanterned roof. Other buildings

**Grotto with a Chinese pavilion
perched on top.** *(opposite)
From the famous gardens of
Saint-James in the Bois de
Boulogne, once one of the
most spectacular of the
jardins anglo-chinois.*

**The Chinese Pavilion at
Chantilly. Watercolour
drawing, 1784.** *This octagonal
kiosk was built in 1770, and
destroyed during the
revolution. The drawing was
sent to Catherine the Great. No
garden seemed immune to the
charms of these ephemeral,
brilliantly coloured and
frivolous structures.*

were dotted about the 65-acre park of the Desert: a Temple of Rest, a Temple of Pan, an icehouse shaped like a pyramid, a Gothic church, and most spectacular, a habitable ruin comprising the gigantic stump of a fluted column, newly built in a state of pleasing decay. Despite its classification as a historic monument in 1941, the vicissitudes of revolution, anti-chinoiserie moralizing, war and neglect have turned Monville's Desert into something more closely approaching its name. Recently the panels of the *maison chinoise* have been retrieved from the undergrowth of the ruined garden. The column survives, but little else.

The garden in which the *maison chinoise* originally stood had a serpentine stream and wriggling paths, and was held to be laid out in a manner which 'an Emperor of China would have acknowledged'. This imprimatur was given by the Prince de Ligne, whose park, Belœil, was one of the largest and most famous in Europe. Its garden which replaced a formal garden laid out in the style of Le Nôtre, was the brainchild of the prince – a zealous believer in the oriental origins of landscape gardening – and Joseph Bélanger, the closest available equivalent to a French William Chambers.

The first stage of the estate's reconstruction into a *jardin anglo-chinois* was the building of a shady garden around a brook. Next, pastoral and literary conventions were served by a Tartar village, a group of rustic thatched shelters with peasants dressed in 'a costume worthy of the dignity and simplicity of nature' and Swiss cows whose demeanour was to be equally regulated. 'My bulls will have a menacing air' the prince declared, although the beasts were fortunate enough to escape the additional

requirements of the luckless herdsmen and their families to provide amusement by singing and playing 'rustic instruments'.

The third stage involved the creation of an English garden, whose purpose was to invite the thinking of sad thoughts; an Indian Temple, where one would go to eat cream; a Chinese Temple to serve as a dovecote; and a mosque, which was an icehouse. Not all of these exotic alternatives to chinoiserie were built, and it is not recorded if it was the Prince de Ligne's opinion that his garden would have been acknowledged by the Emperor of China along with the Desert of Retz. In the end, despite de Ligne's endorsement of China, the specifically chinoiserie elements at Belœil were limited to a few buildings.

The Prince de Ligne was the friend and adviser – a kind of gardening correspondent – to one of the more remote devotees of the *jardin anglo-chinois*: Empress Catherine of Russia. Catherine the Great had enlisted the English landscape gardener, the appositely-named John Bush, to lay out the gardens around her summer palace Tsarskoe Selo, facing the Gulf of Sweden. In these unlikely surroundings she wrote to Voltaire in 1772, informing him of her

The Creaking Pavilion, Tsarskoe Selo. *Exterior view, tower and door detail. Catherine the Great's unbounded passion for the Anglo-Chinese garden brought chinoiserie follies into the grounds of the summer retreat of the Czars of Russia in the eighteenth century.*

feelings: 'I love to distraction gardens in the English style, the curving lines, the gentle slopes, ponds like lakes, archipelagos on dry land, and I hold in contempt straight lines and twin alleys.' The letter concluded with a flourish: '*l'anglomanie domine dans mon plantomanie*'.

While the Prince de Ligne had his Tartar Village, Catherine built a Chinese Village in the extensive grounds of Tsarskoe Selo. The plan was for 18 houses to be built around a temple and a pagoda. When Catherine died in 1786, work on the pagoda remained unfinished, and the scheme – simpler and smaller than originally envisaged – was not completed until 1818. With its brightly painted houses bedecked with Chinese motifs and the dragons on its roofs silhouetted against the snowy wastes of this the most northerly of chinoiserie's dominions, the Chinese village must once have been an extremely pretty toy. But this toy was also put to service: until the revolution members of the court lived in the Chinese village when the Emperor moved to Tsarskoe Selo for the summer. Astonishingly, although battered and down-at-heel, the village has survived all the upheavals that have convulsed Russia since its construction.

The Chinese village was only one of a series of Chinese structures that appeared in the parkland of Tsarskoe Selo. Facing it across a canal is the delightful Creaking Pavilion, while nearby is The Great Caprice, a rugged archway sporting a little pavilion perched on it like a top-knot on a coolie's head. This miniaturization was inspired by a seventeenth-century engraving of a similar structure in Fukien province in China; the original version was so large that ships could pass beneath the arch.

A less authoritative source can be found for the cruciform bridge which spans a canal in the elaborate system of waterways and islands that pattern the landscape. This bridge has an octagonal kiosk perched on a platform supported by a pair of steeply ramped staircases, and is clearly based on a plate in William Halfpenny's *Rural Architecture in the Chinese Taste*. The gardens of Tsarskoe Seloe were not exclusively devoted to China. There were also baths, grottoes, columns, a Palladian bridge, ruins, hermitages, and all the appurtenances of the *jardin anglo-chinois*. Naturally the Prince de Ligne was enchanted, declaring the garden the most interesting in the world.

De Ligne also approved of the early eighteenth-century *chinesische* tea-house at Potsdam, finding it '*superbe et bien entendu*'. This pioneering Chinese pavilion had been built by Frederick the Great before Germany embraced the vogue for informal gardens, and had been placed somewhat incongruously in a formal garden. In the late 1760s a smaller version of the Potsdam tea-house was built at Veitshöchheim, where its peaked roof and palm tree supports still rise above the gravelled walks and trim mazes of the Italianate garden in which it stands. It was only in the following decade that Germany was finally to adopt the *Englischer garten*, with some fairly odd results.

At Rosswald, near Troppau in Silesia, the fashion for exotic villages was taken to its most lunatic extremes when a miniature town, including a church, a *rathaus* and a market was built. The village was intended as a habitation of dwarfs, but a shortage of stunted occupants meant that children had to be pressed into service. The large park contained a

Chinese pavilions, *c.*1763-74. Lustgarten, Veitshöchheim, Germany. *An earlier formal garden with straight walks and clipped hedges is the setting for these symmetrically placed* Chinesische Hausen. *Palm trees with curving fronds, reminiscent of the tea-house at Potsdam, support a ribbed roof decorated with pineapples, the Chinese symbol of hospitality.*

further variety of architectural exotica, including a holy grove, druid caves, a hermitage and a mausoleum in which sacrifices for the dead were ceremoniously conducted. Among such company the presence of the pagoda and the Chinese temple would have elicited little comment. A Chinese village at Wilhelmsohe near Cassel was built by the landgrave, Friedrich II. In an attempt to combine diversion with dairying, the cowsheds, barn, cottages and stables were given a Chinese dressing of bright colours and curved ornament, and grouped around a pagoda, while black dairymaids were employed as surrogate Chinese.

An elaborate but less eccentric *jardin anglo-franco-chinois* – as Georges Le Rouge called it in his 21-volume account of the Anglo-Chinese garden – was laid out in the 1780s for Count Ludwig of Bentheim and Steinfort, at Steinfort, near Münster, in Westphalia. Here structures resembling the *maison chinoise* at Retz, and a Chinese pavilion declared suitable for the eating of strawberries, were placed among patently artificial rocks, hills and islands, while a pagoda-roofed ferry, whose open sides were bordered with criss-cross trellis, cruised the canal. At the gardens of Oranienbaum, near Dessau, laid out in 1795, the assemblage of chinoiserie pavilions is decidedly more conventional: a tea-house on an island, a five-storied pagoda and a couple of Chinese bridges were thought to offer sufficient diversion.

The fashion for landscape gardening spread rapidly throughout Europe in the last decades of the eighteenth century. And wherever landscaping went, pavilions and pagodas followed as an essential part of the baggage of the *jardin anglo-chinois*. They raised their pinnacled heads in parks across Eastern Europe from Prague to Warsaw, and extended their realm into Scandinavia. An English archdeacon travelling in these lands in the 1780s confided: 'We could not avoid feeling extreme satisfaction that the English style of gardening had penetrated into these distant

Chinese Pavilion, Cibalka, Prague, 1818-24. *The country house estate of Cibalka was converted into an English-style summer park in the early nineteenth century.*

Chinese Pavilion, c.1805. In the English Park in the grounds of Wilanow Palace, Poland. *The curious concept of the jardin anglo-chinois extended the realm of pagoda and kiosk right across Europe.*

Das Chinesische Lusthaus.
(top) This late eighteenth-century octagonal summer house, with fretted veranda and bell-hung roof, stood in the Prince of Lichtenstein's estate outside Vienna.

'The Quarters' behind Alresford Hall, painted by John Constable in 1816.
(bottom) Waterside sites returned to fashion for the chinoiserie pavilions of the late eighteenth century, such as this fishing pavilion in Essex. The pavilion still stands.

regions.' Only Italy held aloof. A few examples can be found, but although the Borghese Gardens in Rome and others around the country are nominally landscaped in the English manner, they were laid out late in the day, when chinoiserie was regarded as *passé*, and their winding paths and rank grass are deprived of the ornaments of Cathay.

At the moment when the first landscape gardens were making their appearance in France, the English turned away from the garden of incident. The display of a variety of architectural follies disposed on acres of smooth turf was now viewed with horror as old-fashioned and unromantic, and was overtaken by the wilder, more natural and overgrown look of the picturesque garden. This, together with the controversy caused by William Chambers' *Dissertation on Gardens* which had produced a barrage of criticism against what Walpole called the 'unmeaning fallaballas of Chinese chequer work', and Walpole's own triumphant resuscitation of the Gothic, had all combined to limit the popularity of Chinese pavilions in late eighteenth-century England. Despite the adverse propaganda, however, some notable chinoiserie follies did make their appearance in England in the latter half of the century. One, now known as The Quarters, a Chinese pavilion at Alresford in Essex, still stands. Built originally for fishing parties, it was converted and extended as a residence in the 1950s and is lived in today.

Most of these later pavilions were placed beside or over water. And islands were back in vogue. The trend was started in the 1750s at Virginia Water in Surrey, the lake created by the Duke of Cumberland to provide employment for the soldiers who had served under him. There a Chinese bridge led to a 'Chinese island', while on the lake itself a Chinese junk floated. This 40-foot folly, the *Mandarine*, was towed there by oxen, and formally inspected by the Duke's nephew, George III and Queen Charlotte.

In the late eighteenth century, a Chinese temple erected on an island in the lake at Woburn Abbey in Bedfordshire was large enough to seat 30 diners, whose food was ferried out to them from a kitchen on the shore. This was a separate enterprise from the Chinese dairy, designed by Henry Holland in 1789, which also stood on the shore of the lake. An elegant building, some of whose elements are taken directly from Chambers' *Designs*, the dairy is approached by a colonnade that follows the curve of the lake, and has a trellised porch and an open balcony on the first floor beneath a small octagonal fretted tower. Within, there are marble shelves on painted bamboo supports, and niches filled with porcelain dishes on fretwork shelves. The surrounding gardens were planted with Chinese specimens, newly available in England. This scheme was suggested by Humphry Repton, who had achieved prominence on the death of his father-in-law Capability Brown in 1783, and whose respect for geographical accuracy was typical of the new age.

Although oriental by allusion rather than imitation, and thus a perfect specimen of late eighteenth-century chinoiserie, Woburn's Chinese Dairy was greatly admired in the nineteenth century, an era generally harsh in its judgement of eighteenth-century chinoiserie. These harsh judgements reflected changing attitudes. The nineteenth century was to form a quite different view of China, and of its arts.

Nineteenth-century chinoiserie and the spread to the New World

But the curtain which had been drawn around the celestial country for ages has now been rent asunder; and instead of viewing an enchanted fairy-land, we find, after all, that China is just like other countries.

Robert Fortune, *Wanderings in China*, 1847

The Chinese Gallery, Brighton Pavilion, 1838. *The construction and furnishing of the Royal Pavilion at Brighton, the favourite creation of the extravagant and capricious Prince of Wales, was decided in part by the gift in 1801 of the Chinese wallpaper seen here.*

Dinner-party at a Mandarin's house. Engraving from *China in a Series of Views*, 1848.

As the *ancien régime* perished in the cleansing fervour of the French revolution the golden days of chinoiserie were numbered, although the vogue persisted, in one form or another, through much of the nineteenth century and well into the twentieth. Where frivolity and extravagance – the animating attitudes of the Rococo – persisted, chinoiserie was on safe ground. And as the middle-classes embraced it, chinoiseries appeared in parlours as well as palaces. At Brighton the exuberant and pleasure-loving nature of the Prince of Wales created the Royal Pavilion, the great nineteenth-century monument of the chinoiserie style. Later, along with all the other historical revivals of the nineteenth century, a Rococo revival took place which introduced mass-produced chinoiserie motifs onto wallpaper, textiles and furniture. Many a nineteenth-century porcelain or pottery factory depended for its bread and butter on the continuing popularity of *fleurs des Indes* and blue-and-white tableware decorated with Chinese patterns. For the more adventurous, exoticism, shorn of its rococo aspects, maintained its considerable appeal, and for the aesthetes, shuddering and reeling from the excesses of the new industrial era, the Empire of the Rising Sun provided comfort and refuge from the ugliness of their age.

Until the 1830s chinoiserie continued as a minority taste much as it had in the past. Then attitudes began to change. China was no longer admired in the West, and chinoiserie fell victim to political events. Industrialization, commercialism and imperial interests all ran counter to the pinnacled fantasies of the chinoiserie style. British merchants failed to develop trade with China. Mystery and myth were extirpated by geographers and explorers. The praising of Confucian thought and Chinese government, and the belief in the superiority of Chinese art, all passed into derision. The success of European and British imperialism ensured that everyone knew exactly what was where on the globe, and the clear light of topographical truth was cast onto previously unseen areas of the Celestial Empire. Cathay tottered, and was to vanish completely in the inglorious prosecution of the opium wars.

Disenchantment did not come at once. What was to undermine the old chinoiserie began as early as the 1790s. The revolution and the Terror that followed it in France shattered the hot-house in which chinoiserie had bloomed. Furthermore, increasing penetration of China by the West began to undermine chinoiserie's very foundation, the fantasy of Cathay. But it was only in the 1840s, when events in China threatened the West's commercial interests, that chinoiserie toppled into disfavour.

In 1792 the first rent opened in the veil of mystery surrounding Cathay. Lord Macartney was appointed by the prime minister, William Pitt, to undertake an embassy to China in an attempt to establish an embassy in Peking and to open up trading with Britain. The embassy followed the well-trodden and barren route of all European overtures to the Celestial Empire, and like the others it bore little fruit.

Eight hundred men in three ships sailed up the Chinese coast and on to Peking. They penetrated further, beyond the Great Wall, for the embassy was received by the emperor, Qianlong, at his summer palace at Jehol. The members of Macartney's mission became the first Europeans since the Jesuit

The Mandarin Chow Ta-zhin being carried in his sedan chair. *Engraving from Sir George Staunton,* An Authentic Account of an Embassy From The King of Great Britain To The Emperor of China *(1797). Diplomatic and trade missions conducted throughout the nineteenth century parted the veil of mystery surrounding China's way of life.*

missionaries to see the gardens of Jehol, which had so impressed the early landscape designers of England and France. But this favour of the emperor's did not signify success for Macartney. Gifts and blandishments cut no ice with the emperor, and he said as much – in verse. The emperor composed a poem recording the fact that the king of the red-haired English had sent his envoy, and that:

> *Though their tribute is commonplace, my heart*
> *approves sincerely.*
> *Curios and the boasted ingenuity of their devices*
> *I prize not.*

Several further insulting lines were written before the emperor dispatched Macartney home with an edict acknowledging Macartney's 'tribute', and requiring King George III to swear perpetual obedience to the Celestial Empire. Possibly the emperor had taken umbrage at Macartney's refusal to *kow-tow*, although earlier, more compliant Europeans had gone through the three kneelings and nine knockings of the head without achieving any greater success.

Although the expedition was diplomatically a complete fiasco, far from inspiring anti-Chinese sentiment in England it contributed to a renewal of interest in China and its artefacts, and to a revival of chinoiserie, then in retreat from the calm certitudes of neo-classicism. Georgian England was not yet driven by imperial passions. This only occurred later, in the more commercially-minded world of the Victorians.

Macartney himself had enjoyed his tour of the Imperial Gardens, where he was frequently reminded of familiar sights in England, particularly the gardens at Stowe, Woburn or Painshill. He praised Chinese garden architecture, remarking, 'All the buildings are perfect of their kind, either elegantly simple or highly decorated according to the effect that is intended to arise', although he did go on to compare Chinese architecture in general to 'a person without a single good feature in his face', noting that nevertheless such an individual could have 'a very Agreeable countenance'.

Everybody, including Macartney's valet, published their memoirs of the trip; William Alexander, a draughtsman who had accompanied the mission, exhibited his drawings of the sights encountered annually at the Royal Academy from 1795 to 1800. These detailed, delicate, faithful and beautiful drawings illustrated a two-volume tome,

Sir George Staunton's *An Authentic Account of an Embassy from the King of Great Britain to the Emperor of China*, published in 1797. Engravings ensured their wide dissemination, providing a new source for chinoiserie designs. The architect Henry Holland was to use them in his designs for the Prince of Wales at Carlton House.

In the euphoria that surrounded British foreign policy in the post-Napoleonic era, it was decided to make a fresh overture to the court of China, now ruled by a new emperor, Ch'ia Ch'ing. In 1816 another embassy was despatched, headed by Lord Amherst. It too ended in fiasco. Although he was granted a prompt audience with the emperor, Amherst declined to meet him on the grounds that he was tired and unsuitably dressed, a gaffe that Ch'ia Ch'ing took in bad part. Moreover the letter that Amherst bore from the Prince of Wales hailed the emperor in unacceptably familiar terms as 'My Brother'.

Once more a British diplomat received the Chinese treatment. Amherst returned to England with nothing more than a message to the Prince Regent suggesting that the Prince might continue in obedience to the Dragon Throne but should not attempt to express his feelings any more ardently by sending his representatives to China. Another diplomatic defeat, but it still had no repercussions in the fashinable world. But this was before British interest in China changed its nature.

In 1834 the East India Company's monopoly in the China trade was ended, and a motley horde of free-booters turned their eyes to the profitable business opportunities that now became available. A British envoy, Lord Napier, was sent to Canton to

act as their representative. He died of fever shortly after arriving, but not before managing to antagonize the Chinese authorities with whom he was charged to mediate. The Chinese placed restrictions on British trading, particularly in opium, which was highly lucrative. When these were ignored by the British Hongs the emperor sent a commissioner to enforce them. The commissioner cut off supplies of food and water to the merchants. Worse, he impounded their opium, liquified it and poured it into the estuary, mollifying the Spirit of the Ocean with some incantatory lines composed for the occasion.

The response of the foreign secretary, Lord Palmerston, was to send 16 men-of-war and 27 troop carriers, and in 1840 Canton was captured by the British. Two years later Nanking surrendered without resistance. Under the Treaty of Nanking that followed, Hong Kong was ceded to the British and four ports on the Chinese mainland, including Shanghai, were opened to foreigners. In Nanking, victorious British sailors defaced the Porcelain Pagoda, so richly fabled in the West.

Over the next decades internal dissension weakened the Chinese government further. This gave the British the opportunity to extract further concessions, and the Chinese the chance to break them. By 1860 a British expeditionary force was once more in China. It was commanded by the 8th Earl of Elgin, whose father had so enthusiatically removed the marble sculptures from the Parthenon. By October 1860 Peking was taken, two hundred buildings in the Imperial City were sacked, and British and French forces had plundered Yuan-ming-yuan. Lord Elgin then gave the order to burn the gardens and the palaces. Five palace complexes

Chinese wallpaper. *Presented by Lord Macartney to his London bank, Coutts & Co, where it still hangs.*

Chinoiseries come to town.
View of the Chinese House and
the Rotunda at Ranelagh
Gardens, London. *(above left)*
The *Bains chinois* on the
Boulevard des Italiens, Paris,
*c.*1800. *(above)*
Perspective view of Vauxhall
Gardens, Lambeth, London,
1744. *(left) Adopted first by the
fashionable pleasure-gardens
of the eighteenth century, the
vogue for chinoiseries was
maintained in the public parks
of the nineteenth century.*

and all their subsidiary buildings were destroyed. This brutal piece of despoliation was a fitting endorsement of the new view of China held in the West. In 1839, the year that open hostilities began, a veteran of Macartney's embassy wrote of '[what] was not *then* so generally known as *now* … the proneness to falsehood, the duplicity and knavery of the Chinese, which not only pervade every department of the government, but also, naturally enough, infect the people generally'.

By the time of the desecration of the emperor's summer palace, China was widely seen throughout Europe as a country of liars and fools, whose defences were pitifully weak and whose emperor's claims to universal sway were absurd and meaningless. This view now began to affect the manner in which the West viewed the arts of China. It was symbolically apt that the British conquest of China should end at the gardens of Yuan-ming-yuan, which had been a source of inspiration to the West for over a hundred years and which had stimulated chinoiserie's greatest triumph in Europe, the *jardin anglo-chinois*. However, the heyday of this style of landscape gardening was already past. By the end of the eighteenth century chinoiserie had moved out of the private gardens of the aristocracy and into the urban entertainments of city-dwellers, a place it had first occupied 50 years before when pleasure-gardens were fashionable resorts.

The rococo pleasure-gardens of Ranelagh and Vauxhall in London had received a Chinese dressing as early as the 1750s. Lattice-work fences enclosed the 'Wilderness' at Vauxhall, and society flocked to see and be seen in the supper boxes and Chinese pavilions whose domed kiosks were linked by a colonnade. In Paris there was a *Redoute chinoise* in the Foire St Laurent in 1781, where Chinese pageants, fireworks and illuminations were held, and a Chinese café, where French waitresses wore Chinese dress and a Chinaman acted as porter. The oriental baths in the Boulevard des Italiens turned themselves into *bains chinois*, and in this guise survived the revolution, the only urban chinoiserie entertainment in France so to do. The popularity of chinoiserie entertainments in Paris was celebrated in verse of a kind:

> *Quel pays merveilleux! Sans sortir de Paris,*
> *Dans le Palais-Royal, vous avez des Chinoises:*
> *Un orchestre chinois, arrivé de Pekin,*
> *Execute, en fonflant, un solo de Martin:*
> *Mais dans les Bains chinois c'est un*
>   *autre artifice.*

and so on, until the poet's vein of inventiveness ran dry.

During the ninteenth century chinoiserie continued as the chosen style for places of public amusement. The centenary of the Hanoverian succession, which was celebrated in London in 1814 with a Grand National Jubilee and fireworks in St James's Park, had a Chinese setting designed by John Nash, comprising a bridge with a pagoda in the middle and kiosks on either side from which the fireworks would be launched. A large crowd paid half a guinea each to witness the event. The bridge, pagoda and kiosks were all bathed in light, fire-crackers roared, Catherine-wheels turned and rockets shot from the roof. Unhappily the fireworks proved more spectacular than intended. The pagoda roof caught alight, the top five stages fell blazing into the canal and two people were killed. But not even this disaster discredited the vogue for chinoiserie, which continued to claim pride of place in public gardens.

Places of public entertainment in the nineteenth century no longer attracted the *beau monde* – in the eighteenth century Horace Walpole had complained that at Vauxhall, which he attended nightly, he could not put his foot down without treading on a Prince of Wales or Duke of Cumberland – but the style of architecture of the pleasure gardens continued to reflect the tastes favoured by the rich and fashion-conscious. At Vauxhall Gardens elements of Indian design were incorporated in the early 1820s, when the palm trees and twining serpents of the Brighton pavilion had made this style popular. But by 1826 this style was already out of favour, and a new Chinese entrance to the Gardens testified to a revived interest in Chinese architecture among the arbiters of fashion. The year 1836 saw the erection of a pagoda-like bandstand in Cremorne Gardens which, declared the *Illustrated London News* perhaps somewhat over-lavishly, caused Cremorne Gardens to be 'many times gayer than Vauxhall on its most brilliant nights'. The last appearance of Cathay in an English garden is the Peace Pagoda, complete with gilded Buddha, which stands on the river at Battersea Gardens in London, erected in 1985.

In the landscape gardens of the wealthy, chinoiserie's reign had been checked by the late eighteenth-century cult of the picturesque, which looked on Chinese gardens with horror as artificial. In *The Landscape, A Didactic Poem*, a long and passionate advocacy of the new picturesque style written by Richard Payne Knight, the most articulate

of the advocates of the picturesque, the Chinese style of gardening was damned in couplets as

Light and fantastical, yet stiff and prim,
This child of barren fancy turned to whim.

Somehow chinoiserie survived such condemnation. It was too pretty and too closely tied to the tradition of landscape gardening to be discarded. Even the most picturesque of the picturesques, William Beckford – who built himself a gargantuan folly in the Gothic style, Fonthill – enclosed its 1900 acres of landscaped gardens with a wall like that of the emperor's palace at Yuan-ming-yuan.

Later in the century, gardeners discovered that by using the new specimen plants that were being imported from China as a surround to the chinoiserie architecture, they could keep a foothold among the pagodas and summer pavilions of the eighteenth century while staying faithful to the prevailing fashion for geographical accuracy. While the British were waging war with the Chinese, a botanist, Robert Fortune, was busily collecting specimen plants and seeds in China for the Horticultural Society of London. For 15 years he sent home to England as much of China's varied plants as he could, and wrote four travel volumes, the last published in 1863.

Once he had recovered from the desolate shock of seeing the barren hills above the Canton estuary, Fortune waxed enthusiastic about the flowers, 'the camellias, azaleas and roses of which I had heard so much in England'. The landscape gardeners of England were fired with enthusism by his botanical discoveries. At last they had the chance to move nearer to the real Chinese garden. One of the first gardens to adopt the new vogue for authenticity, Dropmore in Buckinghamshire, stocked a Chinese

**The Dancing Platform at
Cremorne Gardens, London**.
*Painting by Phoebus Levin,
1864.*

garden with the new varieties of oriental flowering shrubs, embellished it with an aviary and a summer house, and provided the visitor with glazed pottery Chinese seats. In the 1820s Prince Pückler-Muskau had visited one of these new-style Chinese gardens, Cassiobury Park in Hertfordshire, laid out by Humphry Repton. Gone were the spacious lawns and terraces, the sparkling pinnacles and gilded dragons of the *jardin anglo-chinois*. In their place he found:

> *a number of vases, benches, fountains and a third green-house – all in the genuine Chinese style. Here were beds surrounded by circles of white, blue and red sand, fantastic dwarf plants, and many dozens of large Chinese vases placed on pedestals, thickly overgrown with trailing evergreens, and exotics.*

It is Robert Fortune *avant la lettre*.

Fortune's own description of the garden of a mandarin – 'old Dr Chang', the very appellation is deflating enough – that he visited in Ning-Po in 1843, would have been heard with incredulity by the gardening Sinophiles of the eighteenth century, although today's suburban gardeners might be more comprehending. For a start, the mandarin's garden 'lies behind the house', and could, in less exalted ownership, be thought of as the back yard. It was reached by 'a subterranean passage', from which Fortune was able to glimpse 'small courts fitted up with rockwork'. He observed that 'dwarf trees are planted here and there in various places, and creepers hang down naturally and gracefully until their ends touch the little ponds of water which are always placed in front of the rockwork.' The garden, Fortune notes, has 'dwarf trees, vases, rock-work, ornamental windows, and beautiful flowering shrubs', but is, he warns, 'very limited in extent', although 'the most is made of it by windings … and arches in the walls, as well as by hiding the boundary with a mass of shrubs and trees'.

The Anglo-Chinese gardens of England, however, were still of a vast scale. When the Earl of Shrewsbury laid out England's last great landscape garden at Alton Towers in Staffordshire he excavated an Indian cave temple, recreated a massive Stonehenge, constructed seven glass-domed conservatories, threw in a Gothic tower for good measure, and planned a pagoda fountain. This was intended to have five cast-iron stories rising 88 feet from a stone base, and was to be illuminated by gas lanterns and festooned with assorted beasts spouting water from every available orifice. Unluckily the Earl's death in 1827 put paid to this sizeable folly, and in its place there stands a more modest three-storey pagoda with diapered paintwork and an upswept canopied roof.

The last pagoda of the century was installed at Cliveden in Buckinghamshire in the 1890s. This was the final resting-place for a much-travelled folly. The pagoda had started life at the Paris Exhibition of 1867, had briefly ornamented the sad remains of the famous eighteenth-century gardens of Bagatelle, and is still to be seen in its present position on a small island in the grounds of Lord Astor's mansion.

In the 1850s the last great Anglo-Chinese garden in England was laid out at Biddulph Grange near Cheshire. Among a dozen different kinds of gardens, the Chinese one featured a joss-house, a Chinese veranda and a long latticed bridge, all placed among appropriately oriental trees and shrubs, some sent back specifically for the project by Robert

Fortune. The garden was bordered by a 'Great Wall of China' and presided over by a Chinese idol, a bull, in an open kiosk. The whole was praised at the time for its 'willow-pattern' effect, a neat example of nature imitating art.

One of the last architectural products of the fashion for chinoiserie was a little temple in the centre of a maze built at Woburn Abbey in 1833 and recently restored. With its cast-iron balustrading, octagonal lantern of trellis-work and brightly coloured red-and-blue glass bells, it is an attractive late essay in the style. But it is completely upstaged by the grandest temple of the times, the Fishing Temple at Virginia Water which King George IV commissioned in late 1825 and which was demolished at the end of the century. It was the king's last fling, elaborate, expensive, with a wealth of chinoiserie detail, a piece of sumptuous frivolity that earned a chorus of popular disapproval. Bigger than any constructed in the eighteenth century, the pavilion was the collaborative effort of two gifted men, Sir Jeffrey Wyatville, the king's architect at Windsor, and Frederick Crace, master of the nineteenth-century chinoiserie interior, who had worked for the king at Brighton. The design of a central octagon, with flanking hexagons and a long covered balcony running along the front, was firmly in the mould of Sir William Chambers. The pavilion stood on the water's edge, with a Chinese boat house alongside and a group of Turkish tents half-hidden in the weeping willows which surrounded it. An aviary and a fountain stocked with silver and gold carp completed the picture. Here, exotic to the end, the king – by now hugely fat and most unromantic to look at – would sometimes dine.

George IV was England's greatest devotee of chinoiserie in the nineteenth century. Indeed on his first public appearance, when he was 12 days old, he was protected from too close an examination by the part of the apartment in which he was exhibited being 'latticed off in the Chinese manner'. (What impression this made on the infant consciousness of the last survivor of the *ancien régime* must remain a matter of speculation.) It was not until he moved into his own establishment, Carlton House, that the young prince was able to indulge his passion for the exotic. Between 1783, when the building was presented to the prince, and 1827, when it was abandoned to the demolition gang, Carlton House absorbed his interests and large amounts of the nation's funds. Building work was subject to recurring crises, financial impasses and a degree of fickleness of taste by the Prince of Wales which bordered on the maniacal.

As was to be the case at Brighton, the prince was closely involved in every aspect of the work at Carlton House. His architect, Henry Holland, who had visited France in 1785, was completely familiar with the prevailing neo-classical taste. Inevitably, there was a strong French influence in the decoration and design. In the design of the Chinese drawing-room, Holland re-imported Chambers' orientalism to England from France, where it had been sharpened with Gallic sophistication and good breeding. Many of its details revealed his familiarity with Chambers' publications: the arrangement of Chinese wall paintings within bamboo screens, the use of a series of thin columns with 'collars' around the room, their decoration of lei-wen spirals hung with bells, and the trellis-patterned dado were all elements of 'Chinese' design advocated by Chambers. This was the testing-ground for the prince's later essays in chinoiserie, anticipating the Brighton Pavilion by ten years. The furnishing of the room was in the hands of a Frenchman, Louis Daguerre, who commissioned and also probably designed the chimneypiece, tables, clock, candelabra and seats.

The year 1790 saw the completion of the Chinese drawing-room. It was revealed as the paragon of Georgian chinoiserie taste. Here fantasy and restraint were balanced, and brilliant craftsmanship and exquisite materials employed with consummate effect. The room had a short life. It was demolished in 1808 when all the rooms on the basement floor of Carlton House were redecorated, but fortunately we know how it looked because of Thomas Sheraton's engravings of the room published in 1793 in his *Cabinet-Maker and Upholsterer's Drawing-Book*. Sheraton, no stranger to ornament, was quite overwhelmed by the room's decoration, writing that 'the whole effect, though it may appear extravagant to a vulgar eye, is but suitable to the dignity of the proprietor'.

The proprietor's demands of dignity were unassuaged. Almost as soon as Holland had done his work, the prince set the whole house in a state of upheaval once again. A trifle wearily Joseph Farington confided in his diary: 'He has ordered the whole to be done again under the direction of Walsh Porter who has destroyed all that Holland has done & is substituting and finishing in a most expensive and motley taste.' Walsh Porter, a connoisseur and dilettante who was a member of the Carlton House set, may have been responsible for another Chinese room at Carlton House. We do not know where this

room was, or how long it survived, but a detailed invoice tells us that the work on it cost £1375 3s 8d. Decorated in 1805-7, principally in black and carmine, with golden pagodas on the walls, a lilac-and-green ceiling painted with Chinese signs of the zodiac, a carpet of the same colours with a bamboo border and a Chinese fishing scene in the centre, the entire scheme sounds like something out of a Hollywood film director's delirium. It is this combination of opulence with a kind of barbaric splendour that was to dominate in the furnishings of that most extraordinary of chinoiserie palaces, the Royal Pavilion at Brighton.

The building of the Royal Pavilion was a result of the Prince Regent's folly; completely in keeping with the character of the man it is no surprise that he considered it his favourite creation. It was at Brighton that the prince's passion for Maria Fitzherbert ripened and deepened until he married her secretly in 1785. In 1784, the year before the marriage, the prince's cook and general factotum, Louis Weltje, rented on his behalf the 'superior farmhouse' which was to be metamorphosed into the Royal Pavilion. All the crowned heads of Europe were then playing at being farmers: the prince's own father, George III, was known as 'Farmer George', and Marie Antoinette was as fond as the next woman of patting butter, but the charms of the rural life held limited interest for the prince.

The qualities uppermost in the prince's character were those of the *ancien régime*. His proud and frivolous nature, irresponsible and self-indulgent personal life and reactionary political views were however countered by an undoubted interest in the arts, and a high-spirited and zestful approach to life

Pair of four-light candelabra. French, *c.*1787-90.
Chinese Drummer Boy Clock. French, *c.*1787-90. *In both of these exquisite chinoiseries, among the many collected by* *the Prince Regent to adorn Carlton House in London, a strong sense of exuberant fantasy is coupled with a typically French finesse of execution.*

in general. It was to be expected that 'Prinny' would transform the rural charms of his newly-acquired property into something wildly original. When the Pavilion was finally completed – and the transformation took 35 years – visitors were completely taken aback. 'I do not believe,' wrote the Princess Lieven in 1821, 'that since the days of Heligobalus, there has been such magnificence and such luxury.' The Prince Regent himself confessed he cried for joy when he contemplated the Pavilion's splendours.

The first changes made were relatively modest. The prince's rising debts did not allow for more. Henry Holland extended the pavilion between 1801 and 1803, and a gift of Chinese wallpaper in 1801 led to the first appearance of chinoiserie in its interiors. The firm of Frederick Crace was used for these first essays in the style, and the decoration was in line with the established tradition of chinoiserie taste. Delicate, light and fanciful bamboo, fretwork, and *treillage* were combined with sophisticated ground colours such as scarlet and purple to provide a scheme that was gay, light-hearted and rather old-fashioned in its air of rococo charm. Simpler furniture was designed for the pavilion, markedly different in style from that for Carlton House. Cheaper materials were used – bamboo and lacquer rather than ebony and ormolu – and consequently the air of opulent extravagance was less powerful.

Brighton was designed to be less a public royal residence and more a place where the prince could put his feet up. But this did not mean that he would be long content with mere tinkering. The exterior demanded attention, and was to get it. At the end of 1802 Holland submitted plans for a Chinese exterior in a style not unlike that of Chambers: rather jolly and colourful with gilded ornaments. A few years later another architect, William Pordern, produced his scheme for a Chinese exterior for the Pavilion. Pordern, who fully earned his nickname of Bold Pordern, was already at work in Brighton on the most grandiloquent Royal Stables imaginable, an edifice not much smaller than St Paul's Cathedral.

The nineteenth century relied less on fancy than previous ages had done. Pordern had studied the well-known topographical drawings of William Alexander and had found there a suitable model for the prince's seaside palace, the Hall of Audience at Yuan-ming-yuan. For the Pavilion Pordern designed an eastern elevation with a blue tiled roof, golden dragons, scarlet columns and railings and painted ornamental friezes. The western elevation was rather simpler and grander in design, with Chinese characters inscribed on the façade and life-size Chinese statues in niches. But the stables were eating money, and this was no moment to ask for fresh funds. Pordern's schemes languished.

Enter Humphry Repton, who in 1806 produced an album of 12 watercolours of his plans to turn the Pavilion into a grand Mughal palace. The prince was enchanted. 'Mr Repton,' he announced, 'I consider the whole of this work as perfect, and will have every part of it carried into immediate execution; not a tittle shall be altered – even you yourself shall not attempt any improvement.' Only the latter part of the statement proved correct. Repton's plans went the way of Pordern's, although the idea of a Hindu exterior lodged in the prince's mind. In 1813 a third architect, James Wyatt, produced plans for unspecified 'improvements' at a cost of £200,000.

Design by the firm of Frederick Crace for the Royal Pavilion, Brighton. Early nineteenth century. *Lively colour combinations were one of the hallmarks of the Crace style.*

Before these had time to be praised and rejected Wyatt was killed in an accident. The prince was desolate. Weeping, he declared: 'he had just found a man to his mind, and was thus unhappily deprived of him'.

Finally, in 1815 – at just the right moment since the Prince Regent had secured the finances and was eager to begin – John Nash appeared on the scene. Nash was well known to the prince; he was responsible for the plans for both Regent's Park and Regent Street, the latter designed to provide a grand link between the park and Carlton House. (It was also generally believed that Nash's wife was the prince's mistress.) His scheme for the Pavilion was dazzling, and it appears that the Prince Regent played a decisive role in its creation. According to

Nash the plans were determined by the great bulk of Pordern's stables, which quite overshadowed the residence of the prince. He recounted:

> It was therefore determined by H.M. that the Pavillion should assume an Eastern character, and the Hindoo style of Architecture was adopted in the expectation that the turban domes and pinnacles might from their glittering and picturesque effect, attract and fix the attention of the Spectator, and the superior magnificence of the Dome of the Stables cease to be observed.

'Hindoo' on the outside, Chinese within: plans were agreed and work started on the remodelling in March 1815. The corridor, staircases and entrance hall were the first interiors to be tackled. By 1817 the basic

Design by Robert Jones for the Saloon, Royal Pavilion, Brighton. *Costs spiralled at the Brighton pavilion as the Prince Regent's fickleness of taste entailed constant changes. This early scheme, since reverted to, has panels of Chinese wallpaper set in brilliant surrounds of red-and-gold fretted designs.*

The Banqueting Room, Royal Pavilion, Brighton. *From a 45-foot-high dome sprouts a gigantic plantain tree, the nest of an enormous carved winged silver dragon from whose talons dangles a lighting device justly described as being of 'unparalleled size'.*

structure of the state rooms was in place. The whole was completed in 1822, after which the king (the Prince Regent had been crowned in 1820) took little interest, visiting it for the last time in 1827.

But while the work was underway the Prince Regent was completely involved. Predictably enough, the vagaries of his taste entailed rising costs and constant changes – the South Drawing Room was altered four times in 1815. The firm of Frederick Crace remained a constant presence in the decoration, and there are numerous references in Crace's accounts to 'attending the Prince in hanging the paper' or 'designing patterns for the approbation of the Prince'. At Brighton Crace's knowledge of the chinoiserie style was augmented by the work of a designer of genius, Robert Jones, who was responsible for much of the designs for the central saloon, and for the remarkable Banqueting Room with its dragons and serpents, its gilded pelmets and mural panels depicting groups of costumed Chinese figures.

Two distinct phases of decoration were embarked on within the six years of Nash's remodelling. Both drew extensively on the vocabulary of chinoiserie. The first was still quite light-hearted and rococoesque, the second much more powerful, with a bizarre but disciplined richness replacing the tinsel and toylike brilliance of the first style. Scaly dragons and metallic snakes, lotus-shaped gasoliers and gilded palm-tree pilasters combined with rich colours and grand furniture to produce an astonishing and exhilarating effect.

Both phases of chinoiserie decoration at Brighton were clearly to be seen in the long low corridor that connects the five state rooms on

The Royal Pavilion, Brighton.
Detail of the hand-painted
dragon wallpaper in the Red
Drawing Room. *(opposite)
Detail of a mural in the Music
Room. (left) Even here, at the
summit of the exotic fantasies
that make up the decoration
at Brighton, the nineteenth-
century regard for geographical
accuracy ensures that the
landscape scenes depicted
are taken from William
Alexander's aquatints in* The
Costume of China, *published
in 1805.*

the ground floor and acts as a spine to the whole
pavilion. It is here that the original stimulus of
the entire decorative scheme, the Chinese wallpaper
given to the prince in 1801, was hung. The simulated
bamboo staircases of cast iron, and the wonderful
pink and blue paper, are both from the first stage
of decoration and have remained in place. The
charming, toylike elements – gay banners and
standing Chinese figures wearing real robes – were
however swept away. In their place came a greater
solemnity. Bookshelves, Indian ivory and
sandalwood chairs, pedestals, a grand central light
fitting – a discard from one of the remodellings of
the Saloon – and a richly patterned carpet altered
the mood. A lavish use of mirrors increased the
scale and brilliance of the whole.

The dramatic finale of the decorative scheme,
the Music Room, represents the summit of the Crace
firm's achievement. At one point Frederick Crace
himself and 34 assistants were involved in its
decoration, often working through the night. Blazing

with crimson-and-gold Chinese landscape murals
framed by gigantic serpents and winged dragons it
resembles a gigantic lacquer box, and was lit by
nine pink cut-glass water-lily and dragon-shaped
gasoliers. Here the king's band, seventy strong, would
play, and the king himself would impress his guests
with his rendering of popular songs.

The Royal Pavilion, so personal a statement
of the chinoiserie style, and so expensive to create,
was unlikely to influence many middle-class
interiors. Both Regent and his extravagance were
unpopular, and this may have contributed to the low
esteem in which the chinoiserie style at the Royal
Pavilion was generally held. A contemporary
publication, *The Decorative Painter's and Glazier's
Guide* of 1827, provides detailed instructions on
technique and colours to be used in attempting the
chinoiserie style. Nevertheless its author, Nathaniel
Whittock, warns of the endless trouble and expense
involved. As to the propriety of such an imitation,
Whittock baldly affirms that 'the civilized mind

revolts at the sprawling dragons, squat houses and a perpetual recurrence of ornament like nothing in nature, or if like anything, making a preference of the most ugly and loathsome, as the toad lizard'. He goes on:

> *The author of this work is aware that he is running counter to the prevailing taste in the highest quarter, by condemning the introduction of the Chinese style. The Chinese apartment at the pavilion at Brighton may be cited as an instance of elegant decoration, and such it indisputably is; and where the building is of sufficient extent to shew all the styles of decoration, one room may, with great propriety, be Chinese; but even in the room above mentioned this style will find few admirers, and time has shown but few imitators.*

But some grand Chinese interiors were attempted. The Dowager Marchioness of Downshire decorated a room between 1812 and 1814 at Ombersley Park in

Worcestershire. The colour scheme was blue and gold; the walls were hung with painted silk framed by feigned bamboo; and the beechwood furniture, also carved and painted to resemble bamboo, bore a striking resemblance to some supplied for the Brighton Pavilion in 1802. A Chinese drawing-room was created by Isabella, Marchioness of Hertford, an ex-mistress of the Prince Regent, in 1827-28. Here the paper was virtually identical to that in the Saloon at Brighton, and was probably a gift to her from the Regent in 1806. Each panel was different, the entire pattern depicting a garden with a balustrade. The Marchioness increased the richness of the effect by adding cut-out birds from Audubon's *The Birds of America*, published in the same year as the drawing-room was being decorated. The furniture was French, with the addition of japanned flowers and twigs, and a Broadwood piano was painted in mock Japanese lacquer too. In a late and rare example of chinoiserie decoration, a Chinese room at Middleton Park in

Déjeune Tables in the Chinese Style by George Smith, 1806. *George Smith, a leading Regency furniture designer, was an eclectic popularizer of the variety of styles then fashionable. The plates in his* Designs for Household Furniture and Interior Decoration *ranged from Egyptian to Gothic and included chinoiserie furniture.*

Plate from *Examples of Chinese Ornament*, Part V, 1867. *By Owen Jones, the English designer, writer and architect and author of* The Grammar of Ornament.

Oxfordshire, dating from 1840, had bamboo and lacquer furniture, Chinese wallpaper and windows painted with chinoiserie scenes. Flickers of interest in Chinese design persisted even when fashionable taste had moved emphatically to the Gothic. A wide-ranging eclecticism was part of the taste of the times, and chinoiserie could still find a place there. The designer Owen Jones, who profoundly influenced High Victorian taste, published his *Examples of Chinese Ornament* as late as 1867.

George IV's taste was eclectic and personal. Like Horace Walpole at Strawberry Hill he collected what he liked, and the furnishing of the Pavilion was as rich and picturesque as its decoration. The furniture comprised a varied assembly of exotica, pastiche and antiques, together with some specially-made pieces. By and large all were of the very highest quality. Flamboyant and unrestrained, they were markedly different in style from those designed for Carlton House. The Pavilion was packed with chinoiserie objects of every kind, gorgeous Sèvres with ormolu mounts, lamps and candlesticks, clocks and china figures. Pitched in among all this were huge quantities of genuine Chinese objects – immense vases, lacquer of every description, paintings, bowls, fans and screens. The prince's agents in the Orient were kept busy 'in bribing the Hoppos and their underlings in China, for conniving at the bringing out of the country sundry prohibited articles'.

The nineteenth century belonged to England. Her economic and political dominance and the power of her industrial production had served to dislodge France from its traditional position as arbiter of the world's taste. For the first time England led the field. High Victorian culture was the flagship,

and industrial techniques the standard. The Prince Regent's championing of chinoiserie was in the tradition of court art, and he collected only the finest examples of the style. But the new industrial techniques, by which chinoiseries were increasingly mass-produced, made possible a wider participation in the taste. Middle-class taste was in the ascendant, and middle-class values of acquisition, ambition, insistence on quality and concern with outward display – coupled with the timidity of uncertain taste and the desire to emulate one's betters – led to conservatism and a lack of courage in the design that catered for this new market.

While the rich dined off imported Chinese porcelain, and the very rich off silver, the rising middle-class used a locally manufactured alternative: Chinese-style designs on table ware, especially decorated in blue and white. Transfer printing on pottery and porcelain was common by the 1830s in England, and became general later on the Continent. Chinoiserie fantasy scenes with landscapes and figures were frequently used to ornament these products. Monochrome printed wares were cheap and, of the single colours, blue-and-white was the most popular. A favourite was the Willow Pattern developed about 1795 by Josiah Spode from an original Chinese pattern known as Mandarin. The design elements – a bridge with three figures crossing it, the willow tree, tea-house, two birds, orange tree and zig-zag fence, all familiar chinoiseries – were put together in a novel way, subsequently employed by many factories in Staffordshire. The landscape depicted was more like the *jardin anglo-chinois* than anything Chinese, and a romantic story was soon attached to it that embellished and explained the significance of the motifs depicted in the scene. The pattern was applied to vessels of all shapes and sizes, and such was its popularity that it was exported to the East and copied by Chinese painters, always eager for a new pattern to ornament their export wares. To this day it remains a staple line in the china departments of shops all over the world.

In 1842 an exhibition of Chinese art removed the last remnants of China's mystery. In the same year as China's humiliating acceptance of the Treaty of Nanking, which as has been seen marked a watershed in the West's view of chinoiserie, a rich American China-trade merchant called Nathan Dunn brought an exhibition of Chinese art to London. A specially built hall erected at Hyde Park Corner housed an immense array of the arts of this newly vanquished nation. Sections of temples, houses, rooms and shops were on display, fully furnished and available for inspection. There were models of Chinese figures from all walks of life, together with the tools of their trades. There were hundreds of Chinese paintings and a number of architectural models. Anyone could walk in and see the real China; over 100,000 catalogues were sold at the door.

'Real' Chinese residences were discussed by Richard Brown, the author of *Domestic Architecture* which appeared in 1841. But the style was not considered worthy of imitation. Indeed it was roundly condemned by the author: 'The apartments are as deficient in proportion, as their construction is void of every rule and principle which we are apt to consider as essential to our architecture.' However Mr Brown did offer as 'a Chinese Residence' a house

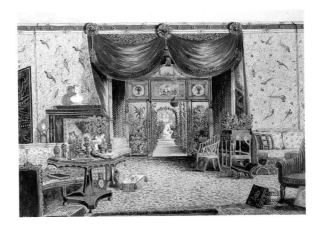

Decoration in the Chinese style. From *The Decorative Painter's and Glazier's Guide* of 1827. *(top) The book's author, Nathanial Whittock, expressly denounced the 'propriety' of such ornament for the ordinary householder.*

The Chinese Room, Middleton Park, Oxfordshire, 1840s. *The extravagance of the chinoiserie interiors of the Royal Pavilion found few counterparts, but some notable Chinese schemes were attempted such as this example.*

A Chinese Residence. From
***Domestic Architecture* by**
Richard Brown, 1841. *The*
nineteenth-century desire
for authenticity of design
led Brown to categorize this
example – spurious as any
eighteenth-century chinoiserie
folly – as 'real' Chinese
architecture.

that would not look out of place along the Thames.
With its sleepy-looking dragons perched on the roof,
bells dangling languidly from their mouths, and
bamboo-shaped supports to an open veranda, the
house is as bogus as any eighteenth-century folly,
and only a certain heaviness in the proportions and
a lack of overall frivolous intent betray its desire
for greater authenticity.

By the time Queen Victoria came to the throne,
the royal tide had turned against chinoiserie. She
herself loathed Brighton and the crowds of trippers
that swarmed along the seafront. Most damaging of
all, on their final visit there Prince Albert caught a
cold. In a pointed rebuke to the profligacy of the
earlier reign, in 1846 Parliament determined that

the Pavilion be sold to pay for improvements at
Buckingham Palace. Under the heading 'Rubbish
for Sale' *Punch* gleefully speculated on a possible
purchaser: 'With a few paper lanterns and a real
native at the door, we feel confident a deal of
business in selling tea, or exhibiting curiosities
might be done'.

The show was over. The Pavilion was stripped
of its treasures. Carriers' carts heavy with chinoiserie
wrapped in blankets transported 137 loads of clocks,
china, furniture and decoration to Windsor and to
Buckingham Palace. Even the kitchen tiles were
removed. In 1850 the empty shell was sold to
Brighton Council for £50,000. A year later, the
catalogue to the Great Exhibition of 1851 carried

only a single illustration of Chinese art: a carved table of a markedly westernized appearance.

But the influence of the Orient was not over. As a source for redemption of European design, then languishing at its lowest ebb, the avant-garde both in Europe and America looked elsewhere, to the Japanese, whose top-hatted appearance in the capitals of Europe heralded the extraordinary interlude of japonisme in the history of nineteenth century taste. The history of japonisme can be seen as chinoiserie's history in miniature, its rise and fall compressed into the latter years of the ninteenth century. However, there are important differences. Apart from the overriding feature of active Japanese participation in the spread of the style, two factors above all others differentiate japonisme from chinoiserie. Chinoiserie was patron-inspired while the impetus for the Japanese style came from the artists themselves. And, unlike chinoiserie, which

mainly affected the decorative arts (already in decline in the nineteenth century), japonisme's influence appears principally in the painting of the period and thus falls outside this book's scope.

In the 1860s notable collectors, artists and patrons began to favour Japanese art. The whole of France's artistic and intellectual classes from Baudelaire to Monet, Degas and the Goncourt brothers, succumbed to the craze. The American artist James McNeill Whistler, whose *Princesse du Pays du Porcelaine* painted in 1864 had done for japonisme what Boucher achieved for chinoiserie, was constantly seen in a kimono; Japanese ballet and opera was praised and patronized. Whistler moved from France to London, where he became famous as the 'Japanese artist' and also made an impact on the architecture and decorative arts.

On a more commercial level, an Oriental Warehouse in Regent Street sold the Japanese

French decalcomania vase, c.1840. *(far left) Successful application of industrial techniques in multi-coloured printing brought chinoiseries within the range of the modest purse in the nineteenth century.*

Minton vase, c.1875. *(left) The impetus for a new interest in the ceramics of the Far East originated with the new breed of artist-potters in France. A French ceramicist, Léon Arnoux, the director of the Minton works in Stoke-on-Trent, was responsible for the Chinese form and vibrant glaze of this simple piece.*

objects which had appeared in the London 1862 Exhibition. Among the eager customers were the architects William Burges, William Nesfield and E.W. Godwin, the painters Dante Gabriel Rossetti and Frederic Leighton, and the seminal interpreter of Japanese art into a modern idiom, Christopher Dresser. The same year a shop selling Japanese goods opened in the Rue de Rivoli in Paris, and five years later, in 1867, the International Exposition held in Paris gave Japanese design a further chance to captivate the artists and connoisseurs of the West. By the late 1860s Europe had become flooded with imports from Japan.

In England commercially-minded designers began to market a crop of fashionable travesties. Bamboo chairs, tables and whatnots rocked on spindly legs, geisha girls simpered on fans, and an indiscriminate clutter of Japanese and Chinese motifs overran the dinner services of the porcelain factories. But from all this confusion and debasement, salvation was at hand.

The retreat by certain aesthetes from High Victorian ugliness launched a vogue for collecting antiques which brought the eighteenth century back into favour. This fanned both the revival of interest in chinoiserie and the new interest in japonisme. In England the Queen Anne revival of the 1870s borrowed elements of Japanese design and led to a new doctrine of interior decoration where no objects of a provenance later than the eighteenth century were valued. Lacquer and japanned cabinets and bureaux, Delft and Nanking China were back in fashion. According to Max Beerbohm: 'Men and women hurled their mahogany into the streets and ransacked the curio shops … Dados arose on every wall, sunflowers and the feathers of peacocks curled in every corner, tea grew quite cold while guests were praising the Willow Pattern of its cup.' A brisk trade in reproduction and fake furniture and furnishings arose as demand outstripped supply.

But a new style – influenced by the freshness and simplicity, both of design and colour, characteristic of Japanese arts and crafts – began to emerge in France, England and across the Atlantic in America. In England the architect E.W. Godwin was so overwhelmed by the novelty of sparseness exemplified in Japanese design that he redecorated his entire house, dressed his wife in a kimono, and went on to pioneer an Anglo-Japanese style, designing furniture of a spindly elegance and uncluttered simplicity of outline. Christopher Dresser went off to Japan, returning in 1877 to design strikingly rigorous and sparse pieces in metal and pottery. His magnum opus, *Japan, its Architecture, Art and Art Manufactures*, appeared in 1882.

While the impact of chinoiserie had declined by the end of the century, the redemptive force of its energy was not yet spent. The arts of the Orient had been integrated into the cutting edge of aesthetic change in Europe. Here they were to assume a position in the vocabulary of western taste far removed from the mystery and fable that had brought chinoiserie into being. As shall be seen, the Modern Movement of the twentieth century has its debt to pay to the ancient civilizations of the East. But we must first move away from Japan to the impact that chinoiserie had in the heart of the new world, America, and to do this it is necessary first of all to step back a couple of centuries and turn our gaze across the Atlantic.

Summer, **by John Atkinson Grimshaw (1836-93).** *The revolt by the aesthetic avant-garde against the ugliness of much industrial design in Victorian England stimulated a general vogue for orientalism, as blue-and-white porcelain, fans and lacquer furniture flourished in the drawing-rooms of the middle-classes.*

The fashion for chinoiserie crossed the Atlantic surprisingly swiftly, although Puritan voices were raised to point out the moral dangers lurking in things of beauty and their acquisition. In 1698 the Philadelphia Yearly Meeting of Women Friends warned against what was crushingly referred to as 'needless things', and urged 'that no superfluous furniture be in your houses wich the Truth maketh manifest to the humble minded'. All the same, the inventories and advertisements of the day show that fancy furniture and fabrics were imported, including the chinoiseries fashionable in Europe at the time. An inventory of 1695/6 of the effects of one Maria van Varick abounds in references to 'chints' and

'Indian callicoes'. There is even a 'flower'd carpet' listed, evidence that, despite the puritanical views of its colonists, the exotic embroideries, painted cottons and silks brought from the Orient by the East India Companies were early arrivals in the New World.

Highly-decorated painted furniture was also much admired by the early settlers who had contracted lacquer-mania in seventeenth-century Europe. The colony kept abreast of this European fashion by importing what they could, and by manufacturing local equivalents. From the 1690s Boston was the main centre for both activities, and much of the japanned furniture that found its way into fashionable homes along the East Coast originated there. There were more than a dozen craftsmen in the Boston area active as japanners between 1712 and 1771. Japanners advertised their services in other parts of the country too, particularly in Connecticut and New York, though not much in Philadelphia, no doubt bringing comfort to the Yearly Meeting of Women Friends.

Many advertisements of the time boasted of the craftsman's great expertise. A typical claim was that of David Mason, who advertised in the *Boston News* in 1748 that he practised 'all sorts of Japanning, Vernishing, Painting and Gilding'. In fact, American craftsmen were not merely unable to match the techniques of the East, they simplified the already simplified process used by English japanners. American japanners dispensed with a gesso base. Instead a painted base, usually black or tortoise-shell in colour, would be decorated with shallow relief ornaments in gesso, smoothed with sharkskin and then varnished. The ornamental motifs would be coloured with silver-leaf, gold-leaf or metallic powder, and their details picked out with a fine brush dipped in lampblack. A few coats of clear varnish completed the process. It was easily done, but the distortion caused by the different drying times inherent in the use of such techniques has made early American japanned furniture among the most fragile of any imitations of oriental lacquer.

Moreover, japanners in America lacked the wide range of oriental models that flooded into Europe, and they freely adapted the few examples available. As a result, the vigorous, rather coarse chinoiserie ornament they produced can be something of a surprise packet; in a notable Boston highboy of 1700, a camel makes an unexpected appearance being placidly led about on a string among the straw pavilions and more easily anticipated exoticisms of flora and fauna. In Connecticut the japanned motifs are even more crudely applied than in Boston – not built up with gesso at all, but simply painted in cream-coloured oil paint on a black or tortoise-shell background – but they have a unique vitality, paradoxically a consequence of the lack of oriental models. Seahorses, a kneeling falconer, giraffes, gazelles and an American Indian shooting a bird with a bow and arrow are all to be seen. Some details may have been copied from crewel work, others, such as the Indian, show that home-grown exotica were as acceptable as anything to be found in the East.

In America, as in England, amateur japanners abounded, and so did their instructors. Professional japanners commonly advertised in newspapers that they stocked materials for amateurs in the field. Like the professionals, the amateur japanners preferred the simplest techniques. From the 1730s, a popular amateur pastime was ornamenting in *lacca povera*, a type of ornamentation also fashionable in Italy at that time, where a ready-made paper pattern is stuck onto an article of furniture and then varnished.

Tinware was an ideal material for japanners, and was available in America from about 1740 when two Irish partners set up a tinsmith shop in Berlin, Connecticut, producing a range of household articles made from small sheets of tin imported from Wales. These were coated with varnish, dried, decorated with oil paint – later stencils – and revarnished. Quite soon the japanned ornament parted company with the Orient as the Pennsylvania Dutch communities began to decorate it with their own characteristic motifs. The same fate overtook painted

Pot based on a Japanese design, by Christopher Dresser. *A prolific and influential designer, Dresser, like Godwin, was fired with admiration for the arts of Japan, visiting that country in 1877.*

Anglo-Japanese furniture designs by E. W. Godwin, c.1860. *While Godwin's furniture designs were wholly unlike anything actually made in Japan, their simplicity, lightness and sparseness epitomized the design values sought by the new devotees of japonisme, and marked a decisive break with nineteenth-century revivalism.*

furniture, where the common use of red, black and white gives much eighteenth-century decorated furniture a japanned air, but no oriental content.

Oriental influences could affect shape and technique as well as decoration. 'Boston chairs', made between 1700 and 1770 and so called because they were exported in large numbers from that city,

Iranistan, Bridgeport, Connecticut. Lithograph, c.1855. *Iranistan – meaning Eastern Country Place – was the mansion built by the great American showman, Phineas T. Barnum, in 1846. Ostensibly modelled on the Royal Pavilion at Brighton, but greatly simplified in outline and detail, it burned to the ground less than ten years after completion.*

had a shape widely believed to be of Chinese derivation, with a single, broad, gracefully-curving back splat, a curved top rail, turned legs and a stretcher. The techniques of chinoiserie decoration were attempted in America almost as soon as they had been tested in Europe. In Philadelphia, the centre of the American textile industry, chinoiseries made their appearance on copper-plated printed textiles from the 1760s, the heyday of the fashion in Europe. In addition block-printing, which imitated the technique used on eastern fabrics, was in use in Philadelphia by the beginning of the nineteenth century for fabrics with oriental patterns, such as the counterpanes with Indian motifs.

Chinoiserie wallpapers were fashionable in the colony too. Once again the American colonies were in step with a fashion current in England. In 1738 a Boston resident, Thomas Hancock, ordered paper from a stationer in London to line two of his rooms. He enclosed a pattern of a paper he had recently seen, remarking: 'The pattern … takes much in the Town. Therefore desire you by all means to get mine well Done and as Cheap as Possible, and if they can make it more beautiful by adding more Birds flying here and there, with some Landskips at the Bottom, I Should like it well.' The request for more birds flying about indicates that the hearty approach to chinoiseries found in japanned decoration was probably widespread.

Both French and English wallpapers in the style of Jean Pillement were imported, some with his delicate chinoiserie vignettes, others with fantastic flowers. Home-produced wallpapers in the early nineteenth century continued the interest in exotica in general and chinoiserie in particular. One

example dating from 1820 features oriental figures and camels, rather as the japanned highboy over a century earlier; on another, parrots and palm trees are charmingly combined. Yet another is cryptically described as being machine-printed with a design of 'Chinese inspiration'.

Chinoiserie interiors made a surprisingly rapid appearance in the southern states. 'New built … after the Chinese taste' was how the James Reid House in Charleston was described in the *South Carolina Gazette* in April 1757, the same year as the publication of Sir William Chambers' *Designs of Chinese Buildings* in the mother country. There was a Chinese Chippendale room at Gunston Hall in Fairfax County, Virginia, in 1758 – roughly the time when the vogue was at its height in England – although the Gunston Hall room, the only one of its kind in Virginia, was less riotous than its English equivalent. A Chinese fretwork trim ornamented its doors and windows, and the cornice carried a scallop-shaped cresting. To complete the picture, the room at Gunston Hall was furnished with trellis-backed chairs and pagoda-roofed pier tables, lined with Chinese wallpaper and decked with oriental porcelain.

Perhaps the oddest American adaptation of an English essay in chinoiserie was Iranistan, the mansion built by the great showman Phineas T. Barnum in 1846. Barnum had been in Europe with his prize exhibit, General Tom Thumb, when he was so captivated by the Royal Pavilion at Brighton that he determined to build something like it for himself. Iranistan, Barnum explained in his autobiography, meant Oriental Villa, or Eastern Country Place. He claimed to have instructed a

London architect to draw up plans that would follow the general plan of the Pavilion but adapt them to the land he had selected – a 15-acre tract near Bridgeport, Connecticut. But the house was no country retreat. Barnum had the mansion sited where it could be boggled at by the passengers carried past it on the New York and New Haven Railroad, the busiest line in the country. Sadly, what they saw quite lacked the high fantasy of the Brighton Pavilion. Iranistan was large, symmetrical, square and unimaginative, a two-and three-storied house with simplified pinnacles, crenellations and roofs. Its ornate interior seems to have been in the High Victorian manner of velvet tablecloths and marble statuary. A house-warming party attended by a thousand guests was held in 1848; ten years later the house had burned to the ground.

As has been discussed, the European chinoiserie garden building *par excellence* must be William Chambers' pagoda at Kew. Its counterpart was to be found in Philadelphia, where a pagoda very closely modelled on Chambers' design was built in 1827. The Philadelphia pagoda stood in a public park, the Labyrinth Gardens. Constructed of coloured bricks, plate-iron and wood and topped by a gilt spire, it stood alongside a long two-storied pavilion with veranda, balcony and Chinese roofs, rather like a sturdy version of a Regency fishing pavilion. An earlier chinoiserie pavilion dating from 1806, and also found in Philadelphia, is a fretted Chinese summer house designed by Benjamin Latrobe – an architect more generally associated with grand works in the Grecian revival style – which approaches the spirit of English eighteenth-century chinoiserie garden designs, if less playful and ornate.

While America was a colony, direct traffic with China was precluded by the monopoly on trade exercised by the East India Company. On 22 February 1784, a week after the signing of the peace treaty with England that brought the American colonies independence, the aptly-named *Empress of China* sailed from New York. She was bound for Canton and carried a cargo of furs, foodstuffs and ginseng, then more highly valued in the East than in America. This was a private venture backed by the Philadelphian financier of the American revolutionary forces, Robert Morris, who ordered a Chinese wallpaper for his house to be carried on the voyage home. There were substantial fortunes to be made from the China trade, not least from tea-importing, a primary purpose of the commerce. The China Trade merchants enjoyed a long reign, lasting until the middle of the nineteenth century, when the development of the steam engine ended the domination of the seas by the fast and profitable clippers. By that time commercial interest was in any case shifting away from trade with China to the new market of Japan.

Wide as it was, the Pacific Ocean alone separated Japan and America. No continent or country stood between to influence or distort the intercourse between the two. It was an American, Commodore Perry, who was instrumental in obtaining the concessions from Japan to trade with the West. With the signing of the Treaty of Peace, Amity and Commerce in 1854, Japan abandoned centuries of seclusion and became involved in new relationships with previously shunned and despised western nations. Japan began to embrace new ideas and attitudes. At the same time the West, not least

Pagoda built in the Labyrinth Gardens, Philadelpia, 1827. *Chinoiserie entered the public arena in America with this belated appearance of a pagoda closely modelled on Sir William Chambers' famous example in Kew Gardens.*

America, was gripped by a passion for all things Japanese. But by contrast with chinoiserie, which had existed as a craze in Europe long before America's emergence as an independent nation, America was not indebted to Europe for japonisme's genesis. The style arrived in the two continents simultaneously, and America would incorporate japonisme into architecture and interiors in more subtle, profound and long-lasting ways than Europe, where the craze quickly flared and as quickly faded.

In America, as in western Europe, japonisme wore two faces. One was very ornamental, the other very bare. Depending on one's preference, the style offered two quite different ways in which to be *à la mode*. In its first phase, japonisme was ornamental. American textiles and furnishing fabrics influenced by japonisme burst with birds, insects, blossoms and patterned discs that overlapped and adjoined one another in a patchwork of designs considered very Japanese. These were often combined with black wood furniture, bamboo or lacquer, in 'aesthetic' interiors. By the end of the century, however, the nation's understanding of Japanese art had undergone a sea-change. The second phase of the style, spareness, came to the fore. As the twentieth century dawned Japan provided the new milennium with a non-classical, unanornamented, functionally-direct architectural model. At the Chicago World Columbian Expositon of 1893, the sparse lines of unrelieved horizontals and verticals, the uncluttered interiors and clear light found in the Japanese pavilion, proved a vital influence on the architecture of the New World. It was from such examples that the Chicago school of architecture developed and that the spirit of Modernism entered American and subsequently European life.

Chinoiserie's last hurrah

China … this vast land which is home to over a quarter of the world's population remains enticing and enigmatic. Over the last decade, standards of accommodation have improved dramatically and the needs of the western visitor are well catered for. The Chinese people are friendly if shy and welcome foreign visitors.

Hayes and Jarvis, *Holidays Worldwide, 1992* (travel brochure)

Chinoiserie dining-room designed by the firm of Rath and Balbach, Cologne, 1919.

Details from English painted silk wallpaper. *One of a range of modern chinoiserie designs currently produced.*

Today we are able to travel everywhere on earth, and we do. The past alone remains obstinately out of reach. Although China has opened its gates to package tours and curio collectors, the West has not discarded the fantasy world of chinoiserie. On the contrary, chinoiserie has flourished in the Occident, retaining the charm and mystery that China itself has necessarily surrendered. Although stylistic movements in the twentieth century have not always worked to chinoiserie's advantage, the taste has remained popular. From Art Nouveau at the turn of the century to the Modern Movement and hippy culture, artists and potters, textile manufacturers and furniture designers, architects and decorators have all raided chinoiserie's repository of colours, techniques and motifs.

Today's 'China' tea-sets are decorated with the 'traditional' Willow Pattern, or the long-legged birds and tidy quails that ornamented Chinese and Japanese porcelains in the seventeenth and eighteenth centuries. Wallpapers flaunt pagodas and mandarins; curtaining fabrics, paeonies and plum blossom. Often these designs are not recognized for what they are, a *leitmotif* of orientalism that has run through much twentieth-century design. And while in some cases chinoiserie designs have descended to pastiche or fallen prey to the chintzy world of nostalgia and 'heritage' interiors, in others the designs stand proud and distinct as legitimate latter-day chinoiseries, the true heirs of Cathay.

This is particularly marked in places of public amusement, a realm where chinoiserie has traditionally thrived. In the course of the twentieth century music halls, theatres, cinemas and hotels, even cruise liners, have all embraced the style, no doubt because of its ability to convey the feeling of opulence and fantasy so important to their architecture and interiors. The 'Chinatowns' found in many of today's western cities are a lively symbol of that interpenetration of East and West which is the life-blood of chinoiserie, and which has become particularly marked in the twentieth century. English potters have studied in Japan, Japanese lacquer masters have worked in Paris. Architects seem ubiquitous. The Imperial Hotel in Tokyo was designed by Frank Lloyd Wright, Hong Kong's Hong Kong and Shanghai Bank by Norman Foster, the National Gallery in Washington by I.M. Pei. This flux and movement of ideas and talent differs from past fashions: it constitues the very heart of Modernism. Like airports and currencies, styles are now international. Lands once considered remote and peculiar are subsumed within the modern world. At a time when everywhere resembles somewhere else, the territory of chinoiserie often goes unrecognized.

The quest for authenticity, so insistent an aspect of the nineteenth century's various revival styles, has been relentlessly extended in the twentieth century. This development has had conflicting consequences for chinoiserie. The desire for authenticity strikes at the heart of a style that thrives on misunderstanding, allusion and re-interpretation. However the pressure for accuracy has led textile and wallpaper companies to reissue document designs of chinoiseries in order to provide verisimilitude to the refurbishment of eighteenth- and nineteenth-century interiors. As a result old chinoiserie designs have now become widely available.

The demand for authenticity has invaded the garden too, though with mixed results. In 1905 a

Smoking Room on *The Empress of Britain, c.*1930. *The persisting images of chinoiserie are given a modern dress. Luxury and travel combine with a whiff of opium to spell out Cathay, and determine the choice of a modern chinoiserie interior for this saloon.*

rich china and glass merchant, Herbert Goode,
imported a Japanese landscape architect to lay out
a Japanese garden at his country house, Cottered in
Cambridgeshire. Along with the architect Goode
imported the garden furniture, bridges and gateways.
The insistence on greater validity, at a time when a
few pale irises, a pond and a cement lantern signified
a Japanese garden to most people, was a signal
success. It brought into being an uncompromising
and accurate translation of a highly organized,
alien concept of gardening. Cottered was, and is, a
most beautiful garden. But it does not follow that
authenticity alone will guarantee the desired result.
Enthusiasts of the felicitous chinoiseries of the
English landscape gardens in the eighteenth century
must blench at the authentic Japanese garden
recently opened in London's Holland Park, where
the very rocks were imported from Japan and
pleasure wilts in the resulting air of empty solemnity.

In the first decade of the twentieth century
japonisme was still tottering about, clutching at the
lilies writhing around the recumbent body of Art
Nouveau, but chinoiserie seemed to have run out
of steam. The Queen Anne style had ebbed away,
leaving a tide-mark of informal, generalized
orientalism lingering in 'Turkish' corners: a divan
with an oriental cover and piles of cushions or
embossed and lacquered wallpapers with 'oriental'
patterns. The Queen Anne revival, coupled with a
shortage of cash, made the renovation of old houses
increasingly popular in the years around the First
World War. As a result the demand for old textiles
grew, and modern patterns were increasingly derived
from eighteenth-century fabrics and wallpapers:
printed cottons with exotic flowerheads, leaves and

**Twentieth-century chinoiserie
wallpaper**. *The popularity in
the 1880s of Japanese 'leather
papers' – heavily embossed
and lacquered wall-hangings
that recalled the luxurious gilt
leather wallcoverings of the
Spanish and Dutch Baroque –
led to twentieth-century
machine-produced versions.*

'Komodie Damask'. *(opposite)
The romance and fantasy of
medieval Cathay lives on in
this modern Swiss fabric. The
pattern is adapted from a
Swiss design of c.1860 for a
block-printed textile but, while
the original is preserved in a
Swiss museum, the modern
version is available worldwide.*

Twentieth-century chinoiseries.

Cathay in Manhattan: a New York morning-room. *Designed in the 1930s, even the radiator cover on the central heating is given a mandarin air.*

'The Mandarin'. *(bottom left) Orientalism and Art Deco come together in this hand-blocked wallpaper which translates the chinoiserie of the eighteenth century to the jazz age.*

Detail of hand-painted silk panel. *(bottom right) Produced today, this fabric imitates not only the technique of Chinese export wallpapers in the eighteenth century, but also the style. The twisting stems of brightly coloured blooms with birds flying energetically among them is an adaptation of one of the most popular of chinoiserie designs.*

birds amid meandering stems. These imitations of Indian chintzes catered well for those with timid oriental or Art Nouveau tastes as well as for the solid middle-classes reluctant to cast aside the naturalistic floral designs of William Morris. The link between Indian designs, William Morris and the reclamation of old houses was extended into the suburban-baronial style of the Jacobean revival – still popular in the 1930s – when 'Jacobean' designs, originally based on the Indian Tree of Life pattern, draped the windows of countless living-rooms.

America, the forcing-house of Modernism, also began to pay attention to its past. A heightened interest in early furniture and room arrangements, spurred by the opening of the American Wing at the Metropolitan Museum of Art in New York in 1924, led to the restoration of colonial Williamsburg two years later. Period rooms burgeoned in other museums, sparking off a new 'Americana' style that included a taste for old fabrics and the creation of new 'aged' fabrics, among them chinoiseries, such as *Mandarin*, hand-brocaded and specially designed for a plantation house in Virginia in 1930.

More original and up-to-date 'Chinese' patterns also appeared on fabrics and wallpapers. The motifs included stylized lanterns, fretwork and exotic birds – a kind of hot-house aviary where peacocks strutted and poppies luxuriated – and were depicted in bright colours, often on a dark background. The new colours were possible because of recently-developed, inexpensive dyeing materials, and were particularly favoured in the United States, where the often stronger light showed brighter colours to advantage.

The vogue for strong colours, present from about 1905, was given a fillip when Sergei Diaghilev brought his Ballets Russes to Paris for the first time in 1909. The exotic richness of the costumes and sets, designed principally by Alexander Benois and Léon Bakst, swung dress and interior decoration eastwards in the years leading up to the First World War, helping to sustain the interest in orientalism into the 1920s. The striking colour combinations, costumes and sets for a ballet such as *Scheherazade* blazed with violent, urgent appeals to sensuality and vigour that made a tremendous impact on artists living and working in Paris, while their timeless appeal to luxury and extravagance captivated fashionable society too. Indeed, the costume designed for Bakst's Chinaman in *The Sleeping Princess* might have been quite at home at the chinoiserie spectaculars held at the Palace of Versailles by Louis XIV.

This is the familiar territory of chinoiserie. But when pre-Ming ceramics, paintings and sculpture began to appear in Europe in the early years of the century, they kindled an interest in true Chinese art. In 1909 the first T'Ang ceramics reached London, treasure trove resulting from the building of a railway line in northern China. So admired were they that within three years fake T'Ang horses, camels and female figures were being turned out. With whoops of delight archaeological scholarship turned away from classicism as the products of new and remote dynasties came to light – Sung, T'Ang, Sui, Eastern and Western Chin, the period of the three kingdoms (Wu, Shu and Wei), Han, Ch'in, Chou, Shang-Yin. Suddenly Chinese art seemed more diverse than had been believed possible.

It took a long time for these objects to reach a wider public. In 1935 an exhibition at the Royal

Academy in London mounted the first representative display of such works in Europe. The critic Roger Fry had no doubt of their effect. The ordinary English art-lover, he pontificated, 'may feel happy enough in the presence of trifling bibelots, the "Chinoiseries" of later periods which have become acclimatized in our drawing-rooms, but the great art, above all the religious art, will repel them by its strangeness'. He was wrong of course, unable to foresee the day when busts of the Buddha would sit on coffee tables, and Tibetan prayer rugs make fashionable wall-hangings.

Potters and ceramicists of the West were the first to feel the profound effects of the newly-discovered Chinese art. They took hold of the idea, common in the East, that the potter ought to be responsible for every stage of the production process, from digging and pugging the clay to personally constructing the kiln, firing, and executing the final decoration. In the West this practice was somewhat incongruously advanced in order to establish the notion of the potter as artist rather than mere craftsman.

In the eighteenth century porcelain masters in the West had admired the elegant forms and exquisite colouring of K'ang Hsi ware. A century later their counterparts were captivated by the beauty of the glazes of eastern porcelain ware. In the twentieth century potters turned to the quest for significant form, which they saw embodied in the noble simplicity of Han, T'Ang and Sung ware. French ceramics, which had already attained high levels of technical virtuosity with the mastery of eastern glazes, were profoundly influenced by Korean and Sung wares. The work of potters like Emile Decœur, Emile Lenoble and George Serré, who had spent a long period in Saigon, was concerned with a synthesis of form and decoration that was quite openly inspired by the design ideals of the Far East.

The chief proponent of this idea in England, Bernard Leach, had been born in China and studied pottery under a master in Japan, where he had lived since 1909. He arrived in England in 1920,

accompanied by a young Japanese potter, Shoji Hamada. The two newcomers founded the Leach pottery at St Ives in Cornwall, where over the years a colony of potters grew up around Leach, influenced by his ambition to amalgamate the quite different traditions of Japanese stoneware and English slipware decoration in a new blend of Orient and Occident. Although this concern with the relationship of function to form was in tune with the contemporary ideas of the Modern Movement, the potters' interest sprang from the practices of the East and was, intellectually at least, impervious to fashion.

Chinoiserie, on the other hand, was a style quite removed from the intellectual preoccupations of the day. It could not be enlisted to march in the colours of the modernists, or the functionalists, the formalists or the expressionists. Nevertheless its techniques, materials and decoration were variously employed by the prevailing fashions, different aspects being re-worked and transformed according to taste. This was nothing new. It had happened with Chinese motifs in textile design as early as the seventeenth century, when chinoiserie was in its infancy.

In the twentieth century the same fate overtook lacquer, or japanning as its western imitation was called. In the past japanners had not confined themselves solely to producing work in a recognized chinoiserie style. In eighteenth-century France the exquisite lacquer known as *vernis Martin* was produced in a wide range of faultless colours. It was often applied plain, with gilded details, sometimes painted with flowers or other naturalistic and rococoesque ornamentation, and only infrequently decorated with gilded chinoiseries. In the twentieth century the largely French-inspired Art Deco style used the lacquer material and technique rather as *vernis Martin* had been used previously, that is as a material in its own right, not simply as a basis for the display of chinoiserie ornament.

Art Deco was born in 1925 at the Exposition Internationale des Arts Décoratifs et Industriels Modernes held in Paris. A movement without a founder, a philosophy or a manifesto, it was all things to all men, able to embrace impartially the high priest of Modernism, the ascetic architect Le Corbusier, and the great exponent of decadent luxury, the furniture designer and decorator Jacques-Emile Ruhlmann. Art Deco had the impact of a new style. Its ostensible concerns were with living in the modern world, and its look seemed new too: all angularity, abstraction and streamlined shapes. On closer scrutiny the Art Deco style appears to be not that new after all, but rather a restatement of the interest in the opulent styles of orientalism and the French Empire which had been part of fashion's concerns since before the First World War.

At one time chinoiserie decoration had been subsumed into the general interest in orientalism. Now it was lacquer's turn to become embedded in a new style. It is not difficult to see how lacquer could be integrated into Art Nouveau. Shiny, brilliant, renowned, lacquer could combine the *grande luxe* of the French Empire style and the exoticism of the East with the vibrant colours of Art Deco. The Paris Expo was a showcase for the re-introduction of lacquer decoration, though in reality the craft's revitalization had begun in the decades preceding the 1925 exhibition.

At an earlier exhibition, the Paris Universelle of 1900 (the so-called Great Bazaar), the main hall of the Japanese pavilion had been consecrated to an exhibition of 'priceless lacquer', while the temple of Art Nouveau, the Bing pavilion, also showed interiors featuring gold finishes 'as soft and subdued as the finest lacquer'. In England too, the Arts and Crafts movement, highly conscious of its debt to Japanese design in general, had occasionally produced

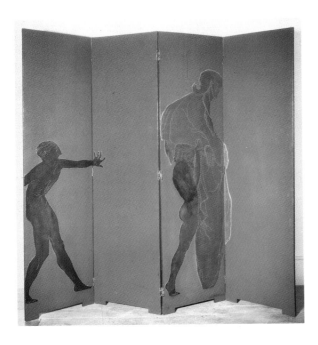

lacquered work. In the early years of the century public interest in lacquer work ensured the survival of lacquer workshops in London and Paris, although these were mainly concerned with repair and reproduction of existing designs.

But lacquer decoration was about to be transformed. The catalyst was a young painter, Eileen Gray, who in 1907 arrived in Paris from London where she had been working as a restorer of old lacquer. In Paris she studied with a Japanese lacquer master, Sagawara, and started to design and lacquer her own pieces using traditional and very expensive techniques, but in an entirely modern idiom. She was patronized by the new taste-makers, the fashion designers, including Jacques Doucet,

who sold his entire collection of eighteenth-century furniture and commissioned a number of contemporary designers to refurnish his apartment. Eileen Gray made tables for him and a screen decorated with symbolist figures. This marked a turning-point in modern lacquer design. Always one step ahead, she exhibited abstract designs for an entirely lacquered room in 1923, two years before the Paris Exposition.

Another French lacquer worker in the contemporary style, Jean Dunand, started out as a sculptor. Intrigued by lacquer, especially when inlaid with other materials, he pioneered the use of crushed eggshells to give a tactile and uneven surface to his pieces. The technique could not have been as eccentric as it sounds because it was exported to Japan, where some of the greatest lacquer masters copied it. At the Paris Expo Dunand was responsible for a black lacquer smoking-room in the French embassy. He also designed lacquer panels for the grand French ocean liners *Ile de France*, *L'Atlantique* and *Normandie*.

Eileen Gray and Jean Dunand were the two greatest exponents of modern lacquer in the West. Their work had always been singular, and very expensive. But lacquer also had a popular side with a more modest mass market appeal. A less exalted showcase for lacquer ware was seen the year before the Paris exhibition, in 1924 at the British Empire Exhibition, which attracted 17½ million visitors to a site in Wembley in London. Oddly situated in the Palace of Industry, the London furniture-makers Waring and Gillow showed a Chinese Lacquer Room, an acknowledgment of the contemporary vogue for chinoiserie catered for by the oriental departments in London shops. The department stores Liberty and Whiteleys both dealt in lacquer along with the familiar litter of orientalia – silks and rugs and ginger jars – and the contemporary fascination of the mysterious East could also be assuaged with chinoiserie gramophone cabinets or wallpapers adorned with mandarins and parasols.

In America lacquer was extensively used by one of the Modern Movement's most successful designers, Paul T. Frankl. European-born, he had travelled in the Far East and was able to combine the exuberant and luxurious use of lacquer in Art Deco interiors with a more explicitly oriental content. In Frankl's hands entire rooms might be lacquered, silvered or gilded; alternatively the lacquered element might be confined to a single piece of furniture: a chair that looked back to the chinoiserie designs of the eighteenth century, or a coffee-table with a mirrored top, whose pierced and fretted frame, low outline and bulbous, curving legs recalled Chinese furniture. Frankl's lacquer colours of red and black were at home in both the Art Deco or chinoiserie styles, and could be used with equally happy results on 'oriental' and completely western furniture designs.

Scandinavia, where the craze for chinoiserie had taken root 250 years previously, is the home of one of the most startling metamorphoses of Chinese design to occur in the twentieth century. Hans Wegner, who trained as a cabinet-maker at the Copenhagen School of Arts and Crafts, and whose furniture designs are the epitome of Danish good taste, has based many of his teak, oak and cane chairs on Chinese models. The debt is openly acknowledged: his so-called 'Chinese chairs', designed from 1944 to 1962, are derived from Chinese models dating back to 1700. These chairs, subtly altered in outline, texture and colour, re-emerge as modern design at its best.

To rediscover the fun and exotic vivacity of earlier chinoiserie, however, we need to move away from the cool refinements of the north and look instead to the fantasy palaces, the settings for fun and entertainment that reach back to the Vauxhall Pleasure Gardens and the early eighteenth century. More recently, chinoiserie decoration enlivened the gin and smoke of the music hall when these resorts of popular entertainment embarked on an increasingly gaudy search for appropriate decor. The Grand Theatre in Clapham, designed by

**A pair of lacquered and
giltwood dining chairs.**
*American designer Paul T.
Frankl's Chinese-style chairs
gave American Modernism
an oriental face.*

E.A. Woodrow at the turn of the century, had a baroque exterior and a Chinese interior, complete with dragons and boxes shaped like pagodas. The theatre has recently been restored to its former glory.

Public parks had traditionally worn an exotic dress. In the early years of the century the New York pleasure gardens at Coney Island, Luna Park and Dreamland, designed in 1903 and 1904, gave pleasure-seekers a chance to see the world – rather like today's visitor to Disneyland – with Venetian, Tudor, Japanese, Indian and classical motifs all breathlessly jumbled together. Even hotels joined in the fun. The Astor Hotel in New York offered a wide variety of styles. There was a Pompeian billiard-room, a Flemish smoking-room, a German Renaissance hunt room, an American Indian grill room and an Oriental room whose purpose was undesignated.

But it was Hollywood and the cinemas that showed its productions that gave the twentieth century its pleasure-domes. The 1920s saw a tremendous boom in cinema building. Many of these houses were extremely large, able to seat between two and three thousand people – and, rather like the films they showed, designed to produce an opulent fantasy world into which the audience could escape, only too well aware of the Depression that lay beyond the walls of the cinema. As with the hotels, the amusement parks, and the theme restaurants, for the designer of cinemas chinoiserie was only one of the options available. But it was an option exercised from La Pagode in the rue de Babylone in Paris, to the Palace in Southall, west London.

Grauman's Chinese Theatre in Hollywood itself is perhaps the most conspicuous example of the style of cinema architecture and exuberant, fantasy-laden and indulgent ornamentation that gave chinoiserie new life in the twentieth century. The mood was set by the publicity that attended the cinema's opening in 1927, when the ushers and usherettes, all dressed in Chinese robes, lined the street outside, affording mild astonishment to the passers-by. Not only was there an entrance that featured a 'huge elliptical forecourt set with tropical trees', and an interior 'resplendent throughout in motifs of early Chinese dynasties' but the very lavatories were thoughtfully screened from vulgar view by a pagoda-like entrance. To this day neon dragons sit atop the marquees advertising the films on offer, while the 'Chinese red antiques-strewn interior' has largely survived drastic remodelling in 1958.

In Seattle the 2400-seater cinema, the 5th Avenue, is a grand example of the subverted authenticity that provided twentieth-century chinoiserie with its richest soil. It resulted from the collaborative effort of two men: an architect, R. C. Reamer, who had built the Old Faithful Inn in Yellowstone Park, and a Norwegian artist, Gustav Liljestrom, an 'expert' on Chinese art and architecture. Weightier authority was at hand too in the form of a German tome, *Chinesische Architektur*, published in Berlin in 1920, and the source book for architect and artist who took no less a model than the Forbidden City for the cinema's interior. The entrance foyer is a latter-day Temple of Heavenly Peace, complete with the dogs of Fo, who stand guard under the mock-timber beams and log roof of the great hall. The auditorium, whose design was based on the audience hall of the Ming emperors, has platoons of five-clawed dragons – knowingly

The Grand Theatre, Clapham, London. *A chinoiserie interior was the obvious choice for the new resorts of public amusement like this turn-of-the-century music hall.*

Dragon decoration on top of column. The Grand Theatre, Clapham. *Slithering across the centuries, the dragon has emerged as one of the most abiding images of Cathay.*

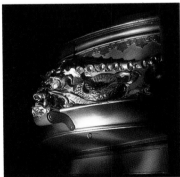

Chinoiserie cinemas in the twentieth century. *The subverted authenticity found in chinoiserie cinema design transported the great palaces of China into the modern world, where they filled public demand for a place of opulent escape from the pressures of contemporary life.*

The 5th Avenue Cinema, Seattle. *Photograph showing the dragon-infested interior. (left) The entrance lobby recreates the Temple of Heavenly Peace in Peking. (bottom left)*

La Pagode, Paris. *(opposite) In the heart of Saint-Germain lies this extraordinary transformation of a nineteenth-century pagoda into a twentieth-century Parisian cinema.*

Grauman's Chinese Theatre, Los Angeles. *(opposite right) Detail of entrance archway. It is not surprising that Hollywood, birthplace of the cinema industry, spawned the most remarkable Chinese cinema of its day.*

introduced as 'symbolic of the emperor' – marching along the walls and ceiling. Infants spawned by a giant parent, the dragons' nest was described in suitably reverential tones in the opening night programme:

> *Its most imposing feature is the great dome. Coiled within an azure sphere and surrounded by glowing hues [rests] the Great Dragon, guardian genius of the place, his presence shadowed and multiplied in varying shapes and forms through the structure.*

From the mouth of this fearsome creature hangs the Pearl of Perfection, the great chandelier that lights the popcorn salesmen and usherettes.

And when the first performance was over, the lights would have come up, the dragon on the asbestos curtain would have writhed for the last time 'in scintillating coils', the first-night audience would have filed out of the Forbidden City and back into the streets of Seattle. But surely the shades of Louis XIV and Catherine the Great, of the Prince Regent and Augustus the Strong, and the legions of less illustrious patrons and enthusiasts, of the architects and decorators, the cabinet makers and porcelain modellers, the travel writers and illustrators, and all the other purveyors of fact and fantasy who constructed the myth of Cathay, must have danced and capered in the starry heavens that night.

Bantam work
A rather rough-and-ready imitation of COROMANDEL LACQUER, made in England in the late seventeenth century. (In the literature of the period the term Bantam work can sometimes refer to true Coromandel lacquer.) Named after the trading port on the west coast of Java.

Bazin
Twilled fabric with a cotton weft and linen or silk warp. Also known as *basin*, or in its earliest form, *bonbasin*. The word, in all its variations, seems to derive from a tropical tree of the West Indies, the bombax, commonly known as the silk-cotton tree.

Bizarre silks
Figured silks, notably produced at Lyons and Spitalfields, and fashionable throughout Europe *c*.1695-1720. The dominant pattern was usually in gold or silver thread, and the background of damask. The silks drew on an extremely wide range of exotic designs influenced by oriental textiles, and were largely composed of floral and foliage motifs, jagged lines and architectural details.

Blanc-de-chine
Type of pure white Chinese porcelain with a lustrous glaze from Te-Hua in Fukien province. The most notable products are statuettes, especially of the Buddhist goddess Kuan-Yin. Imported into Europe from the seventeenth century, *blanc-de-chine* products exerted a very strong influence on the porcelain factories of Europe in the eighteenth century.

Block printing
Method of printing a pattern onto fabric by using carved wooden blocks with a raised pattern area. The process originated in India and was introduced into Europe in the 1670s. Mechanized block printing uses cylindrical surface rollers with raised wooden pattern areas.

Bois de Spa
Generic term applied to the products of the japanning works which grew up at Spa, a watering-place near Aachen, in the seventeenth century. In general, decoration was of gilt chinoiseries applied on a black background, and the items produced ranged from snuff boxes to furniture. The industry flourished throughout the eighteenth century, and its products were dispersed across Europe.

Boiserie
French for wood panelling; usually refers to the elaborate carved and decorated panelling of the seventeenth and eighteenth centuries. In the mid-eighteenth century, boiseries were often decorated with brightly coloured *VERNIS MARTIN*.

Bone china
Type of pure white porcelain made with the addition of bone ash, first patented at the BOW FACTORY in 1748. Durable and inexpensive to produce, its use quickly spread in England. The formula was amended at the Spode factory in the late eighteenth century when a hybrid paste containing china clay and china stone was covered with a lead glaze. This became the standard body for English porcelain production and is still in use today.

Bow porcelain factory
Founded in the East End of London in 1744, the factory's first products were in SOFT-PASTE PORCELAIN. They included cups and bowls decorated in underglaze blue and the KAKIEMON palette, white wares decorated with sprigs of plum blossom and statuettes of pastoral or mythological characters. After 1759 ambition grew and quality declined. In 1775 the factory was acquired by the owner of the Derby factory and ceased to operate independently.

Capodimonte porcelain factory
Founded by Charles III King of Naples in 1743, the factory stood in the grounds of the royal palace of Capodimonte overlooking the Bay of Naples. It produced a translucent, pure white, SOFT PASTE porcelain, which took painted decoration extremely well and was plastic enough to produce delicate and lively groups of figures. When Charles III succeeded to the throne of Spain in 1759, the Capodimonte workers were transferred to a new porcelain factory established at Buen Retiro in Spain.

Cassolette
French word, but commonly used in English, for a perfume burner.

China clay
see KAOLIN

Chinese Chippendale
A type of chinoiserie furniture illustrated in Thomas Chippendale's *Gentleman and Cabinet-Maker's Director* (1754), but generally applied to any chinoiserie furniture which is angular in outline, with spare ornament and prominent lattice-work.

Chintz
From the Sanskrit word meaning variegated; term applied in England in the sixteenth and seventeenth centuries to imported Indian calico and later to European printed cotton fabrics.

Commode
French name for a chest of drawers, used in English for one of French pattern and style, and especially for one that was decorative rather than useful.

Coromandel lacquer
Lacquer decorated with brightly coloured incised decoration made in central and northern China from the seventeenth century onwards, largely for export. It acquired its name from the English East India Company's trading post on the Coromandel coast of India. See also BANTAM WORK.

Coromandel screen
The most highly regarded of the COROMANDEL LACQUER products were large screens of up to a dozen panels which were made in the late seventeenth and early eighteenth centuries. These were manufactured for export only and consequently were very richly decorated. On occasion the panels were used in Europe to line whole rooms. Smaller pieces were used to decorate furniture.

Cresting
Ornamental finish, usually foliate, applied to the top of a horizontal member, such as a chair rail or the top of a cabinet. Pagoda crestings were used on CHINESE CHIPPENDALE furniture.

Delftware
Tin-glazed earthenware; term applied to English pottery products, particularly those of the seventeenth century.

Diaper-work
All-over repeating pattern – usually a chequerwork of rectangles or lozenges, but sometimes floral – forming a background design or used to cover an entire surface.

Ebeniste
French term for cabinet-makers of fine furniture.

Faience
French name for tin-glazed earthenware. The term is derived from the Italian town of Faenza whose maiolica products were popular in sixteenth-century France. The term faience may also be used to describe German, Scandinavian and Spanish tin-glazed wares; Italian products stick to the term maiolica, Dutch to DELFT, but the type of earthenware is in all cases the same.

Famille verte **porcelain**
Type of Chinese porcelain, largely produced for export and decorated in enamel colours, made in the reign of the Emperor K'ang Hsi (1662-1722). The *famille verte* range of colours – a brilliant apple-green and a strong iron-red predominate in a colour scheme that includes yellow, purple and violet-blue – replaced the earlier Ming five-colour scheme in which the blue was not an enamel colour but was painted under the glaze.

Famille rose **porcelain**
The *famille rose* palette was introduced later than the *FAMILLE VERTE*, during the short reign of the Emperor Yung Cheng (1725-35) when a prominent rose pink, introduced from Europe, was added to the existing colour range.

Feldspar
see PETUNZE

Fretwork
Carved geometrical patterns of intersecting lines, sometimes pierced (as in the raised galleries that adorn CHINESE CHIPPENDALE tables) and sometimes in relief, as in much decorative carving of chinoiseries.

Garniture de cheminée
A set of ornaments for a chimneypiece, usually consisting in the seventeenth century of two or three porcelain or earthenware vases. Chinese export porcelain garnitures usually consisted of five vessels, two trumpet-shaped beakers and three covered vases. Silver garnitures were also found in the latter part of the seventeenth century.

Gilding
Decorating with gold. In the early stages of European porcelain production, lacquer gilding was used. This method involved grinding up gold leaf with lacquer varnish and applying it with a brush. As the eighteenth century advanced the preferred method of applying gold leaf to porcelain was honey-gilding, where the gold leaf was ground up in honey, applied with a brush and then secured by a light firing.

Grotesque
Fanciful type of decoration constructed from a series of small, loosely-connected motifs, often formed together into upright candelabra-like components and including human figures, sphinxes, monkeys, vases, trophies, etc. The name derives from the *alla grotesca* decoration found on the grotto-like ruins of Nero's Golden House in Rome, excavated during the Renaissance.

Guéridon
Candlestand or small table suitable for holding a candelabrum.

Guilloche
Continuous scroll pattern, rather like a plait, formed by twisting two or more bands one within the other. Originally used in classical architecture to enrich friezes, it is commonly found as a decorative device from the sixteenth century onwards.

Hard-paste porcelain
'True' porcelain: a blend of white china clay or KAOLIN (which gives plasticity to the paste) and fusible felspathic china-stone or PETUNZE (which gives translucency). This mix is fired at high heat to produce an entirely hard, vitreous, white material, which rings with a sonorous tone if tapped and which fractures with a clean smooth break. Strength and whiteness are increased by ageing the paste; the Chinese stored theirs for decades before use.

Indian work
Most of the goods imported from the Far East came through trading stations established in India or Java. Once the objects reached Europe they were described quite haphazardly as being Indian, Chinese or Japanese.

Japanned ware
LACQUER look-alikes manufactured in Europe, usually decorated with chinoiseries.

Japanning
European attempt to imitate genuine LACQUER. The sap of the lac-tree (*rhus vernicifera*), the vital ingredient in true lacquer, was unobtainable in the West. European imitations were based on a resin called gum-lac, seed-lac, or shell-lac (the deposits of an insect) which were dissolved in spirits of wine. Numerous coats were applied, and decorations were applied in gold size or built up using a composition of gum arabic and sawdust. The process was completed by colouring, polishing, gilding and burnishing.

Japonisme
Nineteenth-century decorative style in Europe and the United States which derived from but did not exactly imitate the arts of Japan, then penetrating the European and American markets in increasing amounts.

Joss
A Chinese idol. The term is probably a corruption of the Portuguese *deos*, meaning god. A joss-house is a Chinese temple; a joss stick, the incense burnt within it.

Kakiemon ware
Japanese porcelain of a highly refined, very smooth and milk-white body, with a flawless glaze over which asymmetric and rather sparse decorations of flowers, figures, birds or animals are painted largely in a restricted palette of orange-red, green and lilac-blue. Named after Sakaida Kakiemon (1596-1666), who is credited with the introduction of both the technique and the style of decoration. In the early eighteenth century the quality and style of decoration of Kakiemon ware set a standard for European porcelain factories.

Kaolin
Also known as china clay. An extremely hard, white clay produced by the decomposition of granite-bearing rock. It is the essential ingredient in the manufacture of HARD-PASTE PORCELAIN, forming about half of the body, and was known in China from the seventh century. The first deposits to be found in Europe were at Aue in Germany and were used at Meissen, the first factory in Europe to produce true porcelain.

Kwaart
Clear lead-glaze used on the earthenware products of Delft in the seventeenth and eighteenth centuries, in order to give the colours an additional glossiness and make them appear more like the porcelain imported from China.

Lacca contrafatta
Italian imitation of oriental LACQUER used mainly in the Venetian states in the eighteenth century. The technique is simple: relief decorations are formed by pasting cut-out prints to the surface of furniture, and applying a final coat of varnish.

Lackcabinett
German term describing a 'Chinese' or 'Japanese' room, generally quite small, with lacquer panels mounted on the walls. (These were often leaves of lacquer screens imported from the Far East.)

Lacquer
Waterproof varnish made from the sap of the *rhus vernicifera* tree which was indigenous to China and later introduced into Japan. Highly resistant to damp, heat and chemicals, chief among lacquer's remarkable qualities is its shiny impermeable crust – formed after the application of numerous coats – which dries so hard that it can be carved in relief. The technique of making small lacquer objects was perfected in China by the beginning of the fourth century BC.

Lattice work
An open fret much used in CHINESE CHIPPENDALE furniture.

Lei-wen spiral
Architectural term used in the West to describe the mast which runs through the centre of a pagoda to form a spire rising high above the roof and carrying nine metal rings or disks.

Marchand-mercier
French dealer in works of art and furniture, prominent in the eighteenth century: a combination of antique dealer and interior decorator who exercised great influence on taste and fashion through the patronage of designers and craftsmen.

Marquetry
A skilled craft used to decorate panelling or furniture. Small pieces of wood veneer, mother-of-pearl, metal or ivory are inlaid in a pattern, often onto furniture with a veneered surface.

Muffle kiln
Covered kiln used for the final firing of enamel pigments on porcelain. The kiln allows the decoration to be fired by radiation without exposing it directly to the flames.

Ormolu
Gold-coloured alloy used to decorate cast- and chased-bronze decorative objects and furniture mounts. The finest work was executed in France in the eighteenth century when mercury gilding, which coated the bronze with an amalgam of gold dissolved in heated mercury, produced a brilliant golden finish but had extremely harmful effects on the gilders.

Pagod
Originally an oriental idol; from the eighteenth century a fat squatting and grinning chinoiserie parody of such a figure.

Palampore
Type of PINTADO or painted cloth from Masulipatam in India, imported into England by the East India Company in the seventeenth century.

Patera
Small, flat, circular or oval ornament often decorated with acanthus leaves and commonly used in the eighteenth and nineteenth centuries to decorate silver, furniture etc.

Pékin
Striped silk brocade with a floral pattern superimposed on the stripes, which are alternately matt and shiny.

Petunze
White china-stone, a silicate of potassium and aluminium, also known as feldspar. It is an essential vitrifying ingredient in the making of *hard-paste porcelain*, fusing with the *kaolin* (china clay) at high temperature.

Pintado
Term used in seventeenth-century England for a painted or printed calico imported from India. The word derives from Spanish.

Plate-printed cotton
Also known as TOILE DE JOUY. Cotton fabric decorated by means of engraved copper plates. The technique was widely used in the eighteenth century when monochrome decoration of chinoiserie designs was particularly popular. Technically, the process is the reverse of BLOCK PRINTING because the colorant is carried in the depressed rather than the raised areas of the plate.

Porcelain
see HARD-PASTE, SOFT-PASTE

Porringer
Small bowl with one or two handles, generally of silver or pewter, popular in England and America from the early seventeenth to the late nineteenth century.

Rinceau
French term for carved, moulded or painted decorative foliage.

Rocaille
French word, originally meaning rockwork and shellwork for decorating grottoes. The term was extended from *c.*1734 to describe a new fashion for such motifs in ornament. From *c.*1796 the slang diminutive of rococo was in use.

Siamoise
Type of striped fabric modelled on the clothes worn by the Siamese ambassadors to the court of Louis XIV in 1686.

Silver-gilt
Silver covered with a thin coating of gold.

Singerie
Decoration in which the main figures are monkeys, often dressed in human clothes and aping the activities of people.

Soft-paste porcelain
An imitation of true (HARD-PASTE) porcelain, invented in the West before the secret of true Chinese porcelain had been discovered. A vitreous frit – normally a mixture of white sand, gypsum, soda, alum, salt and nitre – was melted together in a glassy mass, broken and pulverized, and then ground and mixed with clay. Fired at a lower temperature than hard-paste porcelain the result was a translucent, slightly creamy paste. All enamel decoration was executed on top of the glaze, i.e. after the first firing.

Stoneware
Very hard, non-porous pottery ware made by fusing clay and a vitreous stone, such as feldspar, under high temperatures. Salt-glazed stoneware has a slightly rough, pitted surface. The glaze is achieved by throwing salt into the fire of the kiln when it is at its hottest. Sodium combines with the silicates in the body of the pot to form a thin glaze.

Tenture
French word meaning tapestry or wall-hanging.

T'ing
A small open pavilion in Chinese architecture. Believed by Sir William Chambers to be the correct term for a Chinese temple.

Toile de Jouy
see PLATE-PRINTED COTTON.

Tree of Life design
Tree motif – often large-scale and asymmetrical – commonly employed to decorate textiles, especially bed-covers, imported into England in the seventeenth century. In Indian mythology, the tree symbolized the creative force of life. Indian patterns were taken up in England, shipped out to India, modified there and exported to China, remodified and exported to the West where they were received as Chinese designs.

Treillage
French word for trellis work.

Tulip vase
Tulip- and China-mania combine in this vessel which owes its shape to the Chinese pagoda, and was produced at Delft before the end of the seventeenth century.

Vernis Martin
Generic term applied to French eighteenth-century JAPANNED decoration, named after Guillaume Martin and his brothers who created it in Paris *c.*1730. It is one of the finest European LACQUER finishes, and the only one to reproduce the oriental technique of sprinkling powdered metal into the final layers of lacquer.

Belgium
Spa. Musée de la Ville d'Eaux. Bois de Spa.

France
Few pre-revolutionary chinoiserie interiors have survived, and much of the ephemeral chinoiserie of the *jardin anglais-chinois* has also vanished. However, many of France's museums hold important collections of chinoiserie; the most notable are listed here.
Museums
Besançon. Musée des Beaux-Arts. Paintings include Boucher's oil sketches for the second suite of Beauvais tapestries: Jean Barbault's *The Asian Procession*.
Jouy-en-Josas, nr Versailles. Musée Oberkampf. *Toile de Jouy* displayed in the salons of the modern Château Montebello.
Lyon. Musée Historique des Tissus. Important silk collection from the seventeenth century to the present day.
Marseilles. Musée Cantini. Faience and porcelain.
Nevers. Musée Municipal. Faience and porcelain.
Paris. Every aspect of the decorative arts is represented in the magnificent chinoiseries found in the collections of the Louvre and the Museum of Decorative Arts. Chinoiseries are also to be found at the following museums: Musée Carnavalet, rue de Sevigné. Furniture, including Madame de Sevigné's writing-desk; panelling from Hôtel de la Riboissier in the style of Pillement. Musée Nissim de Camondo, rue de Monceau. Furniture: tapestries in the setting of an eighteenth-century house.
Rouen. Musée des Beaux-Arts. Faience and porcelain.
Sèvres. Musée Nationale de la Céramique. Exceptional porcelain collection, both European and oriental.
Strasbourg. Musée des Arts Décoratifs. Faience and porcelain.
Interiors
Champs-sur-Marne. Château de Champs. Boucher's *Salon chinois*.
Chantilly. Musée Condé. La Grande Singerie.
Haroué, nr Nancy. Château de Crâon. Le Salon Pillement.
Paris. La Pagode, rue de Babylone. Cinema with chinoiserie interior.
Gardens
Boulogne-sur-Seine. Jardin Kahn, a *fin-de-siècle* Japanese-style garden.

Chanteloupe, nr Amboise. Stone Pagoda.
Paris. The parks of Bagatelle and Monceau are open to the public, but both are now shorn of their chinoiseries. There is a so-called *jardin anglo-chinois* at Versailles, near the Petit Trianon. Cassan, at L'Isle-Adam near Paris, has a Chinese pavilion.

Germany and Austria
Despite the devastations of war, and the passing of time, many of Germany and Austria's chinoiserie treasures have survived.
Museums and interiors
Bamberg. Neue Residenz. Chinese room c.1705.
Bayreuth. Schloss Eremitage (Hermitage). Summer palace of the Margravine. Mirror room: small drawing-room decorated with *singeries*.
Berlin. Charlottenburg Palace, Luisenplatz. Great depository of chinoiserie treasure including Dagly furniture: lacquer room; porcelain room; tapestry. Kunstgewerbermuseum, Schloss Köpenick. Decorative arts include Pillement embroidery panel of Lyons silk; porcelain and faience.
Cologne. Lacquer museum of BASF Lacke und Farben AG. Lacquer collection from around the world.
Dresden. Japanisches Palais. Augustus the Strong's Japanese Palace, built to house his porcelain collection.
Frankfurt am Main. Museum für Kunsthandwerk. German lacquer work, furniture and embroidered wall-hangings.
Krefeld. Deutsches Textilmuseum. Textiles include *toile de Jouy*, both French and English; embroidered Lyons silks.
Munich. Bayerisches Nationalmuseum. Decorative arts including eighteenth-century Meissen porcelain. Residenz. Beauvais tapestries, French furniture, period rooms, porcelain. Schloss Nymphenburg. Nymphenburg porcelain, chinoiserie interiors. In the grounds stand the Amelienburg and Pagodenburg pavilions.
Pillnitz. The Wasserpalais. Augustus the Strong's Indianisches Lustschloss.
Potsdam. Neues Palais. Porcelain, furniture.
Sans Souci. The tea-house in the grounds contains Japanese, Chinese and European porcelain.
Vienna. Schönbrunn Palace.

Two rooms with chinoiserie decoration; Austrian and German rococo furniture. Osterreichisches Museum für Angewandte Kunst. Chinoiserie room made for Count Dubsky's palace at Brünn c.1730.
Württemburg, nr Stuttgart. Schloss Ludwigsberg. Lackcabinett, decorated by Saenger, c.1720; Beauvais tapestry.
Würzburg. Residenz. Former residence of the prince-bishops of Würzburg. Decorative arts represented among much else of splendour.
Gardens
Dessau. Situated near Dessau are:
Oranienbaum. Gardens with pagoda, tea-house and Chinese bridges. Wörlitz. Garden with bridge imitating Chambers' Chinese Bridge at Kew.
Potsdam. Sans Souci. The grounds contain the famous tea-house, restored in 1991.
Würzburg. Veitshöchheim. Lustgarten: formal gardens with chinoiserie pavilions.

Great Britain
The persisting importance of the chinoiserie style in so many aspects of the decorative arts means that almost every museum in the British Isles holds some chinoiserie objects. However, a trip to the major collections listed below should reveal enough to satisfy even the most devoted admirer of the style.
Museums
Birmingham. Museum and Art Gallery. Ceramics, orientalia, paintings by George Chinnery.
Bournemouth. Russell-Cotes Art Gallery and Museum. Furniture.
Bristol. Georgian House. Decorative arts.
Cambridge. Fitzwilliam Museum. Pottery, porcelain, textiles, silver, fans. English ceramics etc.
Cardiff. National Museum of Wales. Decorative arts, particularly porcelain.
Edinburgh. Royal Museum of Scotland. National collection of decorative arts from around the world.
Glasgow. Burrell Collection. Textiles, furniture, ceramics.
London. Victoria & Albert Museum. One of the finest collections of decorative arts in the world with unequalled chinoiseries in every field. The Wallace Collection. Major collection of french furniture, porcelain and *objets d'art*.
Oxford. Ashmolean Museum.

Ceramics, porcelain, silver, prints etc.
Port Sunlight, Wirral, Merseyside. Lady Lever Art Gallery. Outstanding collection of English eighteenth-century furniture; Chinese porcelain.
Wolverhampton. Bantock House Museum. Decorative arts; japanning display.
Country houses
Bucks. Claydon House. North Hall and Chinese Room; rococo chinoiserie carving by Luke Lightfoot.
Cambs. Anglesey Abbey. Seventeenth-century porcelain.
Clwydd. Erddig. Panels, porcelain, carpets and fabrics; state beds with Chinese hangings.
Derbys. Calke Abbey. Early eighteenth-century Chinese silk state bed.
Devon. Castle Drogo. Chinese Chippendale furniture. Saltram House, Plymouth. Mirror Room. Chinese Dressing Room. Chinese Chippendale bedroom; porcelain. Chinese mirror paintings and wallpaper.
Gwynedd. Plas Newydd, Isle of Anglesey. Silk bedstead.
Hereford & Worcs. Croft Castle. Chinese Chippendale furniture.
Lincs. Belton House. Chinese bedroom and screen; porcelain.
Norfolk. Blickling Hall. Wallpaper. Felbrigg Hall. Dressing-Room, Bedroom, Chippendale furniture.
North Yorks. Nostell Priory. The State Bed Chamber and Dressing Room.
Northumberland. Wallington Hall, Cambo. Tapestry Room, porcelain.
Oxon. Buscot Park. Porcelain, Chinese Chippendale furniture. Kirtlington Park. English *singerie* decoration.
Powys. Powis Castle, Welshpool. Wallpaper.
Staffs. Shugborough. Mirror paintings, china and Chippendale cabinet.
Surrey. Clandon Park. Porcelain and Chippendale furniture. Ham House, Richmond. Early English japanned furniture.
Sussex. Royal Pavilion, Brighton. Tour-de-force of nineteenth-century chinoiserie, fully furnished and restored.
Warwicks. Charlecote Park. Chippendale pier glasses.
Gardens
Most chinoiserie garden ornaments have not survived into the twentieth century, but

temples and pagodas do still stand on English soil. Among the most noteworthy are:
Beds. Woburn Abbey, Woburn. The Chinese Dairy.
Bucks. Stowe. Original Chinese summer-house reinstated in 1998. Cliveden. Pagoda from Bagatelle, France.
Cheshire. Biddulph Grange. Chinese Temple
London. Kew Gardens. Pagoda.
Middlesex. Osterly Park. Pagoda, recently restored.
Northants. Boughton House, Kettering. Chinese Tent.
Staffs. Alton Towers. Pagoda. Shugborough Park. Chinese Summer House.

Italy
Chinoiserie decorative schemes were found throughout Italy, combining harmoniously – if unexpectedly – with the prevailing classicism. The most notable survivors are:
Naples. Museo e Gallerie Nazionali di Capodimonte. Porcelain room.
Palermo, Sicily. Palazzina Cinese (Villa Favorita). Remarkable synthesis of classicism and chinoiserie. Closed for many years during refurbishment; check current situation with tourist office before visiting.
Rome. Palazzo Braschi. Neo-classical Chinese room.
Stra. Villa la Barbariga. Rococo fresco decoration; one room has specifically Chinese characters.
Turin. Palazzo Reale. Lacquer room which combines Piedmontese and Far Eastern lacquer.
Castello di Rivoli. Neo-classical chinoiserie room.
Venice. Museo Correr. Museum of eighteenth-century Venice.
Palazzo Ca Rezzonico. Venetian lacquered furniture.
Vicenza. Villa Valmarana Vicenza. Sequence of Tiepolo murals; the Foresteria is frescoed with large-scale chinoiseries.

The Netherlands
Amsterdam. Rijksmuseum. Representative collection of decorative arts including porcelain, furniture and lacquer room.
Delft. Museum Lambert van Meerten. Tiles, furniture, Delftware.
Stedelijk Museum. Tapestries, pottery.
Rotterdam. Museum Boymans Van Beuningen. Includes Boucher's painting *The Chinese Fishing Party*.
Sneek. Stadhuis. Town hall has room painted in the style of Pillement.

Russia
Tsarskoe Selo (Oranienbaum), nr St Petersburg. The eighteenth-century 'village of the Tsars' includes: The Chinese Palace of Catherine the Great, now called the China Palace Museum. Original interiors, series of rococo chinoiserie rooms. Katalnaya Gorka. Now a decorative arts museum; original interiors including a Meissen porcelain monkey room.
Garden follies. Landscaped as a *jardin anglo-chinois* in the 1760s, the chinoiserie garden structures have astonishingly survived. The Chinese Village is situated in the grounds of Alexandrovsky, one of two palaces at Tsarkoe Selo. The Creaking Pavilion in the adjoining park of Yevkaterinsky and the bridge designed by William Halfpenny still ornament the elaborate system of waterways and islands, and the Great Caprice stands across the major avenue of the park.

Scandinavia
Copenhagen. National Museum of Denmark. Lacquer; the David Collection of eighteenth-century chinoiserie; Boucher, *The Chinese Lovers*.
Rosenborg Slott. Earliest European lacquered room.
Drammen, Norway. Drammens Museum. Decorative arts.
Drottningholm, Sweden. Kina Slott, Chinese Pavilion. The most complete and perfect example in Europe of a rococo chinoiserie retreat.
Oslo. Museum of Applied Arts. Ceramics, furniture, textiles.
Stockholm. Nordic Museum. Decorative arts.
Royal Palace (Kunglige Slottet). Interiors, porcelain. National Museum. French furniture.
Stürefors, nr Linkoping, Sweden. The English Park, Chinese Pavilion.

Spain
Aranjuez. Palacio Real. Porcelain room.

Switzerland
Bern. Historical Museum. Decorative arts.
Geneva. Château d'Haute-ville. Set of chinoiserie *toiles peintes*.

USA
Little native American chinoiserie has survived, but the style is well represented in museums and collections throughout the country.
Boston, Mass. Museum of Fine Arts. English embroidery, Sèvres porcelain.
Chicago, Ill. Art Institute of Chicago. Decorative arts including tapestries, porcelain.
Fairfax County. Gunston Hall Plantation, Va. The eighteenth-century house displays English and American decorative arts including Chinese Chippendale, designed when the house was built.
Kansas City. Nelson-Atkins Museum of Art. Decorative arts, including japanned furniture and Italian mid-eighteenth-century lacquer room.
New York. The Metropolitan Museum of Art. Representative collections of chinoiserie objects including the earliest extant example of American japanning.
Cooper-Hewitt National Museum of Design, Smithsonian Institution. Engravings by Watteau, preparatory drawings by Boucher; porcelain and textiles.
Ohio. Cleveland Museum of Art. Fourteenth-century Lucchese silk, Beauvais tapestry, eighteenth-century French decorative arts.
Philadelphia, Penn. Museum of Art. European and American decorative arts.
Salem, Mass. Essex Institute. American decorative arts.
Washington, D.C. Freer Gallery of Art. Whistler's Peacock Room and other examples of japonisme.
Winterthur, Delaware. Henry Francis du Pont Winterthur Museum. Decorative arts of Europe and America.

General

Charleston, Robert J., ed., *World Ceramics*, New York, 1990.

Conner, Patrick. *Oriental Architecture in the West*, London, 1979. Comprehensive and scholarly account of the impact of Chinese, Japanese and Indian styles in architecture; particularly helpful on the Anglo-Chinese garden.

Crossman, Carl L., *The Decorative Arts of the China Trade*, Woodbridge, Suffolk, 1991.

Edwards, Ralph, *The Shorter Dictionary of English Furniture*, London, 1964.

Hayward, Helena, ed., *World Furniture*, London, 1965.

Honour, Hugh, *Chinoiserie: The Vision of Cathay*, London, 1961. An incomparable introduction to the subject; scholarly, amusing, and beautifully written.

Huth, H., *Lacquer of the West: The History of a Craft and an Industry 1550-1950*, Chicago and London, 1971.

Impey, O. *Chinoiserie: The Impact of Oriental Styles on Western Art and Decoration*, London, 1977. Covers painting, drawing and engraving, as well as the decorative arts and architecture.

Jarry, Madeleine, *Chinoiserie: Le rayonnement du goût chinois sur les arts décoratifs du XVIIe et XVIIIe siècles*, Paris, 1981.

Reichwein, Adolf, *China and Europe: Intellectual and Artistic Contacts in the Eighteenth Century*, trans., J.C. Powell, London, 1925 (reissued 1968).

Sullivan, M. *The Meeting of Eastern and Western art, from the 16th century to the Present Day*, London, 1973. Scholarly study of influences in both directions.

Chapter One
Contemporary sources

Alvarez, Semedo, *The History of That Great and Revered Monarchy of China*, London, 1655.

Hakluyt, Richard, *The Principal Navigations Voyages Traffiques and Discoveries of the English Nation*, 12 vols., Glasgow, 1903-5.

Mandeville, Sir John, *The Travels of Sir John Mandeville*, Liège, 1371; edition in modern spelling

from the Cotton MS, ed. A.W. Pollard, London 1900, reprint 1964.

Mendoza, Juan Gonzalez de, *Historia … del Gran Reyno de la China*, Rome, 1585; trans., R. Parke, *The Historie of the Great and Mightie Kingdome of China*, London, c.1600.

Nieuhoff, Johann, *An Embassy from the East India Company of the United Provinces to the Grand Tartar Cham Emperour of China*, Leyden, 1665; trans., J. Ogilby, London, 1699.

Polo, Marco, *Travels*, prob. first pub. Paris, as *Divasement dou Monde*, c.1300; trans., Ronald Latham, Harmondsworth, 1958.

Modern sources

Art in Seventeenth Century Holland, exhib. cat., London, 1977.

Clunas, Craig, ed., *Chinese Export Art and Design*, London, 1987.

Devoti, Donata, *La seta, tesori di un'antica arte Lucchese: produzioni tessile a Lucca dal XIII al XVII secolo*, exhib. cat., Lucca, 1989.

Irwin, J., and K.B. Brett, *Origins of Chintz*, London, 1970.

Letts, Malcolm, *Sir John Mandeville: The man and his book*, London, 1949.

Letts, Malcolm, ed., *Mandeville's Travels, Texts and Translations*, Glasgow, 1953.

Trevelyan, G.M., *English Social History*, Harmondsworth, 1967.

Yule, Sir Henry, and Henri Cordier, eds., *Cathay and the Way Thither*, 4 vols., Glasgow, 1913-16.

Chapter Two
Contemporary sources

Le Comte, Père Louis, *Memoirs and Observations … made in a late Journey through the Empire of China*, Paris, 1699.

Evelyn, John, *The Diary of John Evelyn*, 2 vols., 1818; ed., S. de Beer, 6 vols., Oxford, 1955.

Félibien, Jean-François, *Description sommaire du Château de Versailles*, Paris, 1674.

du Halde, J.B., *Description géographique, historique, etc. de l'empire de la Chine, et de la Tartarie Chinoise*, Paris, 1741.

Pepys, Samuel, *The Diary of Samuel Pepys*, Cambridge, 1815; ed., R. Latham and W. Matthews, London, 1978.

Shaftesbury, Anthony Ashley

Cooper, 3rd Earl of Shaftesbury, *Characteristics of Men, Manners, Opinions, Times*, London, 1711 (revised 1713).

Stalker and Parker, *Treatise of Japanning and Varnishing*, 1688; reprinted London, 1971.

Modern sources

Ayers, John, Oliver Impey and J.V.G. Mallet, *Porcelain for Palaces: The Fashion for Japan in Europe 1650-1750*, London, 1990.

Belevitch-Stankevitch, H., *Le goût chinois en France au temps de Louis XIV*, Paris, 1910.

Clunas, Craig, ed., *Chinese Export Art and Design*, London, 1987.

Danis, Robert, *La première maison royale de Trianon 1670-1687*, Paris, 1926.

Fourest, H.P., *La faience de Delft*, Fribourg and Paris, 1980.

Jarry, Madeleine, *World Tapestry*, London, 1969.

Jarry, Madeleine, 'L'exotisme dans l'art décoratif français au temps de Louis XIV', *Bulletin de la société d'étude du XVII siècle*, July-Oct., 1957.

Kendrick, A.F., *Catalogue of Tapestries*, London, 1924.

Kendrick, A.F., *English Needlework*, 2nd ed., revised by P. Wardle, London and New York, 1967.

Oman, Charles, *Caroline Silver 1635-1688*, London, 1970.

Chapter Three
Contemporary sources

Boucher, François, *Diverses figures chinoises*, (9 engraved plates) Paris, c.1740.

Boucher, François, *Figures chinoises et tartares*, (12 engraved plates after Watteau) Paris, 1731.

Huet, Christophe, *Nouveau livre de singeries*, Paris, c.1740.

Huet, Christophe, *Singeries*, (12 engraved plates) Paris, c.1740.

Pillement, Jean, *A New Book of Chinese Ornaments*, London, 1755.

Pillement, Jean, *Receuil de différentes Fleurs de Fantaisie dans le Goût Chinois …*, Paris and London, 1760.

Modern sources

Jarry, Madeleine, 'Eighteenth-century French Tapestry: A Reassessment', *Apollo*, vol. LXXXIX, June 1969, pp.424-9.

Kimball, Fiske, *The Creation of the Rococo*, Philadelphia, 1943.

Schoesser, Mary, and Kathleen Dejardin, *French Textiles from 1760 to the Present*, London, 1991.

Verlet, Pierre, *French Furniture and Interior Decoration of the Eighteenth Century*, London, 1967.

Verlet, Pierre, *Les meubles français du XVIII siècle*, Paris, 1982.

Verlet, Pierre, et al., *La porcelaine de Sèvres*, 2 vols., Paris, 1953.

Watson, F.J.B., *Wallace Collections Catalogues: Furniture*, London, 1956.

Chapter Four
General

Arthaud, Claude, *Dream Palaces*, London, 1973.

Porcelain

Ducret, S., *Porcelain de Saxe et autres manufactures allemandes*, Fribourg, 1962.

Honey, W.B., *European Porcelain of the Eighteenth Century*, New York, 1962.

Lane, E.A., *Italian Porcelain*, London, 1954.

The Queen's Gallery, Buckingham Palace, *Sèvres Porcelain from the Royal Collection*, London, 1979.

Lacquer

Phillips, Phoebe, ed., *Lacquer: An International History and Collector's Guide*, London, 1989.

Strässer, Edith, assisted by Mark Hinton, *Oriental and European Lacquer from the BASF Lacquer Museum*, Cologne, 1977.

Germany

Fauchier-Magnan, A., *The Small German Courts in the Eighteenth Century*, London, 1958.

Hager, L., *Nymphenburg*, Munich, 1955.

Italy

Croft-Murray, E., 'La Favorita, Palermo', *Country Life*, 10 Oct. 1947, pp. 274-5.

Lane, E.A., *Italian Porcelain*, London, 1954.

Succi, Dario, *Capricci Veneziane del Settecento*, Turin, 1988.

Portugal

'Pillement: Six Unpublished Chinoiserie Panels', *The Connoisseur*, Dec. 1956, p.270.

Russia

Craig, Maurice, 'The Palaces of Tsarskoe Selo', *Country Life*, 20 Jan. 1966.

Kennett, Victor and Audrey, *The Palaces of Leningrad*, London, 1973.

Scandinavia

Aasma, Karin, *Drömmen om Kina*, exhib. cat., Göteborg, Konstslöjdmuseet, 1984.

Setterwall, Ake, et al., *The Chinese Pavilion at Drottningholm*, Malmö, 1974.

Spain

Honour, Hugh, 'G.D. Tiepolo and the Aranjuez Porcelain Room', *The Connoisseur*, vol. CXLVI, July 1960, p.183.

Chapter Five
Contemporary sources

Chambers, Sir William, *Designs of Chinese Buildings, Furniture, Dresses, Machines and Utensils*, London, 1757; reprinted Farnborough, 1969.

Chippendale, Thomas, *The Gentleman and Cabinet-Maker's Director*, London, 1754; reprinted New York, 1966.

Darly, Mathias, and George Edwards, *A New Book of Chinese Designs*, London, 1754.

Halfpenny, William, *New Designs for Chinese Temples, Triumphal Arches, Garden Seats, Palings etc.*, London, 1750-52.

Halfpenny, William, *Rural Architecture in the Chinese Taste*, London, 1752.

Johnson, Thomas, *A New Book of Ornaments*, London, 1758.

Lock, Mathias, and H. Copland, *A New Book of Ornaments*, London, 1752; revised ed. 1768.

Sayer, Robert, *The Ladies Amusement, or the Whole Art of Japanning Made Easy*, London, 1762.

Shebbeare, J., *Letters on the English Nation*, London, 1756.

Modern sources

Copeland, Robert, *Spode's Willow Pattern and Other Designs after the Chinese*, New York, 1980.

Crouan, Katherine, *John Linnell: A Centennial Exhibition*, Cambridge, 1982.

Davis, Howard, *Chinoiserie Polychrome Decoration on Staffordshire Porcelain 1790-1800*, London, 1991.

Fastnedge, Ralph, *English Furniture Styles from 1500 to 1830*, Harmondsworth, 1955.

Grimwade, A., *Rococo Silver*, London, 1974.

Hayward, Helena, 'Chinoiserie at Badminton', *Apollo*, vol. XC, Aug. 1969, p.134.

Hayward, Helena and A. Kirkham, *William and John Linnell*, 2 vols., London, 1980.

Hefford, Wendy, *Designs for Printed Textiles in England from 1750 to 1850*, London, 1992.

Honey, W.B., *English Pottery and Porcelain*, London, 1965.

The National Trust, *Claydon House*, London, revised ed. 1984.

The National Trust, *Nostell Priory*, London, 1990.

Neatby, Nigel, *The Saltram Collection*, London, 1977.

Rothstein, Natalie, *Spitalfields Silks*, London, 1975.

Thornton, Peter, *Baroque and Rococo Silks*, London, 1965.

Ward Jackson, Peter, *English Furniture Designs of the 18th Century*, London, 1984.

Chapter Six
Contemporary sources

Attiret, Jean-Denis, *A Particular Account of the Emperor of China's Gardens near Pekin*, 1742; trans., Sir Harry Beaumont [pseud. Joseph Spence], London, 1752.

Chambers, Sir William, *Dissertation on Oriental Gardening*, London, 1772.

Knight, Richard Payne, *The Landscape: A Didactic Poem*, 1794.

Krafft, Johann-Carl, *Plans des Plus Beaux Jardins Pittoresques de France, d'Angleterre et d'Allemagne ...*, 2 vols., Paris, 1809-10.

Le Rouge, Georges, *Détails des nouveaux jardins à la mode*, 21 vols., Paris, 1774-89.

Temple, Sir William, 'Upon the Gardens of Epicurus', 1685; reprinted in *The Works of Sir William Temple, Bart*, 2 vols., London, 1740.

Walpole, Horace, 'The History of the Modern Taste in Gardening', 1775, reprinted in I. Chase, *Horace Walpole, Gardenist*, Princeton, 1943.

Modern sources

Bald, R.C., 'Sir William Chambers and the Chinese Garden', *Journal of the History of Ideas*, vol. XI no. 3, June 1950.

Harris, John, 'Sir William Chambers, Knight of the Polar Star', *Studies in Architecture*, vol. 9, London, 1970.

Harris, John, 'Exoticism at Kew', *Apollo*, vol. LXXVIII, Aug. 1963, p.103.

Jackson-Stop, Gervase, *Follies and Pleasure Pavilions*, London, 1989.

Jardins en France 1760-1820, exhib. cat., Caisse Nationale des Monuments Historiques

et des Sites, Paris, 1977.

de Ligne, Prince Charles J.E., *Coup d'œil sur Belœil*, ed. E. de Ganay, Paris, 1922.

O'Neill, Jean, 'Diversions on the Water', *Country Life*, 1 Aug. 1985.

Pevsner, Sir Nikolaus, and S. Lang, 'A Note on Sharawaggi', *Architectural Review*, vol. CVI, 1949; reprinted in Pevsner, *Studies in Art, Architecture and Design*, London, 1968.

Pevsner, Sir Nikolaus, ed., 'The Picturesque Garden and its influence outside the British Isles', *Colloquium in the History of Landscape Architecture, no.2*, Washington D.C., Dumbarton Oaks, 1974.

Ripa, Matteo, *The Memoirs of Father Ripa*, trans. Fortunato Prandi, 1844.

Sirèn, Osvald, *Gardens of China*, New York, 1949.

Sirèn, Osvald, *China and the Gardens of Europe of the Eighteenth Century*, New York, 1950.

Tompkins, Ptolemy, ed., *Gardens in Central Europe*, Woodbridge, Suffolk, 1991.

Chapter Seven
Contemporary sources

Brown, Richard, *Domestic Architecture*, London, 1841.

Catalogue of the Great Exhibition, London, 1851; reprinted, *The Art Journal* 1970.

Fortune, Robert, *Three Years Wandering in the Northern Provinces of China*, London, 1847.

Jones, Owen, *Examples of Chinese Ornament*, London, 1867.

Nash, John, *Views of the Royal Pavilion, Brighton*, London, 1827.

Whittock, Nathaniel, *Decorative Painter's and Glazier's Guide*, London, 1827.

Modern sources

Aldrich, Megan, ed., *The Craces: Royal Decorators 1768-1899*, London, 1990.

Aslin, Elizabeth, 'The Furniture Designs of E.W. Godwin', *Victoria & Albert Museum Bulletin Reprints*, London, 1970.

Bonham, Joanna, Sally MacDonald and Julia Porter, *Victorian Interior Design*, London, 1991.

Butler, E.M., ed., *A Regency Visitor: The English Tour of Prince Pückler-Muskau described in his Letters 1826-28*, London, 1957.

Dinkel, John, *The Royal Pavilion, Brighton*, London,

1983.

Gardner, Bellamy, 'Duke William's Chinese Yacht', *The Connoisseur*, vol. CXXI, March 1948, p.22.

Le Japonisme, exhib. cat., Paris, Galeries Nationales du Grand Palais, 1988.

Montgomery, Florence M., *Textiles in America 1650-1870*, New York, 1984.

Morley, John, *The Making of the Royal Pavilion, Brighton: Designs and Drawings*, London, 1984

The Queen's Gallery, Buckingham Palace, *Carlton House: The Past Glories of George IV's Palace*, London, 1991.

Singer, Aubrey, *The Lion and the Dragon: The Story of the First British Embassy to the Court of the Emperor Qianlong in Peking 1792-1794*, London, 1992.

Wells-Cole, Anthony, 'Another Look at Lady Hertford's Chinese Drawing Room', *Leeds Art Calendar*, 98/1986, pp.16-22.

America

Barnum, P.T., *The Autobiography of Phineas T. Barnum*, 1855.

China's Influence on American Culture in the 18th and 19th Centuries, exhib. cat., New York, China House Gallery, 1976.

Lancaster, Clay, 'Oriental Forms in American Architecture 1800-1870', *Art Bulletin*, vol. XXXXIX, 1947, pp.186-193.

Sutton, Denys, 'Cathay, Nirvana and Zen', *Apollo*, vol. LXXXIV, Aug. 1966, p.148.

Waterman, Thomas Tilleston, *The Mansions of Virginia*, Chapel Hill, 1946.

Chapter Eight

Klein, Dan, Nancy A. McClelland and Malcolm Haslam, eds., *In the Deco Style*, London, 1991.

Naylor, David, *Great American Movie Theaters*, Washington, 1987.

Schoesser, Mary and Celia Rufey, *English and American Textiles from 1790 to the Present*, London, 1989.

Troy, Nancy J., *Modernism and the Decorative Arts in France*, New Haven and London, 1991.

Woodham, Jonathan, *Twentieth Century Ornament*, London, 1990.

Woods, C., *Sanderson 1860-1965*, exhib. cat., London, 1985.